AUTHORS IN CONTEXT

General Editor: PATRICIA INGHAM, University of Oxford
Historical Adviser: BOYD HILTON, University of Cambridge

OSCAR WILDE

AUTHORS IN CONTEXT examines the work of major writers in relation to their own time and to the present day. The series provides detailed coverage of the values and debates that colour the writing of particular authors and considers their novels, plays, and poetry against this background. Set in their social, cultural, and political contexts, classic books take on new meaning for modern readers. And since readers, like writers, have their own contexts, the series considers how critical interpretations have altered over time, and how films, sequels, and other popular adaptations relate to the new age in which they are produced.

JOHN SLOAN is Fellow and Tutor in English at Harris Manchester College, Oxford. He is a specialist in the literature of the late nineteenth century. His books include *George Gissing: The Cultural Challenge* and *John Davidson: First of the Moderns, a Literary Biography*.

OXFORD WORLD'S CLASSICS

*For over 100 years Oxford World's Classics have brought
readers closer to the world's great literature. Now with over 700
titles—from the 4,000-year-old myths of Mesopotamia to the
twentieth century's greatest novels—the series makes available
lesser-known as well as celebrated writing.*

*The pocket-sized hardbacks of the early years contained
introductions by Virginia Woolf, T. S. Eliot, Graham Greene,
and other literary figures which enriched the experience of reading.
Today the series is recognized for its fine scholarship and
reliability in texts that span world literature, drama and poetry,
religion, philosophy and politics. Each edition includes perceptive
commentary and essential background information to meet the
changing needs of readers.*

OXFORD WORLD'S CLASSICS

JOHN SLOAN

Oscar Wilde

OXFORD
UNIVERSITY PRESS

OXFORD

UNIVERSITY PRESS

Great Clarendon Street, Oxford OX2 6DP

Oxford University Press is a department of the University of Oxford.
It furthers the University's objective of excellence in research, scholarship,
and education by publishing worldwide in

Oxford New York

Auckland Bangkok Buenos Aires Cape Town Chennai
Dar es Salaam Delhi Hong Kong Istanbul Karachi Kolkata
Kuala Lumpur Madrid Melbourne Mexico City Mumbai Nairobi
São Paulo Shanghai Taipei Tokyo Toronto

Oxford is a registered trade mark of Oxford University Press
in the UK and in certain other countries

Published in the United States
by Oxford University Press Inc., New York

© John Sloan 2003

The moral rights of the author have been asserted

Database right Oxford University Press (maker)

First published 2003
Reissued 2009

British Library Cataloguing in Publication Data

Data available

Library of Congress Cataloging in Publication Data

Sloan, John, 1948–
Oscar Wilde / John Sloan.
p. cm.—(Oxford world's classics. Authors in context)
Includes bibliographical references and index.
1. Wilde, Oscar, 1854–1900. 2. Authors, Irish—19th century—Biography. 3. Wilde,
Oscar, 1854–1900—Political and social views. 4. Literature and society—Great
Britain—History—19th century. I. Title. II. Oxford world's classics (Oxford University
Press). Authors in context.
PR5823.S58 2003 828′.809—dc21 2002038160

ISBN 978–0–19–955521–5

2

Typeset in Ehrhardt
by RefineCatch Limited, Bungay, Suffolk
Printed in Great Britain by
Clays Ltd, St Ives plc

CONTENTS

List of Illustrations   vii

A Chronology of Oscar Wilde   viii

Abbreviations   xiii

1. The Life of Oscar Wilde   I
   Irish Beginnings   I
   Oxford and Intellectual Influences   5
   The Aesthete in the Market-place   9
   The Creator of Dorian Gray   16
   Theatrical Success   20
   Prison, Exile, and Last Writings   26

2. The Fabric of Society   31
   The Challenge to Authority   32
   Civilizing Trends   49

3. The Literary Scene   61
   The Growth of New Markets   61
   The Reaction against Realism   75
   Wilde and Censorship   87

4. Wilde and Social Issues   99
   Politics and Political Writings   100
   Sexual Politics: Feminism and Gender   104
   Social Remedies   119
   Prison and Prison Writings   126
   Consumerism: Dorian Gray and Other Collectors   134

5. Wilde and Intellectual Issues   139
   Philosophy and Science   139
   Ethics and Religion   156

6. Recontextualizing Wilde   168
   Reproducing Wilde   171
   Wilde's Changing Image   182

Notes   193

vi   *Contents*

Further Reading   204

Websites   209

Film, Opera, and Ballet Adaptations   211

Index   215

LIST OF ILLUSTRATIONS

'Maudle on the Choice of a Profession.' Cartoon by George
du Maurier from *Punch*, 1881.   12

Reproduced with permission of Punch Ltd.

'A Private View at the Royal Academy' by William Powell
Frith, 1881.   12

Private collection/Bridgeman Art Library

'The Aesthetic Monkey', engraved from a painting by
W. H. Beard in *Harper's Weekly*, 28 January 1882.   70

© 2002 North Wind Picture Archives

'Oscar Wilde at Work'. Caricature by Aubrey Beardsley.   70

Mary Evans Picture Library/Chris Coupland

Punch cartoon, 1892, after the first-night success of *Lady
Windermere's Fan*.   70

Reproduced with permission of Punch Ltd.

Poster for the film *Oscar Wilde*, 1960, starring Robert Morley
as Wilde.   184

Ronald Grant Archive

Peter Finch as Wilde in *The Trials of Oscar Wilde*, 1960.   184

© MGM. Photo: bfi Collections

Edith Evans as Lady Bracknell in *The Importance of Being
Earnest*, 1952.   187

© Carlton Productions. Photo: bfi Collections

Stephen Fry as Wilde with Jude Law as Douglas in *Wilde*,
1997.   187

© United International Pictures. Photo: bfi Collections

A CHRONOLOGY OF OSCAR WILDE

	Life	*Historical and Cultural Background*
1854	Oscar Wilde born in Dublin, second son of distinguished parents, both authors, Dr (later Sir) William Wilde, leading oculist and ear-surgeon, and Jane Francesca Elgee, poet and translator, who wrote for the Young Ireland movement of the 1840s, under the name Speranza.	Outbreak of Crimean War. University College, Dublin founded. Coventry Patmore, *The Angel in the House*.
1857		Matrimonial Causes Act establishes divorce courts in England and Wales; first edition of Baudelaire's *Les Fleurs du mal*: Baudelaire is fined for offences against public morals.
1859		Darwin, *Origin of Species* Smiles, *Self-Help*
1860		Sarah Bernhardt's debut at Comédie-Française; Bishop Colenso denies authenticity of the Pentateuch.
1861		Outbreak of American Civil War.
1864–71	At Portora Royal School, Enniskillen.	
1864		Matthew Arnold delivers from the Chair of Poetry at Oxford the first version of his essay 'The Function of Criticism at the Present Time', which Wilde will answer in 'The Critic as Artist'.
1865		*Pall Mall Gazette* begins publication Ruskin, *Sesame and Lilies*
1866		Matthew Arnold's lectures on Celtic Literature. Swinburne, *Poems and Ballads* (first series)
1867	Death of Wilde's younger sister Isola, aged 8.	Second Reform Act extends franchise for urban voters; abortive Fenian uprising in Ireland; Paris Exhibition; Queensberry rules for boxing.

	Life	*Historical and Cultural Background*
1868		Last public execution in England.
1869		Charity Organization Society founded; Church of Ireland disestablished; founding of Girton College.
1870		Married Women's Property Act gives wives the right to separate property; declaration of Papal Infallibility. D. G. Rossetti, *Poems*
1871–4	At Trinity College, Dublin, reading classics.	
1871		Defeat of Paris Commune. Religious tests abolished at Oxford, Cambridge, and Durham universities. Darwin, *The Descent of Man* Swinburne, *Songs before Sunrise*
1873		Custody of Infants Act; Home Rule League founded; publication of the first edition of Pater's *Studies in the History of the* Renaissance (encouraging 'Art for Art's sake' and an impetus towards the later Aesthetic Movement). Spencer, *The Study of Sociology* Arnold, *Literature and Dogma*
1874	Berkeley Gold Medal for Greek at Trinity: matriculates, with a scholarship, at Magdalen College, Oxford.	Tories win general election; Disraeli forms ministry; First Impressionist exhibition in Paris. Wallace, *The Logic of Hegel, with 'Prolegomena'* Flaubert, *The Temptation of St Anthony*
1875	Summer: visits Italy with Dublin professor J. P. Mahaffy.	
1876	Death of Sir William Wilde. Wilde takes a First Class in Classical Moderations.	Disraeli creates Victoria Empress of India; Lombroso's study *The Criminal* founds the science of criminology.
1877	Visits Greece with Mahaffy, stopping at Ravenna *en route*, returns by Rome.	National Land League founded with Charles Parnell as President. Opening of Grosvenor Gallery in London. *Nineteenth Century* begins publication Flaubert, *Trois Contes*
1878	Wins the Newdigate Prize for his poem 'Ravenna'. Takes a First Class in *Litterae Humaniores*.	Matrimonial Causes Act; Ruskin–Whistler law suit.

	Life	*Historical and Cultural Background*
1879	Settles in London, as 'professor' of aesthetics: regularly lampooned in *Punch* from now on.	Agricultural depression; Irish National Land League.
1880		Charles Parnell demands home rule for Ireland; siege of Kandahar during war in Afghanistan.
1881	*Poems* published. Gilbert and Sullivan's light opera *Patience* produced, satirizing the aesthetes.	Irish Land Act; D'Oyly Carte builds Savoy Theatre, the first public building to be lit with electricity.
1882	Spends year lecturing in the United States and Canada, on such subjects as 'The English Renaissance of Art' and 'The House Beautiful'.	Phoenix Park murders; Married Women's Property Act; Society for Psychical Research founded.
1883	Three months in Paris; lectures in Britain; the early play *Vera* rather unsuccessfully produced in New York.	Sir John Seeley, *The Expansion of England* Mearns, *The Bitter Cry of Outcast London* (exposé of poverty)
1884	Marries Constance Lloyd; settles in Chelsea. Begins regular book reviewing, which continues until 1890.	Third Reform Act; founding of Social Democratic Federation and Fabian Society. J.-K. Huysmans, *A Rebours*
1885	Son Cyril born.	Whistler's 'Ten O'Clock' lecture; passing of the Criminal Law Amendment Act, which for the first time prohibits indecent relations between consenting males, the offence for which Wilde would serve his years in prison. National Vigilance Association founded. Pater, *Marius the Epicurean*
1886	Wilde meets Robert Ross. Son Vyvyan born.	Defeat of first Irish Home Rule Bill in Commons; Guardianship of Infants Act; Charles Dilke appears as co-respondent in divorce suit.
1887–9	Edits the *Woman's World*.	
1887		Parnell accused by *The Times* of promoting political murder; Queen Victoria's Golden Jubilee.
1888	*The Happy Prince and Other Tales* published.	Mrs Humphry Ward, *Robert Elsmere*

	Life	Historical and Cultural Background
1889	'The Portrait of Mr W. H.' published in *Blackwoods*.	London dockers' strike; Cleveland Street scandal. Shaw, *Fabian Essays on Socialism*
1890	The first version of *The Picture of Dorian Gray* published in *Lippincott's Monthly Magazine*.	Parnell–O'Shea divorce case; decline of circulating libraries and the death of the three-volume novel; William Morris founds the Kelmscott Press.
1891	Meets Lord Alfred Douglas. An early play *The Duchess of Padua* produced in New York as *Guido Ferranti*. Publishes the revised *Dorian Gray*, *Intentions*, *Lord Arthur Savile's Crime and Other Stories*, *A House of Pomegranates*. 'The Soul of Man under Socialism' published in the *Fortnightly Review*.	Death of Parnell.
1892	*Lady Windermere's Fan* produced. *Salome* is refused a licence for production in London by Sarah Bernhardt.	
1893	*Salome* (original French version) published in Paris. *A Woman of No Importance* is produced in London and *Lady Windermere's Fan* is published.	Independent Labour Party founded; Second Irish Home Rule Bill, rejected by Lords.
1894	*Salome* is published in English translation, with illustrations by Aubrey Beardsley. 'The Sphinx' and a *A Woman of No Importance* published.	
1895	*An Ideal Husband* and *The Importance of Being Earnest* produced in London. Wilde charges Lord Alfred Douglas's father, the Marquess of Queensberry, with criminal libel. On Queensberry's acquittal, Wilde is arrested for 'acts of gross indecency with other male persons'. The first trial jury fails to agree a verdict: at the second trial Wilde is found guilty and	Liberals lose the general election.

Life   *Historical and Cultural Background*

given the maximum sentence,
two years' hard labour, and
sent to Pentonville. He is
moved to Wandsworth, and
finally to Reading Gaol. He is
declared bankrupt.

1896   Death of Lady Wilde:
Constance Wilde travels from
Genoa to Reading Gaol to
break the news. *Salome*
produced in Paris.

1897   Writes *De Profundis* (a long   Queen Victoria's Diamond Jubilee.
letter to Lord Alfred Douglas)   Havelock Ellis, *Sexual Inversion*
in gaol. On his release Wilde
writes to the *Daily Chronicle*
about the treatment of
children in gaol. He settles
first at Berneval, near Dieppe:
later he joins Lord Alfred
Douglas in Italy, causing a
new rift with his wife.

1898   Moves to Paris. Publishes *The*
Ballad of Reading Gaol, and
writes another long letter
about prison conditions to the
Daily Chronicle. Death of
Constance Wilde.

1899   *The Importance of Being*   Outbreak of Boer War in South Africa.
Earnest and *An Ideal Husband*
published. Travels in Europe.

1900   Visits Rome, returns to Paris.
During serious illness is
baptized a Roman Catholic:
dies 30 November.

ABBREVIATIONS

Ellmann Richard Ellmann, *Oscar Wilde* (Harmondsworth: Penguin, 1988)

Letters *The Complete Letters of Oscar Wilde*, ed. Merlin Holland and Rupert Hart-Davis (London: Fourth Estate, 2000)

CHAPTER I

THE LIFE OF OSCAR WILDE

Irish Beginnings

OSCAR FINGAL O'FLAHERTIE WILLS WILDE (to give him his full name) was born in Dublin on 16 October 1854 into an Irish Protestant family with divided loyalties that spanned both nationalist sentiment and establishment values. The Great Famine in Ireland, which helped to rekindle the desire of separate Irish nationhood, had occurred only a few years before his birth. During the famine, his mother, then plain Jane Elgee, adopted the *nom de plume* 'Speranza' (the Italian for 'hope') and became a national heroine for her impassioned verses and articles in the nationalist journal of the revolutionary Young Ireland movement, the *Nation*. His father, William Wilde, a distinguished surgeon and medical commissioner for the Irish Census in 1851, wrote a report on the devastating effect of starvation and mass emigration which, in his words, had left behind a population that was 'poor, weak, old, lame, sick, blind, dumb, imbecile and insane'.[1] He too held nationalist sympathies, although in his case they found expression in non-political, antiquarian interests. He published several books on Irish places and legends, one entitled *Beauties of the Boyne and Blackwater*, was reviewed by his future wife for the *Nation* in 1849.

Oscar was the second of their three children. His elder brother Willie was his mother's favourite; his younger sister Isola, the 'pet of the house'. There was also in the background an older 'cousin', Henry Wilson—in reality one of his father's three illegitimate children by a previous relationship. Family life at the eighteenth-century house in Dublin's fashionable Merrion Square was cultured, convivial, and sometimes chaotic, with bailiffs at the door on at least one occasion because of his father's financial confusions. His father owned properties near Dublin and on the west coast of Ireland, but this did not count as landlordism, and he earned his living in charge of the St Mark's Hospital for Diseases of the Eye and Ear in Dublin, and from private practice. The Wildes entertained a wide circle of professional and literary friends and welcomed foreign visitors to Dublin. They were an extraordinary couple—he a small, thin, untidy man; she a tall, Junoesque figure, with her hair high on her head, and wearing flamboyant, low-cut gowns with trailing bows that were the fashion in the 1840s and 1850s. She was in fact the daughter of an obscure unsuccessful solicitor, but preferred to reinvent herself, claiming that her maiden name Elgee was a corruption of the name of the great Italian poet Dante Aligheri. She gave prominence in the hallway at Merrion Square to a plaster bust of Charles Maturin, the famous author of the romantic horror story, *Melmoth the Wanderer* and a distant relative by marriage. Oscar inherited his mother's compulsion to romantic self-invention, and her defiant imperviousness to the adversities of the moment.

In 1864, when Oscar was 9, his father received a knighthood from Queen Victoria for his work on the Irish census. That same year Bernard Mulrenin's portrait of his mother was unveiled at the Royal Hibernian Academy Exhibition. There were dinners and celebrations, yet behind the scenes a domestic scandal was about to break that threatened to damage the family's new social prestige. The year before, his mother had broken off relations with Mary Travers, who had been a female helper to the family from the time of Oscar's birth and was one of his father's patients. As his parents were being fêted with invitations, Mary Travers began a campaign to expose them. She alleged that William Wilde had taken advantage of her when Jane Wilde had been pregnant with Oscar, and that she had been chloroformed and raped two years earlier in his consulting-room at Merrion Square. When Wilde's mother wrote accusing her of trying to extort money, she issued a writ of libel claiming £2,000 in damages. The Wildes preferred to face publicity and the courts rather than pay. The sight of Speranza, the spirit of oppressed Ireland become ill-used wife, composed and coolly ironic in the witness box, proved unbeatable. Mary Travers was awarded a derisory one farthing in damages, with disgrace falling on her, not the Wildes.

Oscar and his elder brother Willie were not in Dublin at the time of the trial, having been sent as boarders at the beginning of the year to Portora Royal School near Enniskillen in northern Ireland. Founded 250 years earlier in the reign of James I, Portora in the Protestant north was the favoured school for the sons of Irish

Protestants in the Catholic south. It had strong links with Trinity College, Dublin, which provided examiners for the school's annual examinations. The teaching of history and geography was resolutely English and Unionist in emphasis, with set questions such as: 'Write a brief sketch of the progress of the English House of Commons from AD 1265 to 1509'; 'Name the British possessions in Further (Eastern) India'; or 'Give an account of the origin of Trial by Jury in England'.[2] Oscar was iconoclastic like his mother and was remembered by one of his fellow pupils declaring that he wished to go down to posterity as the defendant in a case of 'Regina versus Wilde' (Ellmann, p. 23). Gossip about his parents' own courtroom success may well have reached the school.

Three years after the trial, tragedy engulfed the whole family when his 8-year-old sister Isola died unexpectedly after a bout of fever. The doctor who attended her remembered Oscar's 'inconsolable grief' and long and frequent visits to his sister's grave.[3] The poem 'Requiescat' written many years later recalls the time of year and his sadness at her early death:

> Tread lightly, she is near
>   Under the snow,
> Speak gently, she can hear
>   The daisies grow.
>
>   . . .
>
> Coffin-board, heavy stone,
>   Lie on her breast,
> I vex my heart alone,
>   She is at rest.

During the long summer vacation, his mother took the two brothers to an exhibition in Paris to help them get over their sister's death. The sights of the brilliant capital with its crowded parks and boulevards made Dublin and Portora seem drab and provincial afterwards. Later, at Oxford, Wilde was amused by the nostalgia of his fellow students for their old schools. He felt no such sentiment for Portora, although it was at Portora that he developed a love of Greek literature and culture, ultimately winning a scholarship to Trinity College, Dublin in 1871.

At Trinity College, Wilde was protected from the rougher,

boisterous side of university life by John Pentland Mahaffy, a Greek classicist and historian, and colourful Dublin figure who promoted himself aggressively as 'that splendid breed of Mongrel, the Anglo-Irishman'.[4] Under Mahaffy's tutelage, Wilde developed as a Greek scholar and a young man of refined wit and conversation in an all-male community in which high-spirited wit was the order of the day. Amid sameness, individuality was all the more important. Wilde attracted notice as a devotee of the English aesthetic movement which was regarded with some ridicule as the avant-garde, 'alternative' life-style of its day. His favourite poet was Swinburne, whose paganism and republican zeal dazzled the youth of Wilde's generation. He also admired the artist-poet Dante Gabriel Rossetti, founder member of the Pre-Raphaelite Brotherhood, whose ideals of the complete artistic life made a stand against the crude materialism of the age. The cult of beauty and art dovetailed naturally with Wilde's love of Greek culture and civilization.

From the 1850s, the clergy and commissioners of education in Ireland had regarded the spread of the classics with suspicion mainly because of its explicitly sexual and homosexual content. In this climate, Mahaffy's rigorously historical account of *Social Life in Greece*, which Wilde helped to edit, was careful to emphasize the platonic, spiritual nature of attachments between men in ancient Greek culture. At this time, Wilde's aestheticism encouraged dangerous inclinations of a very different kind. Although the Wildes were resolutely Protestant, Wilde's mother had had the boys secretly baptized in the Catholic Church when they were children—in empathy, one imagines, with the majority Irish Catholic population. Wilde's father had turned a blind eye, but life at Merrion Square became uncomfortable when he discovered Oscar's attraction to Roman Catholic ceremonies and rituals. It seems to have been Mahaffy who suggested the idea of sending Oscar to Oxford. Anglican Oxford seemed preferable and safer than Dublin with its Catholic clergy and the Catholic University which John Henry Newman had helped to found in the year of Oscar's birth.

Wilde himself was drawn increasingly to England. The path to the 'mother country' had been a well-trodden one for Irish scholars and writers from the time of the early Protestant 'plantations' in the sixteenth and seventeenth centuries. The attraction, as for many in the former British colonies today, was the prospect of a larger stage and greater influence. Wilde's prospects of an academic career seemed more likely to be achieved in the larger world of Oxford. Yet for Wilde initially, the lure was towards a literary ideal of Oxford that stood for resistance to the utilitarian age, and was thus in harmony rather than at odds with his spiritual nationalism. The idea of Oxford as a 'city of dreaming spires', cloistered from the world, had been infused with fresh life in the mid-nineteenth century by poets and educational reformers such as Newman and Matthew Arnold, who saw in the disinterested spirit of university enquiry a moral and aesthetic antidote to the social and religious uncertainties of the times. Wilde was attracted to both thinkers. Newman's Catholic certainties and Arnold's aestheticized ethics acted as a moral counter-measure to Swinburne.

In June 1874, with his father's blessing, Wilde sailed from Dublin to sit an examination for a scholarship in classics (called a Demyship) at Magdalen College, Oxford. The conditions of the scholarships required candidates to be under 20 years of age. Wilde was just two months short of his twentieth birthday. Uncertain perhaps about his technical eligibility, and adopting his mother's cavalier attitude to the truth, he gave his age as two years younger, the average of the other candidates. With his three years of rigorous training in Greek at Trinity College, where he won the Berkeley Gold Medal for Greek, his success came as no great surprise. Wilde enrolled as an undergraduate at Magdalen College, Oxford on 17 October, the day after his twentieth birthday. This time, he registered his date of birth correctly, but questions about his true age would cause problems from that time on.

Oxford and Intellectual Influences

Although celebrated in poetry as 'the city of dreaming spires', Oxford in the 1870s was, and remains today, a place of cultural contradictions. The reforms brought about between the 1850s and 1870s had liberalized the university and diluted the influence of the aristocracy. The demand was for a university that would serve the whole nation, and this meant laicization, improved teaching provision, and the university opening its doors to the sons of the newly empowered commercial and industrial middle classes. Yet the call for competitive scholarships and written examinations based on principles of 'testable knowledge' remained at odds with the trad-itional goal of character formation and sociability that remained the stamp of an Oxford education.[5] Some of Wilde's Oxford friends foundered academically between these two conflicting value systems. That Wilde was so successful in satisfying both was due in large part to the intense classical training he had received at Trinity College. He followed his parents' example of combining hard work and soci-ability. Few were to witness the stolen hours of study that lay behind his appearance of effortless brilliance.

Wilde made an immediate impression at Oxford, with his tall figure, confident manner, and charming laughter. Oxford provided ample opportunities for pleasure and entertainment. For Wilde, the pleasure of Oxford was the absence of the coarseness that had marred life for him at Trinity College. The Encaenia, the yearly meeting of the university, was disrupted in 1874 and 1875 by dis-orderly undergraduates, but generally there was a revolt against stu-dent rowdiness and excessive drinking. Convivial Sunday evenings at Magdalen College included the gentler effects of tobacco and punch, along with music and philosophical talk.

A great deal of consideration has been given to Oscar Wilde's transformation of himself into an Englishman at Oxford. Yeats, a fellow Irishman, believed that by adopting the pose of an English-man, Wilde devised a clever strategy for challenging English preju-dices about the Irish. There is undoubtedly much truth in this. Yet Wilde's lifelong performance was actually that of an Oxonian, which meant a distinct feeling of cultural superiority to the rest of society. A characteristic sign of that superiority was 'the Oxford voice', mocked by D. H. Lawrence as 'so seductively self-effacingly depre-catingly superior'.[6] In his first year, Wilde developed his own lan-guid, melodic version of the intonations of his Oxford friends. In his case the attempt to conceal his origins did not involve the usual betrayal of family loyalties. 'The Irish accent is dreadful,' his mother wrote to him on his return to Oxford for his second year. 'I shudder at *Maurnin, Potric* (Morning, Patrick) . . . How refined *we* are . . .' [7]

In educational terms, that superiority also expressed itself in an adherence to the values of individual educators rather than to the values of society as a whole. Newman and Arnold had already left their mark on Wilde, Newman through his Christian aesthetics, Arnold by his literary evangelism and claims for the importance of

criticism. At Oxford, Wilde came under the influence of other eloquent and celebrated teachers. He studied under the comparative
philologist Friedrich Max Müller, who argued that the origins of
language and imagination were divine. He also attended lectures by
John Ruskin, the champion of the Pre-Raphaelites, who as Slade
Professor of Fine Art was inspiring undergraduates with his moral
vision of Florentine art and culture. Wilde's conscience was stirred
by Ruskin's ethical ideal of art. Later he was influenced by the writings of Walter Pater, then a Fellow of Brasenose College, and a
former disciple of Ruskin, whose preference for Renaissance over
medieval art made a deep emancipatory appeal to individualism,
non-conformity, and the sensuous life. In the notorious 'Conclusion'
to his study of *The Renaissance* (1873), later removed from the second edition out of fears that it would corrupt the young, Pater called
on the young men of his day to 'grasp at any exquisite passion' that
life offered them, and 'to burn always' with a 'hard gem-like flame'.[8]
Pater's *Renaissance* became Wilde's 'golden book' (Ellmann, p. 80).

These influences intensified Wilde's existing aesthetic tendencies.
In his first year at Oxford, he was initiated as a Mason of the Oxford
Apollo Lodge, and delighted in wearing the Masonic costume that
included the velvet knee breeches and silk hose he would later sport
on his lecture tour of America. Yet the aesthetic atmosphere of
Oxford also encouraged a renewed attraction to the Roman Catholic
ritual. The great anxiety at Oxford that had followed the defection to
Catholicism of John Henry Newman and his followers had long
since abated, but the attraction of Rome to young impressionable
minds still caused concern in the university. Wilde shocked the college authorities and his Irish relatives and friends when he published
some pro-Catholic poems in Irish Catholic journals. For Wilde's
Protestant connections and associates, the issue was largely a deep-
rooted resistance to certain aspects of Roman Catholic doctrine and
belief, particularly Papal infallibility; but for Wilde the issue was
essentially one of conscience, of the choice between a sensuous life
and the aesthetic sublimation that Roman Catholicism promised to
satisfy.

Wilde got a First Class in his first Oxford examination and was
suitably grand and celebratory; but behind the scenes, another crisis
loomed. In April 1876, just two months before his examination, his
father died, and the true state of his large debts and liabilities was

revealed. Unknown to the family, his father had taken out mortgages on all his properties during his last years of life, including £2,000 in June 1874, the month Oscar sat for the Demyship. Wilde's peace of mind was further disturbed when his 'cousin', Henry Wilson, died unexpectedly, leaving a will that disinherited him of all benefits from his father's properties in the event of his converting to Catholicism within five years. In a 'Confessional Album' entry at Magdalen in 1877, Wilde gave as his *bête noire* 'a thoroughly Irish Protestant'.[9] He wondered how a man could go before God 'with his wretched Protestant prejudices and bigotry clinging still to him' (*Letters*, p. 54).

Wilde suffered a crisis of confidence in his final years at Oxford. On the surface, he remained defiantly dandiacal. He caused a sensation when he attended the opening of the new Grosvenor Gallery in London in 1877 dressed in a reddish-bronze coat that he had designed in the shape of a cello. The gallery was intended as a showcase of the contemporary art scene, and included paintings by the Pre-Raphaelites and the American-born aesthete James McNeill Whistler's daringly impressionist 'symphonies in colour'. Wilde's review of the exhibition in the *Dublin University Magazine* was his first published critical article. In the battle between the aesthetes and the philistines for the soul of the university, he decorated his Magdalen rooms with blue vases filled with lilies—the recognized symbol of the Pre-Raphaelites—and created widespread mirth among junior and senior members of the university by declaring that he found it difficult to live up to the level of his blue china. He also entered for the university's prestigious Newdigate Poetry prize with an ornate loco-descriptive poem on the subject of Ravenna, which he had visited on his second trip to Italy the previous year.

Wilde's outward appearance gave no indication of the emotional turmoil within. His financial difficulties and Catholic inclinations, fear of doing badly in Finals, and the unlikelihood of obtaining an Oxford fellowship, all weighed heavily on him. On 14 April 1878, a week before Easter, he visited the Brompton Oratory in London, where he made a complete confession of his sins, and prepared to enter the Catholic Church. A confidential letter written by his confessor the following day refers to his 'positive sin' and earnest desire for a holy and pure life (Ellmann, p. 90). The exact nature of Wilde's 'positive sin' remains uncertain, but the source of shame and yearning for an integrity of soul in Wilde's early poetry is invariably sexual. Much of the acute sense of sin felt by the young men of Wilde's generation was associated with the shame attached to masturbation. 'Wasted Days', published a few months before his visit to the Brompton Oratory, is a poem of self-rebuke for wasted intellectual opportunities that are connected with unsatisfied sexual longings. The 'fair slim boy' of the poem is a kind of mirror self, his 'Red under-lip drawn in for fear of Love'. Wilde's writings are filled with images of implied unity, purity, and perfection—children, flowers, jewels, seraphic youths, and pure lily-like madonnas. On the day he was to be received into the Catholic Church, he sent to the Oratory a parcel containing a bunch of lilies, symbol of his continuing devotion to art and beauty in its sensuous as well as spiritual form. The poems that followed in a renewed creative burst express preference for England over Rome ('The Burden of Itys'), faith in humanity rather than in God ('Humanitad'), and joyous pantheism in which sin is seen as being a stage in evolution—'to feel is better than to know' ('Panthea'). His temporary crisis was over.

Wilde was always to remember Oxford as the 'most flower-like time' of his life (*Letters*, p. 1113). The announcement that he had won the Newdigate Prize was followed by a First in Schools. 'I should so like to see the smile on your face now,' his mother wrote from Dublin.[10] However, his Chancellor's Essay Prize submission, 'The Rise of Historical Criticism', failed to impress, and a fellowship continued to elude him. In spite of university reform, Oxford remained a monopoly of the Anglican Church, with clerical fellowships still the majority until 1882. Wilde's behaviour had not always endeared him to the university authorities, and there were others equally qualified. Wilde's answer was to take the message of his new aestheticism directly to society. He had already had some success in placing his poems and first critical reviews. Describing himself grandly in the roll of Oxford Men as 'professor of aesthetics and art critic', he left Oxford for London in 1879.[11] His aim in life, according to his 'Confessional Album' entry, was 'success—fame or even notoriety'.[12]

The Aesthete in the Market-place

Within three years of going down from Oxford, Wilde had become a household name on both sides of the Atlantic. While his celebrity undoubtedly owed much to his flamboyant style and personality, it was also paradigmatic of the kind of fame and notoriety that could be achieved in the new expanding commodity culture. In this the press played a crucial role. In the decades following the Great Exhibition of 1851, the abolition of taxes on knowledge and advertising produced a rapid and unparalleled increase in newspapers and magazines. At the same time, the production and underconsumption of new commodities initiated the modern techniques and practices of advertising. In the process, art was also commodified. The aestheticism that Wilde set out to disseminate was a mirror image of that 'profession of taste' to which the promotional images of commodity culture made appeal. The process also absorbed and assimilated the artist, turning the earlier image of the artist as hero and critic of society into the commodified image of the artist as colourful personality. Wilde's role as aesthete was doubly paradoxical, for not only did his aesthetic opposition to the market encourage the very acquisition of goods and status symbols that he aimed to criticize, but his own role was that of the successful professional who marketed his special knowledge of 'the aesthetic' to an appreciative and paying public.

Wilde's originality lay in the blatant self-consciousness with which he exploited the new methods of advertising in order to oppose the culture in which they were firmly taking root. The 'aesthete in the market-place' was one of the many contradictory roles that Wilde was to play in the course of his life with a sort of deeply earnest frivolity. Wilde's aesthetic, dandiacal pose has frequently been interpreted in psychological, sexual, and racial terms, but there is also a political dimension in its desired extension of a life of aristocratic taste and privilege to the whole of society. This was to be the force of Wilde's most advanced political statement in 'The Soul of Man under Socialism' at the beginning of the 1890s.

It was the social pretensions of the whole 'art for art's sake' movement, as much as the association of art and effeminacy, which inspired contemporary satires of the pretensions and perceived charlatanism of the aesthetes, most notably in George du Maurier's famous *Punch* cartoons of the poet Maudle (Wilde) in the early 1880s when Wilde was an energetic socialite. The mockery of du Maurier's 'Maudle on the Choice of a Profession' and 'Frustrated Social Ambition' was directed in part against the perceived loosening of the traditional basis of entry into fashionable society. English social and cultural class formations had never been impermeable, but the political and economic fusion of upper and middle classes in the mid- to late-Victorian age provided new opportunities for mobility. It was a permeability that helped Wilde to fashion his public image.

Perhaps the very oddness of Wilde's background resulted in his being in every coterie and belonging exclusively to none. In 1879 Wilde settled in London, sharing a flat in Tite Street, Chelsea with his Oxford friend, Frank Miles, a Turner Prize winner. His Oxford credentials resulted in invitations into journalistic circles, while through Miles he was introduced to Whistler, a Tite Street neighbour, whose paintings he had praised in his review of the Grosvenor Gallery exhibition. He mixed with celebrities such as Lillie Langtry, the 'Jersey Lily' of John Millais's famous painting, through whom he came into contact with the world of the theatre and the fashionable set that surrounded the Prince of Wales. To his Fleet Street contacts, he was the scholar and Newdigate poet; to Whistler, a disciple; to the fast set, a man of brilliance and unconventional opinions; and to the wider public, an apostle of the aesthetes who mixed with fashionable society. His visibility is evident in William Powell Frith's painting of the Royal Academy Private View in 1881, where he dominates the crowd, and in the proliferation of images and cartoons of him in the popular press. In all this, Wilde's projected persona was that of the 'success story'. Only a few, such as the Polish actress Helena Modjeska, a stranger to London, cast a glance at his objective achievement. Few knew of the increasingly desperate financial pressures that motivated his public performance.

Wilde attained the height of notoriety with the success in 1881 of Gilbert and Sullivan's comic operetta, *Patience, or Bunthorne's Bride*, which sent up the look and manner of the aesthete in the character of Bunthorne. In the second act, the chorus sings in mock praise of the

> . . . most intense young man,
>   A soulful-eyed young man,
> An ultra-poetical, super-aesthetical,
>   Out-of-the way young man![13]

On the show's transfer to New York, Richard D'Oyly Carte, the theatrical impresario and the show's producer, promptly offered Wilde a series of promotional lectures to provide American audiences with a chance to see the real-life Bunthorne. Wilde's main

MAUDLE ON THE CHOICE OF A PROFESSION.

Maudle. "How CONSUM-MATELY LOVELY YOUR SON IS, MRS. BROWN!"

Mrs. Brown (a Philistine from the country). "WHAT? HE'S A *NICE, MANLY* BOY, IF YOU MEAN THAT, MR. MAUDLE. HE HAS JUST LEFT SCHOOL, YOU KNOW, AND WISHES TO BE AN ARTIST."

Maudle. "WHY SHOULD HE BE AN ARTIST?"

Mrs. Brown. "WELL, HE MUST BE *SOMETHING*!"

Maudle. "WHY SHOULD HE *BE* ANYTHING? WHY NOT LET HIM REMAIN FOREVER CONTENT TO *EXIST BEAUTIFULLY*?"

[*Mrs. Brown determines that at all events her Son shall not study Art under Maudle.*

'Maudle on the Choice of a Profession'. Cartoon by George du Maurier from *Punch*, 1881.

'A Private View at the Royal Academy' by William Powell Frith, 1881. Wilde is easily recognizable among a crowd of other distinguished Victorians.

ambition at the time was to succeed as a playwright, but having had his political costume drama, *Vera: or The Nihilists*, turned down by a succession of leading actresses, he accepted the D'Oyly Carte offer. On Christmas Eve 1881, at the age of 27, he set sail for New York on the SS *Arizona*.

Wilde was later to declare that the two great turning-points in his life were when his father sent him to Oxford, and when society sent him to prison; but his American lecture tour can be seen to mark an equally decisive turning-point in his life. It established a pattern of restless, nomadic existence that, with the exception of a few brief years of domesticity, he was never afterwards to break. From the moment the SS *Arizona* docked at New York he was besieged by reporters, and his sayings became headline news. Wherever he went he was interviewed, photographed, and sketched. American journal-ism had already adopted the personal, popular style of 'new journal-ism' that was only then emerging in England, and liked to feature celebrities in unusual, dramatic settings. Thus we have images of Wilde on board his transatlantic liner; Wilde being taken across the Delaware river for a private meeting with America's greatest living poet, Walt Whitman, in his 'den'; and Wilde in Leadsville in the Rocky Mountains, descending the silver-mine to converse with the miners. He created excitement and curiosity by appearing before his audiences in a spectacularly feminine manner of dress, sporting vel-vet breeches, silk hose, and quilted jacket, and with long flowing hair. Responses ranged from appreciation to laughter, with one ribald cartoon showing Wilde with simian features gazing at a sunflower with the caption, 'The Aesthetic Monkey' (see page 70).[14] Wilde appeared to thrive in the atmosphere that was part vaudeville, part lecture theatre, and betrayed none of that self-loathing which George Bernard Shaw later confessed was the effect of prolonged public exposure. Wilde enjoyed being treated like a 'Royal Boy' (*Let-ters*, p. 126). His was a hotel existence of the celebrity on the road, with its adulation and hangers-on, its excitements and boredom, and its casual pleasures and encounters. The tour, which was originally scheduled to take in a handful of venues, was extended by an extraordinary ten months that saw Wilde zigzag his way across the American continent.

At the beginning of the tour, he had prepared only one lecture, 'The English Renaissance of Art', which drew inspiration from

Ruskin and Pater in advocating the artistic spirit as the only effective means of improving the social and moral life of contemporary industrial civilization. In an attempt to appeal directly to Americans, who already enjoyed a developed consumerist taste for aesthetic design and household decoration, Wilde added two more lectures, 'The Decorative Arts' and 'The House Beautiful', the latter being Pater's phrase to describe those who treat life in the spirit of art. 'Today more than ever the artist and a love of the beautiful are needed to temper and counteract the sordid materialism of the age,' he told his audiences. Wilde's American tour was followed with intense interest by the British press. Success, especially financial success, caused resentment as well as admiration. 'They all say you are making heaps of money, and I smile and accept the notion—for it galls the Londoners,' his mother wrote.[15]

One consequence of his American tour was a reminder that he was 'Speranza's son'. Challenged by expatriate Irish-Americans to justify his claims for an 'English Renaissance' while tyranny threatened his native land, Wilde responded by declaring himself a 'thorough republican' and predicting the revival of Irish art and poetry with the coming of independence (Ellmann, p. 186). Events in Ireland had taken a violent turn with the insurrection of the newly formed Irish Land League, and the imprisonment of Charles Stewart Parnell, the leader of the Irish Home Rule Party. On 6 May 1882 a previously unknown terrorist group, the Invincibles, assassinated the new Chief Secretary for Ireland, Lord Frederick Cavendish, and his Under-Secretary as they walked across Phoenix Park, Dublin. Asked by an American reporter for a response, Wilde replied that England was 'reaping the fruit of seven centuries of injustice' (Ellmann, p. 186). His statement challenged the press statement of the former Chief Secretary for Ireland who blamed Parnell for sowing 'the seed of which this is the fruit'.[16] It was also a version of Irish history created by John Mitchel, an American exile of the Young Ireland movement, and a friend of his mother. Yet Wilde still remained an apologist for empire, and told an audience in the South: 'I do not wish to see the empire dismembered, but only to see the Irish people free, and Ireland still as a willing and integral part of the British Empire.'[17] His support was never for national hatreds which he condemned in 'The House Beautiful' as 'always strongest where culture is lowest'.

Wilde's broad international instincts took him to Paris almost immediately after his return to Europe. There among the French Symbolist artists and poets who gathered around Stéphane Mallarmé and Paul Verlaine, he encountered a more political, theoretically conscious avant-garde than existed in England at that time. The English aesthetic movement was not lacking in historical or social awareness; yet the tradition of English cultural criticism to which he had attached himself was effectively cut off from any genuinely political movement, and indeed often opposed 'mere politics' and theory. By contrast, the 'Symbolists', designated more broadly in their day as 'Decadents', formulated an artistic credo founded upon dreams and intense emotional states that united romantic symbolism with anarchist political aims. The Decadents regarded Charles Baudelaire and Théophile Gautier as the precursors of the movement. Philosophically, the guiding spirit of the movement was Hegel, but it was Hegel reformulated to establish romantic art and individualism in a crucial critical and dialectical role in the onward march of mind. The circles with which Wilde associated were not simply attempting to establish an alternative to the dominance of French bourgeois realism; they were also aligning themselves with resistance to all systems and dogmas in the cause of human spiritual progress. Wilde had already assimilated French influences through Pater, but he began to display more openly than Pater an indebtedness to French Symbolist traditions. In the creative decade that followed, Wilde set out to fuse and develop both traditions in the direction of an English aesthetic avant-garde with himself at the head.

In Paris, Wilde was fond of quoting one of the founding theorists of the anarchist movement, Pierre-Joseph Proudhon's '*La propriété, c'est le vol*' ('property is theft') (Ellmann, p. 205). His own unhappy experience as an Irish landlord gave personal force to his revised version of this, 'Property is simply a nuisance,' in his essay 'The Soul of Man under Socialism' (published in book form as *The Soul of Man* at the time of his trial). Wilde would later describe himself to an English interviewer as 'more than a Socialist . . . something of an Anarchist' (Ellmann, p. 273). To a French journalist, he declared himself with less reserve to be no longer a poet and despot, but an artist and anarchist.[18] To signal his new identity, Wilde dressed in the standard silk hat and black overcoat of the Frenchman of the period, and had his hair cut short in the style of the Emperor Nero. 'The Oscar of the first period is dead,' he said, in response to those who commented on his abandonment of his American costume. 'We are now concerned with the Oscar Wilde of the second period, who has nothing whatever in common with the gentleman who wore long hair and carried a sunflower down Piccadilly' (Ellmann, p. 208).

The Creator of Dorian Gray

Back in England, Wilde's life took several directions: a lecture tour of Britain (1883–5); marriage in 1884 to Constance Lloyd, the granddaughter of a wealthy London QC; the birth of his two sons; and editorship of a Cassells monthly magazine, the *Woman's World* (1887–9). Wilde's reasons for marrying were in part conventional, in part emotional. He was sexually experienced, but his comment to his friend Robert Harborough Sherard after a night spent with a well-known Parisian prostitute, 'What beasts we are, Robert,' suggests his disquiet. In his poem 'The Harlot's House', love 'in the house of lust' is pictured as a grotesque, mechanical coupling of marionettes. Writing to Lillie Langtry to break the news of his engagement, Wilde described his future wife admiringly as 'a grave, slight, violet-eyed Artemis, with . . . wonderful ivory hands' (*Letters*, p. 224). Marriage for Wilde was a new aesthetic experience.

During the years between 1885 and 1890, Wilde produced all of his major essays and fictions. The main event which spurred him to this burst of creative activity was a public quarrel with Whistler. Wilde had already crossed swords on several occasions with Whistler, who liked to keep his disciples in their place. Whistler believed that Wilde's reputation was based on plagiarism of his ideas, and in 1885 he decided to give a lecture at the unheard-of time of ten o'clock in the evening to discredit him. Adopting a mock-biblical lecturing style, Whistler left the audience of his famous 'Ten O'Clock' lecture in no doubt as to the identity of the 'unattached writer . . . the middleman' who had come before the public as a false arbiter of artistic value and taste.[19] Anxious to correct Wilde's 'complete misunderstanding' of his principles of art, he disagreed with Wilde that artistic and social renewal and decay were linked, claiming instead art's indifference to social change or improvement. For Whistler, life and nature simply provided the subject matter for art, and the painter's mission was to find beauty, even in ugliness.

Wilde's prompt reply was published the next day. A series of sharp witty exchanges between the two in the press became the subject of public merriment and debate. On the role of art in life, Wilde's belief that, 'Art is made for life, not life for art' emphasized art's engagement in the real world.[20] For Wilde, beauty existed not as a museum exhibit, but as an active force in life. His disagreement with Whistler that 'only an artist could be a judge of art' found its fullest expression in his dialogue 'The Critic as Artist', which appeared in the liberal periodical, the *Nineteenth Century*, in 1890. 'Art does not address itself to the specialist,' Wilde wrote. 'Indeed, so far from being true that the artist is the best judge of art, a really great artist can never judge of other people's work at all, and can hardly, in fact, judge of his own.' In his high claims for criticism in 'The Critic as Artist', Wilde acknowleged his debt to Matthew Arnold and to the example of Ruskin and Pater, but his complete rejection of the distinction between art and criticism—a claim for criticism as an art form in itself and art as a form of criticism—overturned both Whistler's and Arnold's privileging of the creative over the critical spirit. In this Wilde took his bearings from Baudelaire and the French Symbolists who maintained art's primacy in the unfolding of the critical world spirit. Wilde's aesthetic ideal called for a new kind of reader, one who would look beyond the work of art as a mere reflection of the writer's life or opinions or of existing morality. This is his recurrent refrain in his correspondence through the late 1880s.

Wilde enjoyed a settled home life during the first two years of marriage. He took a lease on a house in Tite Street and had it colourfully redesigned and decorated by E. W. Godwin, one of the leading designers of the aesthetic movement. His two sons were born there, Cyril in June 1885, and Vyvyan seventeen months later in November 1886. Like many Victorian literary celebrities, Wilde also had an adoring circle of young male admirers and disciples. Wilde's ideal male relationship was that of affection and admiration between an older and a younger man. In his *Republic*, Plato has Socrates venerate male attractions and liaisons but condemn them being taken to the point of intercourse or orgasm. Within the conventions of Greek love the older man was expected to be strongly attracted to the young man's beauty and to court him with gifts, while the young man was expected to admire the older man as his model of wisdom and culture. The philosophical quest was for the Form of Beauty or the Good. Wilde's friendship, according to the French poet André Gide, was a form of spiritual domination that often left his admirers feeling exhilarated and imperilled (Ellmann, pp. 333–41). Wilde formed intense friendships of this kind—with Robert Sherard in Paris, and Sherard's friend and New College contemporary John Barlas, described by those who knew him as looking 'like a Greek statue'.[21] Then in 1886, during Constance's pregnancy, there was Robert Ross, the 17-year-old son of a former Canadian Attorney-General who came to stay at Tite Street for several months before going up to Cambridge. Shortly before or soon after the birth of Vyvyan—the most likely date is October 1886—Ross initiated Wilde into homosexual acts for the first time. Inspired by his relationship and conversations with Ross, Wilde wrote his part-essay, part-story, 'The Portrait of Mr W. H.', which sets out to prove that Shakespeare's artistic genius flowered because of his love for a boy-actor.

Wilde and Constance did not resume sexual relations after the birth of their second son. This would not have been entirely unusual, either on grounds of health or economy. Sexual abstinence was a commonly accepted method of avoiding unwanted pregnancy in middle-class Victorian marriages. There would have been no need for him to invent so lurid an explanation as the recurrence of syphilis, as some biographers have speculated. In a letter to her brother Otho dated August 1887, Constance reassured him that 'Oscar and I are very happy together now'.[22] That summer was one of fancy dress balls and fashionable 'at homes' to celebrate Queen Victoria's Golden Jubilee. The warmth and loyalty of the event covered deep social and political tensions following the defeat of the Home Rule Bill in the previous year. Wilde was himself by then leading a double life.

The Picture of Dorian Gray, Wilde's most famous story, owes something to his new way of life. In 1889, he became intimate with John Gray, a carpenter's son who had worked his way up to become a library clerk at the foreign office. A protégé of the Symbolist art couple Charles Ricketts and Charles Shannon, who formed the centre of a bohemian circle of 'Valistes' (Wilde's word) at Whistler's old home, the Vale, Chelsea, Gray was the alleged model for Wilde's Dorian Gray. John Gray contributed a francophile article on the Goncourt brothers to the first number of their coterie magazine, the *Dial*, in August 1889. Wilde visited the Vale after being sent a copy. Significantly, Dorian Gray first meets the Wilde-figure Lord Henry

Wotton in the studio of the artist, Basil Hallward. Wotton, in working his will on Dorian, finds 'something terribly enthralling in the exercise of influence' (ch. III). Wilde himself did much to influence John Gray's career, suggesting him as a speaker at the Playgoers' Club, and arranging to pay for the publication of his first book of poems, *Silverpoints*, to be designed by Ricketts and Shannon. Their relationship coincided with the coming of the 'New Hedonism' in the 1890s, and a new spirit of artistic experiment and freedom of thought that sent a tremor of fear through the heart of the establishment.

There were many in London during the 1890s who would deny anything particularly dangerous about the period; but the feeling of collective defection and a new spirit of modernity among the young at the time was real enough. Urban convergence and technical development saw the emergence not only of popular culture, but also of specialized markets and coteries. Wilde was the presiding spirit of this emerging new culture in the 1880s and 1890s. He lent the force of his presence to a number of budding literary and artistic coteries such as the gathering of Celts at the Rhymers' Club whose membership was swelled by his young Oxford friends and admirers. He also nurtured the personalities and talents of the younger men who helped define the style of the period: Richard Le Gallienne, who as 'Logroller', became the chief publicist of younger poets in the review columns of the *Star* and the *Daily Chronicle*; Aubrey Beardsley whose artistic style more than any other defined the period; Max Beerbohm, as caricaturist and wit; and W. B. Yeats and George Bernard Shaw, who followed Wilde's example in trumpeting the Celtic school of literature. The mood or movement to which they gave expression combined a devotion to artifice with a part-earnest, and at times part-facetious defiance of conventional middle-class attitudes and morality. *The Picture of Dorian Gray* was recognized as an expression of the new hedonism.

The story outraged English critics, who saw it as a dangerous, French-inspired work aimed at corrupting the nation's youth. Gossip about Wilde's flaunted effeminacy of dress and mannerism had already begun to circulate. The Criminal Law Amendment Act of 1885 outlawing homosexual acts between men had resulted in several scandals and prosecutions. Public fears about the threat of immorality; suspicion of foreign influences; hatred of the Irish: the forces that would combine to send Wilde to prison five years later were gathering momentum. Professional resentment and abuse were also in the air, fuelled by Whistler's mischievous accusations of plagiarism. It was no longer possible, as in the early days of the Maudle cartoons and the lecture tours, to laugh the Wilde phenomenon away.

Theatrical Success

Wilde's greatest ambition—to succeed as a playwright—remained unfulfilled. Until 1892 he had not enjoyed much luck in the theatre. *Vera* had flopped in New York in 1883, and English actor-managers failed to show interest in his gloomy costume drama, *The Duchess of Padua*, which under the title *Guido Ferranti* had a brief, unsuccessful run in New York in January 1891. Wilde's breakthrough came when the English actor-manager George Alexander commissioned him to write an original society drama to open his first season as manager of the newly acquired St James's Theatre. Alexander hoped that Wilde's name on the hoardings would attract the smart set. Wilde missed the deadline, but *Lady Windermere's Fan* finally opened at the St James's on 20 February 1892. To first-night cheers and calls for the author, Wilde delighted and outraged the audience in equal measure when he went to the front of the stage smoking a cigarette and congratulated them on having liked the play almost as much as he did himself. Wilde followed *Lady Windermere's Fan* with three other triumphant box-office successes in as many years—*A Woman of No Importance*, *An Ideal Husband*, and *The Importance of Being Earnest*.

Wilde collaborated closely with actor-managers in the design, costume-colour, and arrangement of his plays. Yet, although willing to make concessions to the actors and the public, he argued, in 'The Truth of Masks', that 'a really artistic production should bear the impress of . . . one master only'. His claims for artistic control caused conflict, particularly on the eve of his first play when his comments were printed in a newspaper interview under the headline 'The Poet and the Puppets'. His declaration that 'The stage is only a frame furnished with a set of puppets', appeared to belittle the acting profession (Ellmann, p. 349). Before his theatrical success in the 1890s, Wilde was convinced that English theatre audiences were becoming more appreciative of the subtler elements of performance. His controversial curtain-speech, after the successful first performance, might suggest uncertain relief rather than mockery of the audience, as some supposed at the time. Reviews of his plays that applauded their wit while proclaiming their likeness to the formulaic Parisian melodramas of Victorien Sardou and his English imitators could hardly have pleased him.

Wilde insisted that the only dramatists of his century who interested him were Victor Hugo and Maurice Maeterlinck. Both sought a total 'illusionist stage effect'. Wilde's own plays created a mirror of the fashionable world of his time. Artistically, his aim was not simply to flatter or correct, but to create a critical awareness in the audience through the interplay of seemingly opposing attitudes and styles. In this, Wilde rated Ibsen and Shaw as his nearest rivals. Significantly, the first production of *A Woman of No Importance*—on the face of it the most morally conventional of Wilde's plays— caused the greatest perplexity. The play appeared to show the defeat of old-style patrician values, represented by the seducer, Lord Illingworth (Herbert Beerbohm Tree), by the new puritan middle classes represented by the abandoned mother, Mrs Arbuthnot (Mrs Bernard Beere). Yet some who saw the original production were as disturbed by the sensuous appeal of Mrs Bernard Beere's black velvet gown as they were moved by Herbert Beerbohm Tree's suggestion of the patrician's uncomfortable self-recognition. In Wilde's society plays, both the frivolously comic and the morally earnest are alike revealed as merely masks and surfaces that hint at an unconscious world of human feeling beneath.

Such artistic polarization and codification of complex and finally inadequate forms of feeling is consistent with Wilde's Symbolist aesthetics. Yet, disappointingly for Wilde, his plans to stage his Symbolist, Maeterlinck-inspired drama, *Salome*, in 1892 with designs by Charles Ricketts, and with the French actress Sarah Bernhardt in the title role, had to be abandoned. *Salome* was already in rehearsal when it fell foul of the Censor on the grounds that it contained biblical characters. Wilde denounced 'the narrowness of artistic judgement' in England, and on this occasion defiantly declared, 'I am not English. I am Irish which is quite another thing (Ellmann, p. 352).' In artistic matters, Wilde consistently identified himself with a new 'Celtic school' of literature.

After the success of *Lady Windermere's Fan*, Wilde never returned to a settled home life, preferring to rent out-of-town houses to write his plays. In 1892, after a rest cure at Bad Homburg, he spent the autumn months at a rented farm in Norfolk, writing *A Woman of No Importance*, before moving for the winter to Babbacombe Cliff, near Bournemouth. The following summer he took a house called 'The Cottage' at Goring-on-Thames where he began *An Ideal Husband*, completing it in rented rooms at St James's Place in London. This restless, nomadic existence continued throughout 1894 with periods at Brighton, and trips to Paris and Florence, followed by a stay during August and September at a sea-front house at Worthing, where he wrote his most famous play, *The Importance of Being Earnest*. Even when in town, Wilde preferred to live in hotels, to be near the theatre.

His life of freedom became a strain on his marriage as well as his pocket. As early as 1891, at a garden party at Wilton, Constance appeared to one of the guests to be 'very mad' and 'very miserable', and later that year, during a prolonged absence in Paris, Wilde's mother wrote to him urging him to return home.[23] 'Constance would like you back. She is very lonely,' she wrote.[24] His mother's pleadings went unheeded. A new love had entered Wilde's life.

Wilde had first been introduced to Lord Alfred Douglas in May 1891 by the Oxford undergraduate and poet, Lionel Johnson. Both were among the young Oxford admirers of *The Picture of Dorian Gray*. Douglas, known as 'Bosie' to his family and friends, soon displaced John Gray as Wilde's constant companion, accompanying him to Bad Homburg in 1892, and joining him afterwards at his rented farm in Norfolk. Constance did not suspect their homosexual relationship and treated him as a friend of the family. On being told that Douglas was ill, she offered to come over to Norfolk to look after him. Photographs taken at the farmhouse show Wilde immaculately dressed, pictured cigarette in hand with Constance and Cyril in the garden, posing for the camera like a man who knows how to get through the formalities.

Douglas was later to claim that he was a relative sexual innocent until Wilde seduced him, but the evidence suggests that it was he who tempted Wilde into the dangerous world of pimps, black-mailers, and rent boys. Wilde's relentless quest for casual homo-sexual encounters intensified when he took rooms with Douglas at the Savoy Hotel ahead of rehearsals for *A Woman of No Importance*. He described the feeling later in *De Profundis* as being 'like feasting with panthers. The danger was half the excitement.' In his earlier homosexual affairs, Wilde enjoyed the feeling of influencing and taking possession of a younger man's soul. With Douglas he felt that it was he who was losing his soul. For all his youth, Douglas, an atheist and would-be aristocratic rebel, seemed to have no soul to lose. In marrying, Wilde's mother felt she had sacrificed her bright, vivid nature to his father's nervous, hypochondriacal moods when he was away from the public limelight. In Wilde's later record of his relation with Douglas, he too cast himself in the role of suffering, self-sacrificing victim to Douglas's moods. Their relationship would ultimately lead to Wilde's imprisonment for his homosexuality, and humiliating bankruptcy. Wilde owed £6,000 at the time of his arrest.

During the spring and summer of 1893, with *A Woman of No Importance* attracting crowded houses, Wilde played host and king to his inner circle of Reggie Turner, Robert Ross, Aubrey Beardsley, and Douglas. Through Alfred Taylor, an ex-public schoolboy and pimp, he was also introduced to a widening ring of rent boys who ministered to him in exchange for money, dinners, and presents of his expensive breast-pins and cigarette cases. Wilde's brother Willie believed that he had surrounded himself 'with a gang of parasites'.[25] Even the imperturbable Max Beerbohm was repelled when he saw 'the Divinity' (his nickname for Wilde), overweight and drinking heavily surrounded by his circle of flatterers and hangers-on.[26] The French poet Pierre Louÿs broke off relations with Wilde after seeing Wilde and Douglas together at the Savoy and being present there one morning when Constance brought Wilde his post and pleaded with him in tears to come home.

Wilde tried on several occasions to break with Douglas. They were separated for several months in 1894 when, on Wilde's advice, Douglas's mother, Lady Queensberry, arranged for Bosie to go abroad, to Egypt. The affair resumed when Douglas wrote to Constance begging her to intercede for him. The pair were reunited in Paris that spring, returning together with a box of French and Algerian toy soldiers for Cyril and Vyvyan.

By then, their relationship threatened to become a public scandal. Wilde had already narrowly escaped a scandal in October 1893 when the father of a 17-year-old schoolboy, who had slept with Ross, Douglas, and Wilde in turn, threatened litigation. The matter was hushed up, but both Ross and Douglas had to leave the country temporarily. The police had also begun to keep a close surveillance on the rent boys and pimps who cruised and picked up clients at the Alhambra and Pavilion music-halls, the notorious St James's bar, and the skating rink at Knightsbridge. On Sunday, 12 August 1894 two with whom Wilde happened to have associated were taken into custody following a raid on a drag party in Fitzroy Street—Alfred Taylor, who would later take his place beside Wilde in the dock, and Charley Parker, whose speciality was blackmailing his gentlemen clients. Wilde had himself paid blackmail money for the return of a letter he had written to Douglas containing the sentence, 'it is a marvel that those red rose-leaf lips of yours should have been made no less for music of song than for madness of kisses' (*Letters*, p. 544).

The greatest threat to Wilde came from Douglas's father, the belligerent, litigious ninth Marquess of Queensberry, cyclist, climber, and founder of the rules of boxing. Queensberry blamed Wilde for his son's failure to sit for his Oxford degree in June 1893. On seeing them reunited after Bosie's return from Cairo, Queensberry declared open war against 'the most loathsome and disgusting relationship' (Ellmann, p. 394). His loathing of 'Queers' had intensified to fever pitch when his eldest son Drumlanrig died in a shooting accident amid rumours of a homosexual relationship with the Foreign Secretary, Lord Rosebery. The grieving Queensberry's threats and insults became more violent and intemperate. The worst incident occurred when he turned up unannounced at Wilde's house with a prize-fighter. In an ugly scene, he accused Wilde of being a queer and threatened to thrash him if he saw him again in public with his son. Two weeks later, the police had to be called when the 'Scarlet Marquess', as Wilde now dubbed him, threatened to disrupt the first performance of *The Importance of Being Earnest*. Blocked from entering, Queensberry left a bouquet of vegetables for Wilde at the stage door.

Wilde considered taking out a libel action against him. On 28 February 1895 he received a letter from his solicitor, Charles Humphreys, advising him against prosecuting Queensberry for his threats and insulting conduct, on the grounds that George

Alexander and the staff at the St James's Theatre refused to give evidence about Queensberry's fracas at the theatre. That same day, Wilde stopped in at his club, the Albemarle, and was handed Queensberry's card by the hall porter. It had been left there ten days earlier. The handwriting and a misspelling meant that the message was difficult to make out, but that an insult was intended was clear. Deciphered it read: 'To Oscar Wilde, posing somdomite [*sic*].' That evening Wilde consulted Robert Ross who urged him not to do anything, but at his solicitor's office the next day, goaded by Douglas, Wilde decided he had no choice but to prosecute. He went immediately to Marlborough Street police station with Humphreys and Douglas and swore out a warrant for Queensberry's arrest on a charge of publishing a libel against him.

When the case was finally heard in a packed Old Bailey courtroom on 3 April, Wilde found that he and not Queensberry was on trial. In drawing up his Plea of Justification, Queensberry's defence named ten boys whom Wilde had solicited to commit sodomy, adding two counts relating to the corrupting influence of his writings. Initially Wilde stood his ground in the witness box, vigorously defending his writings against the charge of immorality; but Edward Carson, the cross-examiner for the defence, began doggedly to interrogate him about his alleged homosexuality. At the start of the trial, Wilde's age had been given falsely as 38. Carson, an old classmate from his Trinity College days, made much of this, forcing Wilde to admit that he was in fact 40, thus establishing the case for the defence that Queensberry had acted as any responsible father would to protect his son against a predatory older man.

Wilde was not in court on the third day of the trial, and Sir Edward Clarke, his counsel, indicated their intention to abandon the case before the witnesses were called. Clarke failed to prevent Queensberry being found 'not guilty' on all the counts itemized in his Plea of Justification, which meant that Wilde could now be prosecuted for sodomy. There were cheers in court. At five o'clock that evening a warrant was signed for Wilde's arrest on charges of 'committing acts of gross indecency'. Wilde had taken refuge that day at the Cadogan Hotel with Robert Ross and Reggie Turner who urged him to take the train to Dover and a boat for France. In shock at home, Constance pleaded that he leave the country before the warrant was served. Many reasons have been given for why he did not, then or later. There is no reason to doubt Wilde's own explanation in a letter to Douglas: 'I did not want to be called a coward or a deserter. A false name, a disguise, a hunted life, all that is not for me (*Letters*, p. 652).'

Prison, Exile, and Last Writings

In the trial that followed, the witnesses from the libel action did this time take the stand to testify against Wilde, having been kept at a police house and been offered money and immunity from prosecution. One who refused to 'turn grass', Alfred Taylor, joined Wilde in the dock. The details were unsavoury. Asked sarcastically by the chief cross-examiner to explain to the court the meaning of the phrase 'the Love that dare not speak its name', from a homosexual poem written by Douglas, Wilde temporarily recovered his resolve. His eloquent speech, explaining the nature of love between an older and a younger man, was greeted with a tremendous burst of applause from the gallery. 'It is beautiful, it is fine, it is the noblest form of affection. There is nothing unnatural about it,' he declared. Max Beerbohm, who was at court each day, recalled feelings of anger at 'having to pass through a knot of renters . . . who were allowed to hang around after giving their evidence and to wink at likely persons' (Ellmann, p. 437).

At the end of the trial, the jury failed to reach a verdict, and a new trial was ordered. Wilde was allowed bail but could not return to Tite Street. By claiming the £600 costs for Wilde's libel action, Queensberry had forced a sale of Wilde's possessions. The bailiffs moved in, and Tite Street was looted and vandalized, with the panelling stripped from the walls, and all the family possessions sold in bundles at knock-down prices: first editions of his father's books, the Newdigate Prize bust, even the box of toy soldiers he and Douglas had brought back from Paris for the children.

Wilde's second trial opened on 22 May. The verdict was this time a foregone conclusion. On 25 May Wilde was sentenced to the harsh term of two years in prison with hard labour. Some sections of the press gloated on his misfortune. A leading article in William Henley's *National Observer* expressed a 'deep debt of gratitude to the Marquess of Queensberry for destroying the High Priest of the Decadents . . . the obscene imposter, whose prominence has been a social outrage ever since he transferred from Trinity College, Dublin to Oxford his vices, his follies, and his vanities.'[27]

Many at the time considered Wilde to be a scapegoat of the Liberal establishment. The name of Rosebery and other prominent figures had come up in the course of the trial, and with an election looming, some felt a conviction had been secured to appease public outrage. Others like Yeats regarded Wilde as a victim of irrationality complicated by 'the Britisher's jealousy of art and the artist'.[28] For Charles Ricketts who suffered persecution and stress by association, Wilde's imprisonment was a 'tragic event, in which the fibre of the nation seemed of poor quality'.[29] For the prisoner himself what followed was a modern-day 'stations of the cross'. At Pentonville prison, he was put on the treadmill for six hours a day, and made to sleep on a plank bed. Sanitary arrangements consisted of a small tin vessel that the prisoner emptied three times a day. In November, handcuffed and in convict's dress, he was jeered and spat at on the platform of Clapham Station as he waited under guard for the train to transfer him to Reading Gaol. Three months later, having had little contact with the outside world, he received a visit from Constance, who had been living abroad with the boys under the name Holland. Notified by Willie, she had travelled from Italy to be the one to break the terrible news to him in person. His mother was dead. The authorities had refused her dying request that her son be allowed out of prison to visit her. In the concluding passages of 'The Soul of Man under Socialism', Wilde connects Christ's acceptance of pain to the realization of perfection, but qualifies this by adding: 'It has reference to wrong, unhealthy, unjust surroundings. When the wrong, and the disease, and the injustice are removed, it will have no further place.'

Although Wilde always flaunted a feminized side and was sometimes indiscreet, he generally sought to conceal his homosexual liaisons. Before his trial and imprisonment, he was far from being the champion of sexual freedom that history has sometimes made him. His contributions to homosexual undergraduate magazines, to the *Spirit Lamp*, edited by Douglas in 1892, and its successor the *Chameleon*, would have gone unnoticed in the larger world if he had not persisted in his libel charge against Queensberry. He and his entourage wore green carnations to the first nights of his plays, the secret badge of French homosexual circles, but its true significance was not universally understood. On one occasion, at the height of his homosexual life-style in 1893, he fled in fear to France to escape, as he records in *De Profundis*, 'the impossible, terrible, utterly wrong state my life had got into'. Wilde's sexual openness and militancy really began in the last days of his imprisonment.

In his final year at Reading Gaol, Wilde was allowed books and writing materials. Between January and March 1897 he wrote the confessional letter to Alfred Douglas that became known as *De Profundis*. In it, he justified his sins as a source of evolutionary development, and accepted suffering as the means to the fulfilment of the complete individual. Douglas's situation is contrasted to his own. 'To you,' he told Douglas,

the Unseen Powers have been very good. They have permitted you to see the strange and tragic shapes of Life as one sees shadows in a crystal. The head of Medusa that turns living men to stone, you have been allowed to look at in a mirror merely. You yourself have walked free among the flowers. From me the beautiful world of colour and motion has been taken away.

On 18 May, Wilde walked free from Reading Gaol. He left the next day for France, travelling incognito under the name of Mr Sebastian Melmoth, after the name of his favourite martyr, St Sebastian, and the cursed wanderer of his great-uncle's horror story, *Melmoth the Wanderer*. In writing *The Picture of Dorian Gray* Wilde had already borrowed some elements from Maturin's tale, which begins with the young student Melmoth's discovery in an unused room of a portrait of an evil Melmoth ancestor. Like Wilde's Dorian, the figure in the painting has made a bargain with the devil whereby he can live without showing signs of ageing. In a melancholy ending, Melmoth returns to his native Ireland to die after more than a century of restless wanderings, having failed to find a kindred soul to share his fate. Wilde imaginatively identified his own situation in Maturin's homeless Anglo-Irish exile. He himself was not to see either England or Ireland again. He settled near Dieppe where he wrote the first of two letters of protest to the *Daily Chronicle* on the terrible conditions of prison life. He also composed *The Ballad of Reading Gaol*, his moving, grimly realistic account of the execution of Charles Thomas Wooldridge, a trooper in the Royal Horse Guards, hanged at Reading Gaol in July 1896 for the murder of his wife. The poem was published in 1898, giving the author's name as C. 3. 3, Wilde's number in Reading Gaol, his cell being the third on the third floor of Block C.

Wilde wrote to Constance begging for a meeting with her and the boys, but Constance hesitated. He was reunited with Douglas at Rouen that summer, after which the two travelled to Naples together, but the relationship foundered when Lady Queensberry stopped Douglas's annual allowance, and Constance simultaneously cut off the £3 a week that was paid to Wilde from her estate. Wilde returned alone to Paris in February 1898, with his allowance restored, but having alienated Constance and lost all chance of meeting his sons. Wilde and Constance were never to meet again: that April Constance died in Genoa at the early age of 40, following a spinal operation. Wilde visited her grave in February the following year. The inscription carved on her tomb read just, 'Constance Mary, daughter of Horace Lloyd Q.C.', making no mention of her married name. 'I was deeply affected,' Wilde wrote to Robert Ross, 'with a sense, also, of the uselessness of all regrets' (*Letters*, p. 1128).

Wilde's remaining days were to be spent travelling between Italy and France, relying for money mainly on selling and reselling the copyright of his works and on hand-outs from his friends. He avoided attracting attention, although there were frequent indignities and snubs. His was a furtive existence of cafés and casual sexual encounters. He was often unhappy and down at heel, but he was also resilient and became a spirited exponent of 'Uranian love' (as homosexuality was called in those days) which he held to be 'more noble than other forms' (*Letters*, p. 1019). He could also still rise to the big event. There was a touching histrionic reunion with Sarah Bernhardt at Nice following her performance in *La Tosca*. 'I went round to see Sarah and she embraced me and wept, and I wept, and the whole evening was wonderful,' he wrote to Robert Ross (*Letters*, p. 1116). He also had the satisfaction of seeing the publication in book form of *The Importance of Being Earnest* and *An Ideal Husband*. In his last days, writing only to friends, Wilde believed that his artistic achievement would finally be recognized by future generations, who would also come to accept all that he had been.

Wilde was staying in Paris when he died in November 1900 of cerebral meningitis following an unsuccessful ear operation carried out in his hotel room the previous month. On 29 November, the day before his death, Robert Ross went in search of a priest, having vowed to bring a priest to him when he was dying. After great difficulty he found Father Cuthbert Dunne, a Dubliner then attached to the Passionist Order, who came at once to the hotel and administered baptism and the last rites. Wilde died at about 5.30 the following morning. Requiem mass was said for him at Saint-Germain-des-Prés, and he was buried at Bagneux cemetery on 3 December with Douglas among the fourteen mourners present. A simple gravestone, with an iron railing round it, bore his name and dates of birth and death, with a quotation from the Book of Job, chapter 29: 'After I spoke they did not speak again, and my word dropped upon them.' Found among Wilde's few personal possessions was an envelope with the words 'My Isola's Hair' written on the outside.

CHAPTER 2

THE FABRIC OF SOCIETY

'REALLY, universally, relations stop nowhere.' Thus Henry James described the novelist's difficulty in constructing a narrative of human relationships. In mapping the social fabric, the historian faces a similar lack of boundaries, particularly in the British Isles which engage different national histories. Wilde was of the generation born in the mid-Victorian period known to historians as 'the age of equipoise'.[1] The phrase is used of a period, roughly between 1850 and the early 1870s, when the forces that make up society—the old and the new, the progressive and reactionary—appeared to achieve a satisfactory balance. With the failure of the Chartist movement and the revival of Irish agriculture after the tragedy of the Great Famine, the conflicts of the 'Hungry Forties' appeared to recede. The Great Exhibition, held at the Crystal Palace at Hyde Park in 1851, was a triumphant symbol of British industrial and economic power. A utilitarian mix of *laissez-faire* capitalism (from the French meaning 'non-interference') and legislative reform ensured the triumph of the entrepreneurs. By 1870, Great Britain was producing a third of the world's total manufactured goods, and was known proverbially as 'The Workshop of the World'. Through a process of industrial expansion, Britain became the world's first predominantly urbanized society.

The period after 1870 saw the continuation of these trends, with the emergence of the suburbs, technological progress such as electric lighting, the creation of new products, and the beginnings of mass culture and communications. By 1901, the year of Queen Victoria's death, 75 per cent of the total population lived in towns, as opposed to 32 per cent at the beginning of the nineteenth century. Yet despite manifest national prosperity, Britain began to lose its position of economic pre-eminence. The United States and Germany emerged as powerful rivals in the world's markets, helped by an extended rail network and coal-propelled steamships. By 1870 Germany had a globally competitive iron and steel industry and was the world's leading producer of synthetic dye, while North America had begun exporting vast supplies of cheap machine-harvested grain from its central prairies. In Britain a series of economic slumps from 1873 to 1896 meant periodic reductions in profits and dividends for entrepreneurs and investors. British farming was particularly badly hit. A series of cold summers—according to records, every year between 1877 and 1882—resulted in bad harvests and an influx of cheap imported wheat from North America. This in turn meant a fall in prices and low rents. The first strike in England of agricultural workers took place in 1874. Rural revival was not to come until the mid-1890s. The prolonged agricultural depression had a profound effect on British political and social life. Although the landed aristocracy continued to maintain its majority in the House of Commons until 1885, the new industrial classes were assimilated into the ruling classes, while in Ireland the agricultural slump was coterminous with the emerging political force of the Home Rule Party. A remark of Wilde's Lady Bracknell in *The Importance of Being Earnest* announces the demise of the traditional basis of political and economic power in England: 'Land has ceased to be a profit or a pleasure. It gives one position and prevents one from keeping it up.' By the 1870s, the 'earnestness' that had been the defining characteristic of Victorian society—embracing hard work, high principle, and duty—began to give rise to the opposing tendencies of Tory high imperialism and a new spirit of revolt against *status quo* subservience and compromise. It was the end of equipoise.

The Challenge to Authority

POLITICS

In 1874, the year of Wilde's arrival in England, the Tories under their leader Benjamin Disraeli achieved the first Tory majority in Parliament for thirty-three years. Their victory was proclaimed as a triumphant return to Conservatism, following a successful campaign in which Disraeli had demonized the leader of the reigning Liberal Party, William Gladstone as 'an ally of the republicans'.[2] In reality, the Tory triumph was the consequence of increasing factionalism among Liberals, and the stirring of a new radicalism in English life.

During the 1860s, British radicalism both inside and outside Parliament remained tied to the Liberal Party. Lobby groups such as the Reform Union, led by the wealthy and respectable, and Edmond Beales's Reform League, with its largely working-class membership, co-operated in the battle for democratic franchise.[3] The Parliamentary Reform Act of 1867 was a victory for the reformers. It added a million new voters to the rolls. In practice, a series of restrictions served Conservative interests, and decided many secularists, religious Nonconformists, and Irish nationalists against voting in the 1874 election. Gladstone's difficulty in satisfying all interests, combined with Disraeli's opportunism, cost the Liberal Party the election.

The renewal of class antagonisms in the 1870s was in part inspired by events abroad. The insurrection of the people of Paris in 1871, known as the Paris Commune, following Napoleon III's catastrophic defeat in the Franco-Prussian war, inspired the founding of clubs up and down the country to further the republican cause. In 1871 Sir Charles Dilke, a radical Member of Parliament, attacked the seclusion of the widowed Queen Victoria and the high cost of the monarchy, and called for her deposition. The Queen responded by appearing in an open landau at St Paul's cathedral early in 1872, for a special Thanksgiving Service following the Prince of Wales's recovery from typhoid fever. The carefully stage-managed public occasion created a wave of national sentiment and sympathy for the monarch. From Dublin, Wilde's mother, with her Irish republican sympathies, recognized that the Queen had effectively killed the republican campaign in England stone dead.[4] Having listened to her palace advisers, Victoria was learning the value of the big event.

In France, the Paris Commune was quickly suppressed, but the alliance of workers and intellectuals remained for the Left a powerful symbol of revolutionary action against large-scale financial and industrial state control. Many of the heroes and intellectuals of the Commune (known as 'Communards') escaped to London to join earlier political exiles from Europe, prominent among the latter the socialist revolutionary Karl Marx. Among the English middle classes, some answered the stirrings of radical revolt with a return to the paternalistic spirit that underpinned the Charity Organization Society. Others were inspired by Carlyle's and Ruskin's feudal notions of society to join the middle-class Settlement Movements in the 1870s and 1880s, with their belief in the need for the presence of gentlemen among the working classes. This was the route followed by many Oxford men of Wilde's generation. Many previous dissenters were reconciled to the Establishment. Dilke, the republican bogeyman, was admitted to the Cabinet in 1880 as Under-Secretary of State for Foreign Affairs on condition that he repudiate his republican views, and convert to the imperialist gospel (as set out later in Sir John Seeley's opinion-forming *The Expansion of England*, 1883). Wilde who dined with him a year later in 1881, mocked him as 'a lion who has clipped his radical claws and only roars through the medium of a quarterly review now—a harmless way of roaring' (*Letters*, p. 108).

If the 1870s proved to be a false dawn for British radicalism, the spirit of utopianism and corporate action was far from crushed. Although the Victorian gospel continued to absorb and assimilate the challenge to utilitarianism and individualism during the 1870s and 1880s, some intellectuals looked beyond the 'new Feudalism' to more scientific and socialist theories of society. New independent political clubs and associations came into being during the 1880s. With this growth in left-wing activity, there was increasing agitation for the removal of the limits on franchise imposed by the 1867 Act. Many demanded even more radical changes. In 1882 Henry George, the American land reformer and author of the popular *Progress and Poverty*, kindled a socialist revival during his lecture tour of Britain. Working-class orators like John Burns and Tom Mann took to the platform to demand the abolition of private ownership of land. Many opposed co-operation with the Liberal Party. William Morris joined the Marxist Social Democratic Federation (SDF), but defected in 1884 with Marx's daughter Eleanor to found the breakaway Socialist League, when the authoritarian Henry Mayers Hyndman proposed standing in parliamentary elections. The passing of the Third Reform Act that year extended franchise and redrew the constituency boundaries in favour of large towns, but socialist agitation continued, particularly when the House of Lords attempted to block the Bill. Throughout 1886 there were fears of insurrection in the capital. Tensions came to a head in 1887, the year in which Queen Victoria's Golden Jubilee was celebrated. On 13 November, a day that became known as 'Bloody Sunday', police with batons dispersed a mass protest rally of socialist and anarchist groups in Trafalgar Square. Among those injured and imprisoned were R. B. Cunninghame Graham, a Liberal Member of Parliament and passionate supporter of Home Rule for Ireland, and John Barlas, an ardent member of Hyndman's Social Democratic Federation, both known to Wilde.

The events of Bloody Sunday convinced many socialist leaders that the hopes for a revolution in England were premature, and intensified the split between the parliamentarians and the anarchists. The term anarchism, from the Greek meaning 'without a ruler', had been adopted by the French socialist leader Pierre-Joseph Proudhon in 1840 to describe his ideal of an ordered society without government authority. Proudhon opposed violence, but disciples and followers such as Peter Kropotkin endorsed violent methods and 'propaganda by the deed'. Kropotkin arrived in England in 1886 and founded the journal *Freedom*, the organ of the anarchist Freedom group that included among its members the Russian dissident Sergei Stepniak, a visitor to Wilde's house in Tite Street. A ban on demonstrations after the riots of Bloody Sunday drove the anarchists underground, but despite periodic scares in the press, the threat they posed to the state was never a serious one. The fate of Wilde's young admirer John Barlas is instructive of changing attitudes to revolutionary action after 1887. Barlas was arrested in 1891 and eventually sent to an asylum after firing a revolver at the House of Commons to mark, as was reported in the press at the time, his 'contempt for the constitution of Parliament'.[5] By then his continuing loyalty to 'propaganda by the deed' appeared an embarrassing anachronism to his friends. Among prominent middle-class sympathizers like Wilde and Morris, support for anarchy usually tended towards theory rather than political action, and to a convergence with the ultra-individualism of bourgeois *laissez-faire* attitudes.[6]

In one area at least, the trade union movement, direct action continued unabated after 1887. Trade unionism in the skilled crafts had been a feature of British industrial life from mid-century. Their role as self-help associations and as vehicles for peaceful collective bargaining was acknowledged by the Trade Union Acts of 1871 and 1875, which recognized the right of workers to conduct strikes and engage in peaceful picketing. In the 1880s and 1890s the 'new unionism', as it was called, extended the battle for rights for unskilled as well as craft workers against the resistant paternalism of employers. The fiery trade union orator Tom Mann claimed more than 'material necessities to lift us above worrying for food and shelter . . . —we yearn for culture'.[7] His campaign for a legal eight-hour day was taken up by union leaders such as Will Thorne of the newly formed National Union of Gas Workers in 1889. That was also the year of the famous London dock strike for the right of unskilled workers to unionize. Constance Wilde with Oscar by her side attended a Hyde Park demonstration on 1 September in their support. With the continuing spate of strikes and lockouts, the demand for the representation of labour interests outside the Liberal Party was accommodated by the birth of the Independent Labour Party (ILP) in 1893. Encouraged by the Fabian Society's doctrine of the inevitability of gradualism, the Independent Labour Party became the vehicle for the smooth incorporation of working-class identity and interests within the existing political system. This was to become a source of frustration and puzzlement to socialist theorists with larger international hopes.

It is against this background of political rebellion and assimilation that the collective bohemianism of the 1880s and 1890s—including art nouveau, decadence, and Wilde's aesthetic individualism— emerged as a distinctive social phenomenon. It has been argued that Britain, unlike its continental neighbours, failed to produce a genuinely radical intelligentsia or avant-garde that challenged the traditional basis of English social and cultural life. Certainly, campaigning socialist groups like the Fabian Society, founded in 1884, and boasting G. B. Shaw among its chief trumpeters, remained wedded to the idea of the gradual reform of existing society. It can be argued that the claim of late-Victorian oppositional writers and intellectuals to avant-garde status rests upon their unconventional use of traditional forms and concepts. This is a literary issue that must be considered elsewhere. Within a historical context, what is important is the perception in the 1880s and 1890s that the followers of the aesthetic movement formed a fashionable community that posed a threat to tradition. This is the force of Holbrook Jackson's recognition that Oscar Wilde 'bridged the chasm between the self-contained individualism of the decadents and the communal aspiration of the more advanced social revolutionaries'.[8] Conservative journals like *Blackwood's Magazine*, the *Edinburgh Review*, and the *National Observer*, waged war against what they saw to be degenerate and unsavoury. It was the very ubiquity of the aesthetic mood that caused alarm. The new aestheticism no longer promoted itself as a moral refuge from mechanical civilization, in the tradition of English social critics such as Carlyle, Ruskin, and Matthew Arnold, but served as a model for life itself. Hugh Stutfield, writing in the relaunched *Westminster Gazette* in 1895, lamented that: 'Carlyle is out of fashion, for Israel has taken to stoning her older prophets who exhorted to duty, submission, and suchlike antiquated virtues, and the social anarchist and the New Hedonist bid fair to take their place as teachers of mankind'.[9] The new go-as-you-please bohemianism appeared, from an Establishment viewpoint, as an amorphous, unassimilated body. The display of foreign, particularly French influences, made it doubly alien and repulsive, and overlapped with irrational fears about the presence of anarchists and destitute foreigners in London in the 1890s. After 1895, the dissident temper of the 1880s and 1890s bohemian life-style was ostensibly dispelled and dispersed, but the unassimilated tendencies of that collective defection were arguably to work themselves out, on a sexual and cultural level at least, in the century that followed.

NATIONALISM

Among those that took part in the Trafalgar Square rally of 1887 were groups of Irish nationalists, whose cause had become linked with the goals and grievances of other marginalized groups. The Trafalgar Square riots were to some extent fuelled by an earlier demonstration at Mitchelstown in Ireland at which three protesters against land eviction had been killed. Although no less equal a part of the United Kingdom than Wales or Scotland, Ireland, with its largely Catholic population, continued to be governed like a British colony, with a Lord Lieutenant and a large number of troops backed by the paramilitary Royal Ulster Constabulary. The failure of the 'Young Ireland' movement of the 1840s temporarily silenced the call for national separation, but the desire for an end to British rule did not evaporate. Many of the leaders and supporters of the Young Ireland movement escaped penal servitude and found refuge in America. There an organization dedicated to the overthrow of British Rule in Ireland, the Fenian Brotherhood (a name derived from the legendary Gaelic warrior Fionn Mac Cumhail's élite legion, the Fianna), was secretly formed. Many Irishmen, among them the Young Ireland leaders John Mitchel and Thomas Meagher, supported the Confederate cause during the American Civil War—a

sympathy that Wilde cautiously applauded during his lecture tour of
the south in 1882. With the help of American money and arms from
the Civil War, the Fenians began a campaign of guerrilla warfare in
1867. Wilde's mother, whose nationalist poems had been inspir-
ational during the Young Ireland campaign, wrote disapprovingly of
Fenianism: 'It is a decidedly *democratic* movement and the gentry
and aristocracy will suffer much from them—their object is to form
a *republic* and heaven keep us from a Fenian republic!'[10] The rising
failed, but in England three Irish rebels were hanged at Manchester
following the death of a policeman, and the explosion of a Fenian bomb
at Clerkenwell prison which left twelve Londoners dead, decided
many on the urgency of a new political solution to the Irish problem.

Fenianism has been described as 'mass nationalism in an epoch of
triumphant liberalism'.[11] It would be more true to say that it
emerged at a time when the Victorian gospel of liberalism and paternalism was already on the wane. In significant ways Irish militancy
matched the aggressive nationalism of other emergent nation states
(Italy and Germany politically unified in 1861 and 1871 respectively,
the United States after the Civil War), as well as the rising tide of the
new British imperialism to which Irish nationalism was a challenge
and affront. In the 1870s and 1880s, Irish Protestant politicians such
as Isaac Butt and Charles Stewart Parnell tried in vain to gain
acceptance for the idea of limited Irish self-government within a
more federalized United Kingdom. Even with Gladstone and the
majority of the Liberal Party behind it, the Irish Home Rule Bill of
1886 was defeated.

Most Fenians and many non-Fenian nationalists had in any case
wanted more complete separation, among them John Mitchel who
expressed hostility to 'the helpless driftless concern called "home
rule"' when he was allowed to return to Ireland in 1874.[12] It was on
this occasion that Wilde was dazzled by the personality of Mitchel,
the returning *émigré*, whom he met at his parents' house. The
arguments for Irish Home Rule also failed to convince Unionists.
Anglo-Irish landowners, and Unionist strongholds such as Trinity
College, Dublin, suspected further assaults on Protestant Ascendancy of the kind represented by the disestablishment of the Church
of Ireland in 1869, and the Land Act of 1871, limiting the power of
landlords to evict tenants.[13] To Protestants and Presbyterian farmers
in Ulster, with its long history of sectarianism, 'Home Rule' was

identical with 'Rome Rule'.[14] Staunch Unionists like Edward Carson, who was cross-examiner at Wilde's first trial, believed the interests of Ireland were best served by a British Parliament. They dismissed the nationalist view of the Irish as a conquered race, even in the face of systematic denigration and racial stereotyping in the English press. Racial abuse was a characteristic of nineteenth-century imperialist discourse, and in its humorous form was viewed as bracing and harmlessly robust. During Wilde's American tour, the *Oxford Magazine* reported of E. A. Freeman, the Regius Professor of History at the University, that 'the only people to whom he is distinctly unkind are the negroes, Irish, the Chinese and Mr Oscar Wilde'.[15] Humour aside, racial targeting of this type reflected and fed popular hatreds and prejudices, and reinforced the view that the Irish were 'troublesome subjects' who were unfit to govern themselves.

Hostility to the Irish intensified in England in the late 1870s and 1880s, when Irish Members used obstructionist tactics in Parliament to draw attention to the demands for Home Rule. There was bitterness on both sides. The agricultural slump of the late 1870s was particularly severe in Ireland, where the flood of cheap grain from America forced down farm prices and led to the mass eviction of tenants. Anger gave birth to the National Land League in 1879, with Parnell as its President. Its posters announced provocatively, 'The Land War! No Rent!' Although Parnell was careful to deplore violence, the 'land war' of 1881–2 was marked by mass boycotts (from the name of an evicting land agent, Captain Boycott), and underground violence culminating in the murders of the Chief Secretary and Under-Secretary for Ireland in Phoenix Park, Dublin, in 1882. Retaliatory action included the suppression of the Land League and the imprisonment of Irish leaders, including Parnell, by the British government. The Wildes were among those Irish families who supported Parnell, even though for them it meant loss of rent from their estate at a time of serious financial difficulty after the death of Sir William Wilde. Wilde was critical of the Irish Secretary, A. J. Balfour's coercive regime in Ireland. Balfour's Irish Crimes Act of 1887, which made it illegal for Irish tenants to resist eviction, sparked a return to violence. When *The Times* tried to discredit Parnell over letters he had allegedly written condoning violence, Wilde showed his support for Parnell by attending the meetings of the Royal Commission set up to investigate the allegations. Parnell was completely vindicated when it was proved that the incriminating letters had been forged by a needy Irish journalist called Richard Pigott, but within a year Parnell was brought down by the scandal of his long-term affair with a married woman, Kitty O'Shea. He died in 1891, abandoned by Gladstone's Liberal Party and condemned by Catholic Ireland. It was with Parnell painfully in mind that Wilde, in 'The Soul of Man under Socialism', expressed contempt for journalists who 'drag before the eyes of the public some incident in the private life of a great statesman, of a man who is a leader of political thought as he is a creator of political force, and invite the public to discuss the incident . . . to dictate to the man upon all other points, to dictate to his party, to dictate to his country.' Many, like Wilde's mother, regarded Parnell as a nationalist hero, destined 'to strike off the fetters and free Ireland'.[16] With his fall from grace and sudden death, in James Joyce's eloquent evocation of the event in *A Portrait of the Artist as a Young Man*, he became in some eyes a sacrificial victim. In 1893 the second Home Rule Bill was rejected in the House of Lords. Without Parnell's guiding presence and political skill, Home Rule was dead, and was to remain buried for another twenty years.

WOMEN'S RIGHTS

During the passing of the Reform Bills in 1867 and 1884, the attempt to secure an amendment giving women the vote failed on both occasions. Queen Victoria's views on 'Women's Rights with all its attendant horrors' as a 'mad, wicked folly' reflected age-old patriarchal and religious beliefs as to the inferiority and subordination of women to men.[17] Traditional beliefs concerning women's natural physical and intellectual inferiority were given new credence in the latter half of the nineteenth century with the rise of evolutionary biology, and the manly cult of empire. Women were entitled to vote on local and school boards from the 1870s onwards, but suffrage for women was not achieved until 1918, and then only for those over 30; full suffrage was achieved only in 1928. In the late-Victorian age, change and improvement in women's legal status came about largely through gradual legislation conceding a woman's rights over her property and her body.

The 1857 Divorce and Matrimonial Causes Act, which made civil divorce a possibility, was a decisive challenge to male authority over women. Though initially proposed simply as a tidy legal measure to abolish the jurisdiction of Parliament and the old ecclesiastical courts on matters of separation and divorce, the bill was quickly seized upon by campaigning feminists and lobbyists such as Mrs Caroline Norton, and Mrs Barbara (née Leigh Smith) Bodichon.[18] Lord Broughton and the Law Amendment Society supported their desire for a change in the law governing divorce. The major achievement of the Act was in enlargement of the grounds for divorce from adultery aggravated by bigamy or incest to include adultery aggravated by cruelty, although there was still inequality before the law as husbands had only to prove adultery. The Act did protect the property and earnings of separated wives from seizure by the husbands. The extension of the protection of property and earnings to all wives proved too radical a threat to age-old patriarchal attitudes, and to middle-class notions of men and women's 'separate spheres'. In 1854, the year of Wilde's birth, Coventry Patmore published his poetic tribute to the Victorian ideal of domestic womanhood, *The Angel in the House*. His codification of manly action and female passivity was sanctified in John Ruskin's appeal to Victorian conscience, *Sesame and Lilies*, in 1865: 'The man's work for his own home is . . . to secure its maintenance, progress, and defence; the woman's to secure its order, comfort, and loveliness.'[19] In reality, many middle-class Victorian women found themselves in the bitterly humiliating situation described by Oscar Wilde's mother as having only the 'provision for a wife's personal expenses called pin money . . . the husband reserving all the rest for himself and giving the wife no account of it'.[20] Her husband had used her own settlement to buy property, leaving her without claim or income after his death. The right of married women to ownership and control of their own property and earnings was not finally secured until the landmark Married Women's Property Act of 1882. Even then, women like Constance Wilde married, as the English upper classes had always done, under a settlement agreement by which the wife kept control of her property through trustees.

Male prerogatives were further dented during the 1880s by two significant pieces of legislation. The Matrimonial Causes Act of 1884 granted a woman some rights over her person in cases involving her refusal to comply with the demand for the restitution of conjugal rights. Many clung stubbornly to the popular belief that it was a man's right to beat and keep a non-compliant wife at home by force. In a famous appeal case of a Lancashire woman called Emily Jackson in 1891, the Lord Chancellor and the Master of the Rolls ruled emphatically that the idea was based upon 'quaint and absurd dicta'.[21] The popularity of the English Punch and Judy show as jocular wife-beating entertainment dates from that time, while what constituted a good husband became a popular topic of the day. In a second important piece of legislation, the Guardianship of Infants Act of 1886 established the principle of a mother's rights to custody of the children following a separation or divorce. The harshness of the Common Law, which gave the husband legal rights to keep a mother from seeing her children, had been softened earlier in the century, in 1839, when the court was given power to grant a mother access to her children, and in some cases custody of infants. The miserable situation in which Wilde found himself after his release from prison—forbidden from ever seeing his children again—would have been unimaginable earlier in the century. Paradoxically, the principle of a woman's natural rights to custody over her children had gained legitimacy from the association of 'home' with woman's biological destiny, so often denigrated by present-day feminists. With international rivalry, Darwinian theories of biological selection, and the perceived effects of agricultural depression and urban growth fanning fears of the 'deterioration of the race', the nurturing of infants had by then become a national concern. Ruskin's sanctification of the good mother as a stable moral centre within a restless, competitive male world was extended to include the patriotic duty of raising a healthy nation.[22] The new value put on motherhood came paradoxically at a time when more and more women were questioning assumptions about women's natural destiny. A conflicting attitude to marriage, motherhood, and women's sexual and social identity was to become characteristic of 'New Woman' writers such as Olive Schreiner, Sarah Grand, and George Egerton.

The phrase 'New Woman' came into vogue through its use by Sarah Grand in a debate with the novelist 'Ouida' about sexual stereotypes in the *North American Review* in 1894. The emancipated 'New Woman' was largely a literary and journalistic invention, whether promoted by feminists, or lampooned by journalists and cartoonists. Male writers of the period tended to present her as either neurotic, over-educated, and a poor mother—Thomas

Hardy's Sue Bridehead in *Jude the Obscure* (1895) is an example of all three—or alternatively, as 'mannish' and hearty.

'New Women' of the more militant type were nevertheless a tangible fact. They found their voice in middle-class drawing-rooms, in socialist and feminist circles, and in the unconventional milieu of literature and the theatre. Although inevitably entangled in the relationships of a male-dominated world, actresses were often among the most advanced women of the day. Ellen Terry, after her separation from the artist G. F. Watts, chose six years of domesticity and children with the architect and designer E. W. Godwin before returning to the stage, while Lillie Langtry transformed herself from a society beauty into an actress and international celebrity. During his brief spell as editor in late 1880s, Wilde used the Cassells magazine *Woman's World* as a forum for advanced woman who were seizing opportunities in education and public life in order to overturn traditional attitudes to women.

In the nineteenth century, sexual laxity and marital infidelity continued to be tolerated among aristocratic circles. This was true of wives as well as husbands. The Prince of Wales's many mistresses included a string of noble ladies as well as actresses. He and his 'Marlborough House' set developed a code of conduct in extramarital affairs that aimed to keep marriages together and avoid scandal. This may have been as much out of regard for Queen Victoria's earnestness as out of respect for public morality. Public attitudes towards adultery can be seen in the response to the Parnell–O'Shea affair. That many in authority, including Gladstone, appear to have known about the relationship for some years could not prevent a scandal that succeeded in uniting, as nothing else had done, Catholic Ireland and Protestant England. 'Nonconformist conscience' (a phrase coined to describe prudish reaction to the affair) delivered the deathblow to Parnell's political ambitions. Sir Charles Dilke's political career similarly ended in ruins after his appearance as a co-respondent in a divorce case in 1885. The new drama of Ibsen and Wilde in the 1890s reflected daring attitudes to such social and sexual issues of the day as independent womanhood, parenting and child custody, and what constitutes a good husband. The challenge of Wilde's plays to his Victorian audiences was not so much their *risqué* themes, but their indulgent attitude towards sexual indiscretion.

THE LOOSENING OF SOCIETY

The fear of scandal that pervaded life and relations in the late-Victorian period can be explained to some extent by the dominance of middle-class morality and by the need to maintain traditional authority and control in a period that saw the weakening of aristocratic 'high society'. It speaks for the confidence of middle-class Dublin that the Wildes continued to be accepted in respectable society after the public scandal of Sir William Wilde's trial for the alleged rape of one of his patients, Mary Travers. The uncertainty of clear social boundaries in England made such toleration more risky. In England, 'society' had ceased to be an exclusive, close-knit circle that was a law unto itself.

Until the second half of Victoria's reign, titles of honour remained almost exclusively the monopoly of the landed establishment. With the democratic extension of political and economic power, the honours system was inflated and widened in order to grant peerages and titles to a greater number of recipients from more diverse social backgrounds. The 1880s saw a dramatic rise in presentations at court. The resistance of Nonconformist Liberals such as John Bright to 'snobbery' and deference was a stand against the norm.[23] Those who gained a political or economic foothold in society avidly sought acceptance by their 'betters'. In one of the great *causes célèbres* of the period, the Tichborne Case (1867–75), Arthur Orton claimed to be the baronet Sir Robert Tichborne, the heir to the Tichborne estate. Orton was discredited and imprisoned, but the trials focused attention on the fragility of traditional claims of heredity and privilege. In fact, the English ruling classes had been decisively infiltrated by banking, mercantile, and professional new money since the 1780s. Yet to the old guard, the traffic in titles and the power of money over patronage suggested the threat of scandal and corruption in public life. The fourth Marquess of Salisbury advocated 'the supreme importance' of keeping 'our public life pure and free from reproach'.[24] From above, the infiltration and pretensions of the *nouveaux riches* also meant the dilution of London society. In the 1880s society ladies like Lady Dorothy Nevill still looked nostalgically, if somewhat mistakenly, to the 1850s as a vanished age of *grandes dames* and exclusivity when the ruling English aristocracy still maintained a distance from 'a mob composed of persons whose only claim to social consideration consisted in money-bags'.[25]

The dilution and fragmentation of London society was reinforced in the 1880s by the Home Rule crisis. The Home Rule controversy split families and friends, Liberal Unionists and Gladstonian Loyalists, into separate social as well as political 'sets'. The situation was not helped by the defeat of the Home Rule Bill by only forty votes in June 1886. The following year, Queen Victoria's Diamond Jubilee resulted in a show of unity, but society remained deeply divided. Wilde's own entry into society was restricted mainly to Gladstonian Loyalists (Lord Acton, the Kendals, and James Knowles, editor and founder of the *Nineteenth Century*), and to the theatrical fringes of the Prince of Wales's smart 'fast' set.

The Prince of Wales's attraction to the modish, the raffish, and the rich showed a manifest disregard for aristocratic protocol. Whispers of financial and sexual scandal surrounded his immediate entourage. Stories of scandals and fraud involving the 'quality' were followed in the new popular press. Sensational reports of upper-class leisure, permissiveness, and crime arguably reinforced rather than questioned traditional perceptions of the difference between 'them' and 'us', but they also weakened social and moral respect for authority. With the passing of the Criminal Law Amendment Act in 1885, upper-class homosexuals could no longer expect immunity from prosecution, although aristocrats like Lord Ronald Sutherland Gower, the supposed model for Wilde's Lord Henry Wotton in *The Picture of Dorian Gray*, could always escape to the Continent whenever scandal threatened. In the last quarter of the nineteenth century Europe and the continents of Africa and Asia were no longer simply stops on the aristocratic Grand Tour, but the regular home of a motley group of titled fugitives and wealthy dropouts from English society.

SCIENCE AND MORALITY

To a large extent the challenge to authority in many areas of social life and relationship in the second half of the nineteenth century was the consequence of a weakening of belief in basic religious orthodoxy. The erosion of religion by science had been one of the deepest concerns of theologians, philosophers, and imaginative writers in the early Victorian period. To Tennyson, the evolutionary scientific findings of Sir Charles Lyell's *Principles of Geology* (1830–3) posed a terrifying threat to the possibility of any spiritual significance to life at all:

> O life as futile, then, as frail!
> > O for thy voice to soothe and bless!
> > What hope of answer, or redress?
> Behind the veil, behind the veil.

> (*In Memoriam*)

The claims of John Henry Newman and the Tractarians that the real grounds of Church authority rested upon apostolic descent (that is, Christ's original instruction to his disciples) were an attempt to stem the tide of religious 'liberalism' that might one day reach the shore of secularism. Such religious anxieties and counter-moves remained a feature of English life in the late-Victorian period. Some opponents of the Divorce Law in 1857 argued mistakenly that the Act meant that the State had abandoned the Church's principle of the indissolubility of marriage. What the Act did do was transfer jurisdiction in matrimonial matters from the Church Courts to a new civil authority.

The lessening of ecclesiastical authority was felt in many areas of social life. In 1871 university officials were, technically at least, no longer required to take religious tests. The encouragement of speculative enquiry in the universities gradually divested learning of its 'religious clothing'.[26] Among educated young men in the 1870s and 1880s, teaching or social work (known as 'slumming') replaced Holy Orders as favoured vocations. The theme of warring curates that had amused readers of Charlotte Brontë's novel *Shirley* in 1850 had become dated by the 1880s, compelling W. S. Gilbert to adapt his idea of rival curates to the more topical theme of rival aesthetes for his comic opera *Patience* in 1881. For all its moral earnestness, Matthew Arnold's ethical crusade in the 1860s and 1870s on behalf of literature and culture rested on an acceptance of the impossibility of traditional religious dogma. This is what more sanguine scientific and rationalist adversaries like T. H. Huxley and Frederic Harrison recognized in dubbing Arnold the 'Jeremiah of Culture'. Arnold's idea of culture was an aesthetic version of liberal theology, or 'modernism' as it was called, which sought to reconcile the essential truth of religion with the facts of the modern world. Wilde's contemporary, George Tyrell, an austere Dublin Protestant turned Catholic 'modernist', dismissed Arnold's aesthetic, secular religion of culture as 'the preservation of the ancient and beautiful husk after the kernel had been withered up and discarded'.[27]

The English poets who most exhilarated Wilde and his generation were those like Robert Browning and the pre-Raphaelite D. G. Rossetti, in whom the fleshly and the spiritual were at war, or like Algernon Swinburne, who explicitly rejected Christian dogma. Swinburne's début volume of verse, *Poems and Ballads* (1866), intoxicated the young with passages of heretical lyricism such as:

Though the feet of thine high priests tread where thy lords and our forefathers trod,
Though these that were Gods are dead, and thou being dead art a God,
Though before thee the tanned Cytherean be fallen, and hidden her head,
Yet thy kingdom shall pass, Galilean, thy dead shall go down to thee dead.

('Hymn to Proserpine')

Society could still respond harshly on occasions to anti-religious attitudes. George William Foote, editor of the *Freethinker* and President of the National Secular Society, was sentenced in 1883 to three months' hard labour at Holloway under the blasphemy laws. Religion continued to have an important place in people's lives that cannot confidently be measured simply in terms of falling church attendance. Indeed, according to one historian, the widely accepted assumption that various secular world views replaced shared traditional beliefs gives 'no explanation for the outbursts of the miraculous in the midst of the unprecedented nineteenth-century advance in scientific knowledge and technology'—the claims for healing through prayer at the time of the Prince of Wales's recovery from typhoid in 1872, for example.[28] Wilde himself believed in the importance of the miraculous in keeping alive man's progressive, myth-making spirit.

The undoubted decline in ecclesiastical authority in the period was the result of economic prosperity and urban freedom rather than of biblical controversies and the findings of science. The attempt by the Evangelicals to limit Sunday trading and the sale of alcohol caused riots on Sunday afternoons during the summer of 1855. In *Little Dorrit*, published that year, Charles Dickens has his hero Arthur Clenham reflect with bitterness in chapter 3 on the dreary

Sundays of his evangelical childhood, 'when he sat with his hands before him, scared out of his senses by a horrible tract which commenced business with the poor child by asking him in its title, why he was going to Perdition'. The strict Sunday Trading Bill, which the secularist George Holyoake described scornfully as 'a mere Church monopoly act, for the protection of religion from competition', was subsequently withdrawn.[29]

Reaction against the old Victorian Britain of sin and sabbatarianism also encouraged more open attitudes to sexuality. In the campaign for sex reform, the rationalists and the morally 'progressive' were not always in agreement. When the secularist campaigners Charles Bradlaugh and Annie Besant were prosecuted in 1877 for distributing a pamphlet on birth control—at that time virtually a taboo subject—they received little support from the feminists, who feared that contraception would expose women even more to male carnality. When diverse groups of radical feminists and evangelicals campaigned side by side for the reform of the sex laws the impact on people's lives could be repressive. The first signs of this became evident in the late 1870s during the campaign to abolish the Contagious Diseases Act, which had been introduced in the 1860s to ensure that prostitutes in garrison towns and ports were checked regularly for evidence of venereal disease. Then in 1885, a sensationalist exposé of child prostitution in the *Pall Mall Gazette*, 'The Maiden Tribute of Modern Babylon', fanned the flames of moral panic. Its author, W. T. Stead, was a convert of the 1859–60 evangelical revival turned pioneering 'new' journalist and editor. The extent of prostitution and the visibility of vice within the city began to be viewed as a threat to social order. Such anxieties were fed by related concerns in the early 1880s about national decline in the face of working-class organization and electoral expansion. The Criminal Law Amendment Act, which raised the legal age of sexual consent to 16, contained clauses outlawing brothel keeping. Vigorous enforcement through the courts by the newly formed National Vigilance Association meant that large numbers of prostitutes were made homeless. Although committed opponents to the acceptance of prostitution by the state, some leading feminists were alarmed by the coercive policies of social purists among their ranks. 'Beware of "Purity Societies",' warned Josephine Butler, a leading feminist campaigner, 'ready to accept and endorse any amount of inequality in the laws, any amount of coercive and degrading treatment of their fellow creatures in the fatuous belief that you will oblige human beings to be moral by *force*.'[30]

Clause II of the Criminal Law Amendment Act, introduced almost as an afterthought by the Liberal backbencher, Henry Labouchere, made sexual acts between men, in private as well as public, a crime. Lesbianism escaped the prosecution of the law chiefly because homosexuality was generally viewed in the nineteenth century as an aspect of uncontrolled and indiscriminate male lust. The aim of Clause II was the protection of boys as well as girls from sexual exploitation, but the consequence was to stigmatize homosexuality along with prostitution as a contagious and corrupting plague within society. This was the atmosphere in which Oscar Wilde was tried and sentenced for gross indecency in 1895. To supporters of the Act, Clause II was a weapon in the class as well as the sex war, as it was commonly believed that homosexual exploitation had spread from the decadent aristocracy to London's fashionable and artistic circles. Wilde in the dock came to define the public image of degenerate and outlawed homosexuality, until then vague and undefined in the minds of the majority. The Revd Richard Armstrong of the Social Purity Alliance denounced Wilde as one of those 'writers of elegant and glittering literature, glossing over vice'.[31] To others, Wilde was a heroic martyr to the prejudices of the new puritanism. According to Havelock Ellis, Wilde's trial and imprisonment encouraged others 'to take up a definite stand', and contributed ultimately to greater discussion and understanding of gender and sexual identity.[32]

Civilizing Trends

The Criminal Law Amendment Act is an example of the way in which humanitarian, civilizing intentions led to conduct which many would now regard as repressive and even inhumane. The Victorians, with some justice, thought of themselves as a 'kindlier', more civilized people than their eighteenth-century ancestors. Philanthropy and voluntary help societies flourished long after responsibility for poor relief and education had passed into the hands of the state. By the 1860s, the degrading, publicly inflicted punishments of Hanoverian times—the pillory, the convict ship, and the gallows—had been done away with. New penalties against prostitution and public drunkenness in the 1870s and 1880s attempted to banish from sight the more ugly and unpleasant aspects of city life. In this process of purification, there was a characteristic Victorian split between sentiment and reason. Readers of Dickens's *Oliver Twist* (1837–8) might share Dickens's outrage at the draconian callousness of the new Poor Law (1834), but most, like Dickens himself, adhered to the belief in individual responsibility and personal moral development that helped to frame it. The idea of character-building directs the action and ethos of such classic Victorian novels as *David Copperfield*, *Great Expectations*, *Jane Eyre*, and *Adam Bede*, with their prevalent images of redemptive suffering, ennobling work, and the mastery of passions. The challenge to traditional authority, and the consequent widening of individual freedom of action was accompanied by anxieties about the need to enforce new forms of discipline and social control. On the level of social policy, the face of individualism and political *laissez-faire* looked away as the arm of the law extended utilitarian moral concerns about discipline and foresight to every area of social life.

Belief in pain and punishment as a necessary requirement for reformation was a deeply entrenched Victorian attitude. George Eliot spoke on behalf of her age when she wrote in *Adam Bede*: 'Deep unspeakable suffering may well be called a baptism, a regeneration, the initiation into a new state' (ch. XVII). In a letter to Florence Nightingale in 1860 John Stuart Mill expressed the belief that punishment was 'the sole means available for beginning the reformation of the criminal'.[33] When Wilde's London contemporary, the poet John Davidson, commended Wilde's harsh sentence as an opportunity for redemptive suffering,[34] he was merely repeating Wilde's own celebration of necessary pain 'as a mode of self-realisation' in the closing passages of 'The Soul of Man under Socialism'. Yet, crucially, Wilde sees suffering and pain as indexes of a society gone wrong. They are 'a protest' and 'provisional' stage in society 'whose saner, healthier, more civilised' goal should be leisure and happiness for all. Wilde's counter-argument to suffering is an emergent feature of late-Victorian society. It is evident in the growth of pills and remedies designed to eradicate discomfort. The related view of want and work as latent evils is the anti-Victorian ethos that unites George Gissing's struggling lower-class heroes and Thomas Hardy's Jude in *Jude the Obscure*.

PENAL REFORM

The emphasis on personal responsibility and moral reformation was written starkly in the reform of the Victorian penal system. Successive Prison Acts in the 1860s and 1870s established new institutional rules aimed at promoting uniformity, fairness, and moral influence in the treatment of criminals. In the 1850s and 1860s the huge reduction in the number of executions and the end of transportation to Australia meant that prisons had to deal with a much more 'hardened' class of criminal. The 1865 Prison Act introduced a system of separate cells and rules of silence in order to isolate and calm prisoners, and prevent a 'promiscuous mingling' of the good and the bad. Sir Edmund Du Cane, the Chairman of the Prison Commission, was dedicated to deterrence and disciple. His stated goal was a condition, 'where all facilities for moral and religious improvement are cared for, but where labour is exacted from all, and where a disagreeable sense of personal restraint and real punishment is brought home to each offender'.[35] Attitudes may have been kinder and more humane, but the emphasis was on orderliness and organization. During his regime, from 1878 to 1894, the treatment of offenders in local prisons was especially severe. The Du Cane years, according to Sidney and Beatrice Webb, saw 'a uniform application of cellular isolation, absolute non-intercourse among the prisoners, the rule of silence, oakum-picking, and the tread-wheel'.[36] The tread-wheel, or 'mill' as it was known to the prisoners, had been introduced in 1817 as a prison deterrent. Prisoners were consigned to fifteen 'quarter hour spells' of walking on a revolving cylinder used in the grinding of prison corn. Oakum-picking, which alternated with the tread-mill for those serving hard labour, put prisoners busily to work tearing up old tarry rope for use in the caulking of wooden ships. The development of industrious habits and moral instincts was also encouraged by sermons and of Bible reading. Reading Gaol, where the Bible was the only book allowed to prisoners, was known as 'Read, Read, Reading Gaol'. Prisoners were not protected by various laws against flogging, which was used as a means of punishment and discipline until the end of the century. Suspected malingerers were fastened to a 'triangle' to prevent the movement of hands and feet, and then beaten with a 'cat of nine tails'. L. O. Pike's historical study of crime, published between 1873 and 1876, questioned the moral effects of flogging and other prison disciplines and deterrents.[37] A Committee of Inquiry into the state of prisons in 1895, headed by Herbert J. Gladstone, William Gladstone's youngest son, recommended a more humane approach to prison discipline and treatment. In a letter to the *Daily Chronicle* in 1897, Wilde drew public attention to the brutal realities of prison life, particularly with regard to children in prisons. In a second letter the following year he gave voice to the overwhelming contempt felt by prisoners themselves towards the pretended pieties and benevolence of the prison regime. Little was done to change the conditions of prison life until the First World War.

A moral agenda is also evident in the abolition of public execution. The 'civilizing moment', in 1868, was achieved not through objections to the sufferings of the condemned, but through the evident failure of the scaffold to serve as a moral warning to the rowdy, drunken crowds that gathered to watch 'the drop'. Criticism of public executions went back to the eighteenth century. Henry Fielding, a police magistrate as well as novelist, believed that the scaffold drama made heroes of condemned criminals. Fielding advocated more private and solemn executions on the grounds that 'they would be much more shocking and terrible to the crowd without doors . . . as well as much more dreadful to the criminals themselves'.[38] Charles Dickens waged war on public executions in precisely the same terms almost a hundred years later. 'From the moment of a murderer being sentenced to death, I would dismiss him to the dread obscurity,' he wrote in 1849. 'I would place every obstacle in the way of his sayings and doings being served up in print . . . His execution within the walls of the prison should be conducted with every terrible solemnity that careful consideration could devise.'[39] Dickens's arguments for private execution outraged the abolitionists with whom he had previously sided—Charles Gilpin, Richard Cobden, John Bright, William Ewart—but reform when it finally came was within the framework of deterrence and moral discipline he proposed. Yet significantly, the Capital Punishment Within Prisons Bill went through Parliament in the wake of two controversial multiple executions that threw into question the efficacy of deterrence. The first followed the sensational trial of the 'Five Pirates' in 1864 for the murder of their captain and five crew members; subsequently three Fenians were executed together for the accidental killing of a Manchester police-man in 1867. The last public execution in England took place on 26 May 1868, just three days before the Capital Punishment Within Prisons Act received the Royal Assent. The condemned man was Michael Barrett, a 27-year-old Irish stevedore, convicted contro-versially of causing the Fenian explosion at Clerkenwell prison which left seven dead and many injured. In the history of the gal-lows, the power and authority of the state was always made to appear heartless and oppressive whenever protesters or political radicals were sent to the scaffold.

The first execution under the new Act was carried out five months later without the crude carnival atmosphere of public executions, which had been a magnet to prostitutes, pickpockets, and ballad-hawkers of the prisoner's 'last confessions'. Most Victorians were relieved to see the end of a practice that seemed primitive and ana-chronistic in an age of advanced technology and the Crystal Palace. The popular press continued to exploit morbid interest in murderers and their executions, while the crusade against capital punishment continued. In the eyes of the abolitionists, the prison walls merely curtained the barbaric and unpleasant from public gaze. At the hang-ing of the victim-heroine in Hardy's novel *Tess of the D'Urbervilles* (1892), the Victorian prison wall is the terrifying 'blot', the warning to onlookers that the reformers intended, but ironically the only people interested in the execution are members of the family. By the 1890s it had become something of a paradox that the moral solem-nity of private executions and prison punishment should coincide with biological and sociological theories that moved away from vol-untaristic to more deterministic and mitigating explanations of human behaviour and motivation. It is with this firmly in view that Wilde composed *The Ballad of Reading Gaol* (1899). Wilde's ballad exploits morbid interest in murderers and their executions to cor-rective ends. It returned the sordid reality of prison and private execution back to the streets, as the cry not of a ballad-hawker's 'come-ye-all', but of a suffering insider.

WELFARE AND EDUCATION

The Victorian commitment to self-reliance that helped shape penal reform also influenced welfare policy and education. In all these areas of social improvement, one can see seemingly conflicting tendencies at work—on the one hand, a continuing commitment to minimal state intervention and individual responsibility; on the other, an extension of social responsibility.

This is strikingly apparent in the framing of the deterrent 1834 Poor Law which discouraged those seeking relief by making it dependent on entry into the workhouse, with loss of dignity and human rights.[40] Recognition of the social causes of poverty in the second half of the nineteenth century did not undermine the Victorian encouragement to self-reliance. Samuel Smiles's *Self-Help* (1859), published in the same year as Darwin's *Origin of Species*, gave expression to the spirit of the age in suggesting that self-help 'is the root of all genuine growth in the individual; and, exhibited in the lives of many, it constitutes the true course of national vigour and strength.'[41]

Throughout the nineteenth century, relief for the poor came largely from individual donations to the hundreds of voluntary organizations and charities that existed across the nation. By 1861 there were 640 charities in London alone. It was in order to bring greater order and organization to this spreading network of relief, and to combat the feared effects of indiscriminate almsgiving, that the Charitable Organization Society (COS) was formed in 1869. The COS remained true to the Victorian spirit of self-help, convinced 'that the poverty of the working classes in England was due, not to their circumstances . . . but to their own improvident habits and thriftlessness'.[42] In this, the COS was in fact behind the times. The long-term unemployment resulting from economic depression in the 1870s and 1880s made the real causes of poverty all too plain. By the end of the 1870s, the combination of scientific purposefulness and encouragement to self-reliance, displayed by the COS, in particular the attempt to separate the 'deserving' from the 'undeserving' poor, was already discredited.

In Ireland, the experience of the Great Famine in the 1840s had long before impressed on the national consciousness that poverty was involuntary, rather than being the effect of personal weaknesses. Accounts of the devastating effects of hunger and want on the country and its people were not to be matched in England until the 1880s when a series of frank surveys and studies brought home to people the true extent of poverty in England, most notably Andrew Mearns's *The Bitter Cry of Outcast London* (1887), and the founder of the Salvation Army, William Booth's *In Darkest England and the Way Out* (1890).

The last quarter of the nineteenth century also saw the rebirth of socialism and more collectivist ideas of society. The militant voices of the SDF, the Socialist League, the Fabians, and the ILP in the 1880s and 1890s challenged philanthropy and sympathy as remedies for social misery, and called for more radical collective state action and control. Henry George, in his best-selling *Progress and Poverty*, declared that 'a social state is possible in which poverty would be unknown, and all the better qualities and higher powers of human nature would have the opportunity for full development'.[43] Yet it remained the case that commitment to self-help continued to shape public opinion despite the emergence of these alternative viewpoints.

Victorian attitudes to education from the mid-century onwards displayed a similar conflict of values. The reform of public and endowed schools in the 1860s; the passing of the enabling Elementary Education Act of 1870; and the ending of the exclusively Anglican character of the older universities in the following years: all of these measures appeared to be radically democratic in extending educational opportunities. In reality, voluntary and denominational control continued long after the 1870s. At the same time, the ethos directing the whole process of educational reorganization was based on the notion of equality of opportunity that transferred responsibility for failure from society to the individual, while at the same time accepting existing inequality. Reforms were carried out in a way that established different kinds of schooling for different classes. The burden of failing educationally became particularly crushing on the individual in a climate of opinion in which one's place in society became a measure of one's social worth.

Competitive examinations and the notion of 'testable knowledge' also ran into conflict with a traditional educational ideal of character development. In Wilde's Oxford, Mark Pattison, Rector of Lincoln College, objected to the obsession with examinations that had taken root in the university.[44] Wilde himself met these potentially conflicting demands, achieving competitive academic success while remaining an ardent follower of Newman and Arnold, with their claims for the intrinsic value of education. According to Wilde's *De Profundis*, 'to acquire the "Oxford temper" in intellectual matters' meant being 'one who could play gracefully with ideas'.

In his essays and plays, Wilde's response to practical education and practical philanthropy was invariably scornful. He enjoyed exposing philanthropy not simply as ineffectual, but for all its kindly intentions, religious or otherwise, as a form of social control. 'We are trying at present to stave off the coming crisis, the coming revolution, as my friends the Fabianists call it, by means of doles and alms', Gilbert declares in 'The Critic as Artist'. Wilde remained a proponent of absolute self-reliance, but in an imagined utopianism in which freedom from want and freedom for leisure and self-development were possible for all.

LEISURE, CONSUMERISM, AND MASS CULTURE

The old moral framework of discipline and work appealed less to a new generation that preferred the luxuries and relaxation of the new consumer culture. The Great Exhibition at the Crystal Palace in 1851 launched a new era in conspicuous consumerism and mass culture. A million bottles of Schweppes soda-water, lemonade, and ginger-beer were sold across the counter of the refreshment stand during the Exhibition. French visitors were astonished by the mass production in England of luxury goods. One French journalist wrote, 'It is very odd. An aristocratic country like England is successful at supplying the people, whereas France, a democratic country, is only good at producing goods for the aristocracy.'[45] The Great Exhibition encouraged a new 'habit of enjoyment' and leisure to no purpose that discomforted the evangelicals and puritan-minded. The Crystal Palace was re-erected at Sydenham in South London, and remained a permanent place of popular amusement and holiday recreation down to the twentieth century. To *The Times*, in 1861, the frantic search for enjoyment and diversion that had become a feature of modern 'holidays' was simply tiring work.[46] In his mock-epic account of the Crystal Palace in his poem of that title, John Davidson described ironically the 'business-like' pursuits of the invading crowd on gala day, culminating in the Epicurean enjoyment of

> Lunch in the grill-room for the well-to-do,
> The spendthrifts and the connoisseurs of food.

Entertaining guests at extravagant dinner parties in the later nineteenth century was a sign of rising consumption and refinement. The middle classes developed an elaborate array of cutlery and codes of etiquette. Cigars and coffee remained an after-dinner custom, but cigarettes also became fashionable after they were introduced to British solders by the French during the Crimean War.

The cult of the 'good life' reached to all levels of society. The extension of the railway network in the 1850s opened up the coast and countryside to visitors and day-trippers from the city. For the artisans and working classes in the south, there were annual trips in August to Brighton, Margate, and the south coast, while Blackpool and Llandudno became favourite resorts for the workers of the new expanding industrial cities in the Midlands and the north. For the middle classes and the well-to-do, posh hotels and rented cottages replaced the old-fashioned watering places as favourite holiday destinations. In the 1860s, the Temperance reformer turned travel magnate, Thomas Cook, introduced tours to the Continent, the United States, and the Middle East, to promote a healthy life-style. The English upper classes enjoyed rest cures at Homburg, but crossings to North Africa and Egypt usually had more pleasurable motives. Interest and curiosity were stimulated by advertising and by the vogue of travel articles in the new popular press.

The promotion of the outdoor life also reflected concerns about public health. By mid-century, the life expectancy of those born in large cities was about half that of those born in the countryside. By the 1860s, the situation began to change, and more care was given to the layout of houses and streets. By the century's end, the modern city aspired to be a place of culture and civilized living, with electric-lit theatres, department stores, and accessible residential suburbs. Bedford Park where Yeats and other artists and writers lived inspired Frederick Bowyer's 'An Artistic Colony: A Song of Bedford Park', with the refrain:

> Oh come and live at Bedford Park,
>   Where culchaw [culture] reigns Supreme!
> Where vulgarity is NOT, in the most exclusive spot
>   And Art is our one good theme.

In architectural design, the more relaxed Queen Anne style was in fashion, or at least an eclectic architectural amalgam of Elizabethan Tudor Gothic that passed for it.

The brutal, more violent aspects of early Victorian life and recreation were gradually eradicated. Prize fighting and dog fighting were driven underground in the mid-Victorian period. The Marquess of Queensberry became the originator of the famous Queensberry rules that govern fight contests to this day. Organized games and physical exercise were encouraged. Ice-skating was a popular activity for the meeting of the sexes. Lawn tennis replaced croquet in the 1880s as the sport in which women could play against men. Activities such as 'pedestrianism' (walking tours), cycling, and golf became national pastimes while informal local sports like football were taken off the streets and organized by professional associations with codified rules. Women too travelled, and by the end of the century, rode bicycles and played team games. New hobbies and life-styles required new clothes, with increasing distinction being made between formal and informal wear. Women's fashions in particular became less fussy and more functional by the end of the century. Wilde was a leading advocate of freedom from constriction in women's dress, and encouraged his wife Constance to put theory into practice. During the 1880s Constance edited the *Gazette* of the Rational Dress Society which advocated divided skirts instead of petticoats for everyday wear. In his own dandified designed dress, Wilde attempted to combine colour with comfort in the nineteenth-century male costume.

The growth in the market for clothes, entertainment, and household goods was matched by the growth of advertising. The 'cultured' objected to the puffery and ubiquity of wall hoardings, while the puritanical found the linking of pretty girls with a product morally offensive. Lillie Langtry earned a large sum of money for a poster with the caption, 'Since Using Pears Soap I Have Discarded All Others'.[47] Energetic agents—such as Thomas Barratt of A & F Pears Ltd. and S. H. Benson of Bovril's—showed the way in creating new markets through advertising. No trade was unaffected. In creating a market for decadence with the launch of the *Yellow Book*, John Lane of the publishers Mathews and Lane resorted to the techniques of advertising, although the product itself was more froth than substance. George Gissing's *In the Year of Jubilee*, published in 1894 and set at the time of Queen Victoria's Jubilee of 1887, is ambiguous in its response to the bewildering expansions and excitements of market advertising and consumerism. The novel's 'coming man' is an advertising agent, Luckworth Crewe, who dreams of a future of seaside piers covered end to end with coloured advertising posters. The Jubilees were themselves stage-managed advertisement campaigns for monarchy. Queen Victoria had learned a lesson about the dangers of exclusion in the 1860s and 1870s, and had listened to her advisers. The Jubilees were both advertisements of progress, and symbols of traditional value. The combination proved a winner. In Whitehall in 1897 an exhibition, equipped with modern lavatories and telephones, celebrated the material progress of 'the longest reign'. The promotion of new goods as embodiments of wholesome traditional values was to be a favourite technique of slick, successful advertising.

One consequence of the emerging world of images was the creation of a climate of conformity that attempted to suppress the older diversities of public opinion. This was particularly true of the Empire, which claimed to unite all sections of political opinion and social background under the banner of one nation. The 'new imperialism' emerged as a positive idea during Disraeli's political campaigning in the 1880s. The word 'imperialist' had first been coined in the 1840s in France to describe the nostalgic glorification of the Napoleonic era by *'le parti impérialiste'*.[48] It passed into British political discourse in 1876, and doubled with 'Beaconsfieldian' as a smear word to express opposition to Disraeli conferring on Queen Victoria the status of 'Empress of India'. Disraeli, with characteristic opportunism, annexed the term during the 1880 election campaign, in raising the spectre of Irish Home Rule as 'a challenge to the . . . imperial character' of the United Kingdom.[49] In the event Disraeli's election defeat meant a massive endorsement of Gladstone's anti-imperialist crusade (called 'Midlothianism'). Yet the new imperialism remained aggressively nationalistic. Exponents like Joseph Chamberlain preached its 'civilising mission' while advocating the need for the violent 'pacification' of recalcitrant tribes. Chamberlain was one of the leading Unionists responsible for the split within the Liberal Party over the issue of Home Rule for Ireland. Many resisted the jingoistic fever that overrode other cultural and political allegiances. Among them was R. B. Cunninghame Graham, the staunch supporter of Irish Home Rule and convert to William Morris's socialism, whose spoof sermon 'Bloody Niggers'

(1897) satirized the rhetoric of the British Empire's 'civilizing mission'.[50]

The civilizing ethos of healthy sport was increasingly annexed to the rhetoric of aggressive imperialism and the idea of competition between nations. The link between athleticism and manly nationhood can also be found in the early- and mid-Victorian age; it is a feature, for example, of Thomas Hughes's popular novel of a boys' public school, *Tom Brown's Schooldays* (1857), which celebrates Thomas Arnold's attempt to civilize and tame brutal manliness. Yet the cult of athleticism remained yoked to the Victorian ideal of masculinity and attendant fears of effeminacy and over-refinement. In 1861 a mid-Victorian Pepys recorded with satisfaction in his diary that, 'The affected Dandy of past years is unknown. If he exists, he is despised. The standard or average English gentleman of the present day must at least show vigour of body.'[51] With the culture of leisure and urban refinements in the last two decades of the nineteenth century, such masculine anxieties, if anything, intensified. The imperialist romances of Rudyard Kipling and Rider Haggard produced the defining images of British manliness. 'Mankind won't stand it much longer, this encroachment of the humane spirit,' announces an admirer of Kipling in the final chapter of Gissing's novel *The Whirlpool* (1897). 'See the spread of athletics. We must look to our physique, make ourselves ready . . . [Women] must breed a stouter race.' In popular illustrated magazines like *Black and White*, bare-breasted beauties and men in uniform, the home front and the frontier, provided respective representations of male and female destiny. The Royal Procession of Imperial Troops during Jubilee celebrations on 22 June 1897 moved the reporter of the *Daily Mail* 'to understand, as never before, what the Empire amounts to. . . . We send a boy here and a boy there, and the boy takes hold of the savages and teaches them to march and shoot . . . and believe in him, and die for him and his Queen.' It was in this mood of scientific racism and belligerent masculinity that raillery against the aesthetes in the 1880s turned to revulsion and fear of effeminacy in the 1890s. On the announcement of Wilde's conviction and prison sentence for homosexuality in 1895, the London prostitutes—victims of an earlier purity campaign—danced patriotically in the street.

CHAPTER 3

THE LITERARY SCENE

WHEN Wilde decided on a literary career, rather than a career in the Civil Service or in politics, he was under no illusions about the difficulty of making a living as a writer. The rise in literacy and cheaper methods of production and distribution had produced a rapid and unprecedented expansion of the literary market-place. Yet this growth coincided with a fragmentation of the readership, and a perceived division between literature and journalism, and between 'good' literature and 'cheap' literature. 'It is impossible to live by literature. By journalism a man may make an income,' Wilde wrote in 1885 (*Letters*, p. 264). As an added difficulty, many late-Victorian writers felt that it was their duty to set about changing the attitudes and expectations of the general reading public. Theirs was the legacy of the Victorian social critics—Carlyle, Arnold, and Ruskin—and the idea of a cultured élite opposed to contemporary civilization. Their credo was at once radical yet traditional, in form as well as content. Like the leading writers of his day, Wilde hoped to appeal to the general public while at the same time educating them against the sentimental, the conventional, and the predictable. The perception of Wilde's career as a writer has passed through several stages in this respect. In contrast to the established views of Wilde as an exceptional personality and dilettante, or as a conformist rebel or subversive, there has been an important revaluation of Wilde as a versatile professional writer, tuned to the necessary compromises and realities of literary production.

The Growth of New Markets

POPULAR READING

The growth of the press after 1870 is usually explained as the effect of the Elementary Education Act passed that year which enabled local authorities to provide elementary schooling for everyone. This is perhaps over-simplistic. Certainly the proliferation of newspapers and new reviews can be attributed to the rise of the reading public. From the beginning of the century, the population doubled, while the overall level of literacy increased by 30 per cent. However, these developments themselves do not account for the explosion of printed stuff, which was made possible by urbanization and a reduction in the costs of production. Mass circulation dailies such as the *Daily Chronicle* were already a reality by the mid-1860s. For the large circulation newspapers, the capital expenditure involved in the introduction of new web rotary machines in the 1860s, and new mechanical typesetting in the 1890s, was offset by a large reduction in labour costs. In the production of periodicals and small evening sheets, falling paper prices and the repeal of the 'taxes on knowledge'—the newspaper tax in 1855, and the tax on paper in 1861—provided opportunities for expansion and diversity.[1] Among the journals to which Wilde contributed, *Blackwood's Edinburgh Magazine* (known as 'Maga'), the *Nineteenth Century*, and the incongruously named *Fortnightly Review*, were traditional heavyweight monthlies; others like the newly established and short-lived *Court and Society Review*, and the *Dramatic Review*, were of the populist 6d. or 1s. weekly variety.

The growth of the press coincided with the growth of cities. The flood of printed material served a new expanding class of urban and suburban readers avid for entertainment and diversion, news and comment. In the eighteenth century and for much of the Victorian age, the spread of journalism was seen by the literary world as a threat to social order and hierarchy. Many felt a real sense of discontinuity between the society they lived in and the society of their predecessors. To Thomas Carlyle, J. S. Mill, John Ruskin, and Matthew Arnold, it was one of the disintegrating forces of modern urban life. Against such social fragmentation, they sought to reinstate some older concept or spirit of community. Carlyle, who clung tenaciously to the heroic ideal of the 'Man of Letters', railed against journalism as 'just ditch water'.[2] Ruskin no less rancorously compared art critics in the press to a heap of dung, 'content if . . . they may attract to themselves notice by their noisomeness, or like its insects, exalt themselves by virulence into visibility'.[3] All four men of letters hankered after a system whereby works of literature would carry a certificate of authority. In calling for a literary tribunal in England on the lines of the French Academy, Arnold quoted approvingly the French philosopher and historian Ernest Renan's view: 'All ages have had their inferior literature; but the great danger of our time is that inferior literature tends more and more to get the upper place.'[4] The literary ideal that Wilde and his generation inherited from Ruskin and Arnold was one that contrasted the aesthetically disinterested spirit of the university with the philistinism and partisanship of the metropolis—the new Jerusalem with the new Babylon. The preface to *Modern Painters* contains Ruskin's most sustained attack on the way journalists gain credit by pandering to the prejudices of their readers. On the title page, Ruskin identifies himself simply as 'A graduate of Oxford'.

Wilde became familiar with *Modern Painters* while he was an undergraduate at Oxford. He adopted Ruskin's scorn of journalism. In his prose dialogue, 'The Critic as Artist' (1890), the dreamy Ernest's ideal aesthetic world is devoid of art-critics: 'By the Ilyssus there were no tedious magazines about art, in which the industrious prattle of what they do not understand. On the reed-grown banks of that little stream strutted no ridiculous journalism monopolizing the seat of judgement when it should be apologizing in the dock.' In agreement for once, the more urbane Gilbert is equally savage: 'As for modern journalism, it is not my business to defend it. It justifies its own existence by the great Darwinian principle of the survival of the vulgarest.' The clamour of the opinion-forming press is a running joke in *The Importance of Being Earnest*. Algernon, for instance, is of the opinion that literary criticism should be left 'to people who haven't been at a University. They do it so well in the daily papers' (Act 1). By the mid-1890s, under constant attack from the press, Wilde occasionally let the mask of urbanity slip. In September 1894, for example, he objected angrily in the letter pages of the *Pall Mall Gazette* about the 'great license of comment and attack . . . allowed nowadays in newspapers', acknowledging sarcastically that 'it would be too much to expect any true literary instinct' among their staff (*Letters*, p. 614). In his provocatively titled 'A Few Maxims for the Instruction of the Over-Educated', in the *Saturday Review* that same month, his disparagement of public taste and the journalists who feed off it is again pure Ruskin turned into venomous aphorism. In Wilde's version, 'The only thing that the public can see is the obvious. The result is the criticism of the journalist.'[5]

Wilde's early career coincided with the rise of the 'New

Journalism', a term first coined by Matthew Arnold in 1887 in an article in the *Nineteenth Century* denouncing the appeal to sentiment rather than intelligent argument in the popular press.[6] The New Journalism was at first condemned as 'the Americanization of English journalism'. As pioneered by W. T. Stead, the 'crusader in Babylon' of the *Pall Mall Gazette* in the 1880s, the 'New Journalism' introduced a strong personal note that had in fact to some extent existed before Victorian respectability had stifled unorthodoxy.[7] The intimate interview and the personal paragraph became standard features, even in respectable sections of the British press; news stories were dressed out with vivid dramatic or melodramatic detail; moral and social enthusiasms were paraded; articles were signed. In claiming to take its mandate from the 'average man', the New Journalism could satisfy its twin aim of profit-making venture and 'journalism with a mission'.

Wilde took full advantage of the opportunities for self-advertisement in the popular press. Even before he could claim to have achieved any real success, he featured in the popular annual, the *Biograph* and in Edmund Yates's society magazine, the *World*. According to George Bernard Shaw, who was taken on as drama critic at the *World* in 1884, Yates gave the middle classes what they wanted—the dirt on society made 'perfectly presentable' and socially correct.[8] Wilde and Yates made natural allies. The *World* took Wilde's side against the unpleasant ridicule by letter-writers and correspondents in some sections of the British press during Wilde's lecture tour of America; it also made the rivalry and witty exchanges between Wilde and Whistler the talk of London in 1886. Faced with the inquisitive personal style of the American press—where the methods of the New Journalism were already common practice— Wilde appeared to be in his element. He thrived in an atmosphere of attention and adulation. In conversation with Wilde, American journalists were able to fill their columns with 'Oscariana'. Yet in England, where sensationalism and moral rectitude made hypocritical bed-fellows, Wilde was sometimes wary. 'The newspapers seem to me to be written by the prurient for the Philistine,' he wrote to Arthur Conan Doyle when *The Picture of Dorian Gray* was condemned as an immoral book (*Letters*, p. 478). In full flow against English puritans and hypocrisy, Gilbert in the second part of 'The Critic as Artist', identifies the 'new Journalism' as 'the old vulgarity' writ large. Wilde's most savage satire of tabloid journalism is voiced by Mrs Cheveley, the blackmailer of Sir Robert Chiltern in *An Ideal Husband*:

Sir Robert . . . Suppose that when I leave this house I drive down to some newspaper office, and give them this scandal and the proofs of it! Think of their loathsome joy, of the delight they would have in dragging you down, of the mud and mire they would plunge you in. Think of the hypocrite with his greasy smile penning his leading article, and arranging the foulness of the public placard. (Act 1)

Editors often stirred controversy by soliciting a response to critical or abusive letters and articles prior to their publication. This was a favourite technique of editors like Augustus Moore of the scurrilous sheet, the *Hawk*, and W. T. Stead while editor of his own *Review of Reviews*. In spite of feelings of 'self-loathing', Shaw could never resist rising to the bait.[9] Wilde, by contrast, sometimes resisted the lure. When the American-based Irish dramatist Dion Boucicault and the editor of the New York *World* urged Wilde to respond to an attack on his mercenary motives by the British journalist and lecturer, Archibald Forbes, Wilde 'thought it wiser to avoid the garbage of the dirty-water-throwing in public' (*Letters*, pp. 135–6). When provoked into making a public statement, Wilde, like Arnold and Ruskin before him, followed the gentlemanly practice of expressing his views through letters to the press. Like them, he was aware of the paradox of reaching an audience through the very organs that were the object of his scorn.

Wilde saw nothing contradictory in earning his living in a trade he publicly despised. In 'Half an Hour with the Worst Authors', for instance, one of his many reviews for the *Pall Mall Gazette* during the 1880s, Wilde shows evident enjoyment in using journalism to denounce lapses of style and taste 'of our ordinary magazine writers'.[10] The *Pall Mall Gazette* was itself a strange hybrid among literary magazines. First issued in 1865, it took its name from the fictional paper, 'written by gentlemen for gentlemen', in Thackeray's novel *Pendennis*. As an evening paper of news, political comment, and articles on literature and current affairs, the *Pall Mall Gazette* had enjoyed a respectable place within the self-styled 'Higher Journalism'. Even during the sensation-mongering W. T. Stead's editorship from 1883 to 1890, as a flagship of the New Journalism, the paper retained some of its distinction. Stead did not always get everything his own way, and had to apologize to the paper's owner, Henry Yates Thompson, in 1886 when advertising revenue fell in the six months following his 'The Maiden Tribute of Modern Babylon' crusade on child prostitution.[11] Although he treated the Oxford men on his staff—the 'University tips'—with good-natured condescension (among them Edward T. Cook, the paper's future editor, and Alfred Milner, his chief assistant), Stead respected their critical acumen and worked in close co-operation with them.[12] He appears to have commissioned Wilde as a contributor to the paper following the controversy in October and November 1884 surrounding Wilde's lecture on dress. Wilde's earliest contributions date from that time. His sense of superiority to 'tradesmen journalists' lay in the fact that he remained an independent writer rather than a university graduate who had joined the staff.

Journalism as a profession, rather than as an occasional activity, attracted a large number of Oxbridge undergraduates in the last decades of the nineteenth century. The Oxbridge recruits brought to Fleet Street a subdued air of culture that contrasted strangely with the brash rough and tumble of Stead and the 'new journalists'. Among Wilde's contacts was W. L. Courtney, who combined a career in journalism with his duties as an Oxford don, and who joked of his Jekyll and Hyde existence in the 1880s, writing serious stuff for the heavyweight quarterlies and persiflage for society magazines like the *World*. Wilde invited one of Courtney's students (and later second wife and biographer) to contribute an article of life in 'The Oxford Woman's Colleges, by a member of one of them' for the first number of Wilde's relaunched *Woman's World* in 1887.

The offer of the editorship of the 1s. monthly *Woman's World* came from the hard-nosed newspaper man, Thomas Wemyss Reid, general manager of the expanding publishing firm of Cassell and Company. Reid, who had begun his career as innovative and highly successful editor of the *Leeds Mercury*, always kept an eye out for fresh talent and new ideas. He was also, like Wilde, a Gladstonian Liberal. Wilde was to transform the magazine. He altered its title from the *Lady's World* to *Woman's World* after some market research and extended its range to include sections on literature, art, travel, and social study, with dress and fashion left to the end of the magazine. He worked hard to make it a success, soliciting contributions from prominent women writers, activists, and actresses on both sides of the Atlantic. To Helena Sickert, sister to the painter and a female activist and former student of Girton College, Cambridge, Wilde set down his aim as editor: 'The magazine will try to be representative of the thought and culture of the woman of this century, and I am very anxious that those who have had university training, like yourself, should have an organ through which they can express their views on life and things' (*Letters*, p. 301). Wilde himself undertook to write the 'Literary Notes'. His standpoint was not that of a scholar, but of what was pleasant to read. His name on the cover ensured a successful launch. His target readers were educated middle-class women. One of Wilde's motives in taking on the editorship was clearly financial. His salary of £6 a week might seem modest in comparison with Stead's of more than three times that amount at the *Pall Mall Gazette*; but it was fair payment for a magazine with a steady but modest circulation. Shaw at the time was by comparison earning three guineas a week as dramatic critic for the *World*.

It would be simplistic to conclude that in meeting market forces in this way Wilde was therefore more a conformist than rebel. In accepting the editorship, Wilde's aims were also avowedly radical. His constructed woman reader was no longer the Victorian 'angel in the house'. Serious feminist articles such as Laura McLaren's 'The Fallacy of the Superiority of Men' and S. William Beck's 'A Treatise on Hoops' sought to change conventional attitudes to women's history and women's lives. Features on women in education and in traditionally male professions such as medicine also set out to challenge the popular conception that educated women were dowdy.

Circulation figures for *Woman's World* were never high, and soon began to fall off. In October 1888 Wemyss Reid and John Williams, chief editor at Cassells, recommended in their end-of-year review that 'more prominence' be given to 'distinctively feminine subjects' (*Letters*, p. 363), by which they meant beauty and fashion. Wilde defended the political aspirations of his female contributors, but bowed to financial realities. He agreed to remain for another year, but he began to lose interest in the magazine and left decisions increasingly to his sub-editor, Arthur Fish. He resigned without acrimony in November 1889, leaving *Woman's World* to return to its old format before it eventually ceased publication altogether. Although an effective editor and reviewer, Wilde neither adopted the noisy overbearing style of the successful new breed of journalists such as Stead and Frank Harris, nor inclined temperamentally or stylistically to the miscellaneous style of other Oxonians turned journalists such as Courtney and Andrew Lang. When asked to provide the literary 'Causerie' column for Wemyss Reid's new journal, the *Speaker*, in 1890, Wilde declined with the frank confession: 'I know I write best on a definite subject and have not much discursive journalistic faculty' (*Letters*, p. 417). The lively 'Causerie' column was in fact to be written with great success for many years by the young Cornishman and Cambridge graduate, Arthur T. Quiller Couch. Wilde continued to write articles and reviews. He was fastidious in his 'taste' and drew a clear line between literature and journalism, but he stopped short of the literary snobbery that prompted his impoverished contemporary, George Gissing, to turn down an offer to write for the *Pall Mall Gazette* under John Morley because he considered journalism degrading. Wilde's essays in the *Nineteenth Century*, and the *Fortnightly Review*, turned back to the style and manner of the 'Higher Journalism', transforming and unsettling the methods and authority of Victorian social criticism in the process.

Wilde invariably combined literary fastidiousness with practicality. In his agreement with the American actor-manager Lawrence Barrett he arranged that his verse drama, *The Duchess of Padua* (with its American title, *Guido Ferranti*) should appear anonymously in New York in 1891 in order to have the play 'judged entirely on its own merits' (*Letters*, p. 464). He was well aware of the value of publicity in an age when 'brand names' sold consumer products, including literary ones. He consistently traded on his name in selling his writings in the late 1880s and 1890s, and again in the 'leftover years' following his jail sentence. He also stage-managed the entry of his disciples—Richard Le Gallienne, John Gray, Aubrey Beardsley—onto the London literary and artistic scene. Yet he also knew that celebrity could have a negative effect on a writer's career if it relied upon transitory modishness and news value. Well-known writers were lionized in the popular press. The most fashionable could earn large fees for giving interviews. Wilde often gave interviews for nothing. By the mid-1890s he more often resisted the intrusion. Asked to give an interview for *McClure's Magazine* in November 1894, he declined with the confession, 'I am sick of my name in the papers' (*Letters*, p. 624). The following January, in reply to those who criticized his curtain-speeches, he stated in a pre-planned interview with his friend Robert Ross that 'The artist cannot be degraded into the servant of the public.'[13]

The image of the writer's life reflected in interviews and personal columns in the popular press was generally that of the 'good life'. Thus in Wilde's early profile in the *Biograph*, the reader learns of his recent trip to Florence, of his new passion for Florentine art, and of the aesthetic arrangement of his rooms, with their Blake drawings, Burne-Joneses, and blue china. The ideal of aristocratic ease was a fantasy of writers themselves—hence the prevalence in fiction and plays of the writer as a glamorized, tweed-jacketed man of leisure. Hence too the founding in 1892 of the Omar Khayyam Club whose epicurean dinners Hardy, Conan Doyle, Gissing, and H. G. Wells all at one time or another attended. In resisting George Alexander's request that he drop a scene from *The Importance of Being Earnest*, Wilde allegedly protested that 'it must have taken fully five minutes to write!'[14] Insouciance was the assumed posture of the new aestheticism. The workaday realities of a writer's life were usually far more prosaic. George Gissing's candid novel of the literary life, *New Grub Street* (1891), shows writers facing the difficulties of composition, and the emotional and economic hazards of marketing and publishing their work. Wilde himself worked hard at his desk. He kept to a punitive timetable in order to fulfil contracts and make up for missed deadlines. During his 'holiday' to the Lake District in 1891, he wrote *Lady Windermere's Fan*. While staying in Norfolk in 1892, he successfully drafted *A Woman of No Importance*. At Goring-on-Thames in 1893, he worked on *An Ideal Husband*, and at Worthing in 1894, *The Importance of Being Earnest*. He kept up an appearance of effortless creativity, but sometimes found writing difficult. While working on *Lady Windermere's Fan*, he made the following confession to George Alexander: 'I am not satisfied with myself or my work. I can't get a grip of the play yet: I can't get my people real. . . . artistic work can't be done unless one is in the mood; certainly my work can't. Sometimes I spend months over a thing, and don't do any good; at other times I write a thing in a fortnight' (*Letters*, p. 463). Max Beerbohm, one of the few people to see Wilde at work, depicts him as an 'early riser', up sharpening ideas that will appear to be spontaneous.[15] The drawing of 'Oscar Wilde at Work', attributed to

'The Aesthetic Monkey', engraved from a painting by W. H. Beard in *Harper's Weekly*, 28 January 1882.

'Oscar Wilde at Work'. Caricature by Aubrey Beardsley.

FANCY PORTRAIT.

QUITE TOO–TOO PUFFICKLY PRECIOUS!!

Being Lady Windy-mère's Fan-cy Portrait of the new dramatic author, Shakespeare Sheridan Oscar Puff, Esq.

["He addressed from the stage a public audience, mostly composed of ladies, pressing between his daintily-gloved fingers a still burning and half-smoked cigarette."– *Daily Telegraph.*]

A *Punch* cartoon from 1892, after the first-night success of *Lady Windermere's Fan*.

Aubrey Beardsley, shows Wilde in shirt-sleeves at his desk, sur-rounded by open volumes—most prominently, Gautier, Flaubert, Swinburne, and the family Bible.

The romantic myth of the writer was concurrent with the emer-gence of literature as a trade. By the late nineteenth century, the literary world was not immune to the pressures of the new con-sumerism that affected all branches of commerce. The traditional image of Victorian gentleman-publishers such as William Blackwood and John Murray at the centre of a friendly circle of distinguished authors concealed the reality of a fiercely competitive trade in the mid-Victorian period.[16] The later Victorian age saw the absorption of many small family firms into large companies, and the develop-ment of newer, more commercially aggressive publishing practices. In 1884 the Society of Authors was founded under the leadership of Walter Besant to protect the professional writer against the abuses of publishers. The Society clashed publicly with publishers in 1887 and 1890 over the issue of disadvantageous contracts. Publishers retali-ated by establishing the Publishers' Association in 1896. Some authors were slow to assert their rights. Many continued to sell their manuscripts outright, thereby relinquishing any claim to future profits. Although condemned by the Society of Authors, outright sale was often considered a more reliable way of ensuring some financial return, than in trusting to the accuracy of publishers' accounts.[17]

Wilde's transactions with publishers and theatre managers reveal his astute, business-like approach to the sale and marketing of his writings.[18] He felt he had been cheated by Ward, Lock and Co. in agreeing to let them have *The Picture of Dorian Gray* for £120 advance on royalties of 10 per cent. He was to strike better deals with James R. Osgood, McIlvaine and Co. in selling the copyright of *Intentions* and *A House of Pomegranates*. In assigning the perform-ance rights of his plays, he made detailed arrangements for advances and a percentage of box-office takings. Such above-board, con-tractual agreements were becoming increasingly standard by the 1890s, but evidence of Wilde's professional vigilance is demon-strated in his dealings with John Lane at the publishing house of the Bodley Head. Wilde's letters during February 1893 show an increas-ing weariness and frustration at Lane's procrastination over con-tracts, and failure to pay proper royalties. Lane charmed and flattered the authors on his list, but many quickly discovered that the appearance of generosity and of old-fashioned relations between publisher and author was a cover for sharp business practice and profiteering at their expense. Lane's behind-the-scenes record as a publisher is one of double dealing, lost balance-sheets, and broken promises. Wilde, who had sexual relations with Lane's office boy, Edward Shelley, was not taken in by Lane's respectable front. He was to have his revenge by calling the manservant in *The Importance of Being Earnest* Lane after him.

Wilde's industry, and practical approach to writing, is also reflected in his willingness to revise his work. When the publisher Ward, Lock and Co. suggested that he enlarge *The Picture of Dorian Gray* from the periodical to the book version to help sales, he complied by adding six new chapters. For some readers, the enlarged version, and in particular the melodramatic development of the Sibyl Vane affair weakens the original; for others, the polished satire of the book version is an improvement. The fact that Wilde added a Preface in answer to his critics suggests that he himself did not consider there was any loss of artistic integrity or intention. The same is true of his constant revisions of his plays. He sometimes disagreed with the changes proposed by the actor-managers with whom he worked. He resisted point blank George Alexander's wish that the identity of Mrs Erlynne in *Lady Windermere's Fan* should be revealed to the audience by the end of the second act, rather than during the final act, only to relent after the first performance. On seeing Alexander's version of *The Importance of Being Earnest*, cut from four to three acts, he reportedly commented: 'Yes, it is quite a good play. I remember I wrote one very like it myself, but it was even more brilliant than this' (Ellmann, p. 406). The fact that he kept to Alexander's alterations in the published versions of his plays indicates that he finally accepted the artistic superiority of the acted versions. Unlike Henry James, who failed disastrously as a dramatist in the 1890s, Wilde was genuinely a man of the theatre. He may have quarrelled with Alexander, and even on one occasion been ordered out of rehearsals, but, like Shaw, he understood that a successful play was a collaborative effort, not a work that emerged from the head of the playwright, like Minerva fully formed from the head of Jove.

ART AND LITERATURE

The publishing history of the mid- and late-Victorian period was not exclusively one of populism and mass markets. The *Germ*, launched by the Pre-Raphaelite circle in 1850, inspired a succession of avantgarde 'art and lit' magazines later in the century. In the book world, the founding of the Kelmscott Press by William Morris in 1890 established the vogue of the book as art object. Wilde played an important part in both of these developments in late-Victorian publishing history. He encouraged Herbert Horne and Arthur Mackmurdo when they began publishing their quarterly, the *Century Guild Hobby Horse*, in 1884. The Century Guild association was founded by Mackmurdo in 1882 as a branch of the Arts and Crafts Movement dedicated to the unification of the arts. Its influences were Ruskin, the Pre-Raphaelites, Arnold, Pater, Morris, and the new aestheticism. The *Hobby Horse* proclaimed its 'art for art's sake' credentials: 'Art must exist for its own sake, as an expression or ornament of life'. Wilde allowed the *Hobby Horse* to reproduce a facsimile of the manuscript of Keats's 'Sonnet in Blue' given to him by the poet's niece during his tour of America. He also enthusiastically reviewed the lectures on modern art delivered in 1887 by Selwyn Image, a Century Guild artist and poet, who co-edited the *Hobby Horse*. It was the promise of Wilde's presiding presence at Herbert Horne's house on Fitzroy Street in 1890 that brought together the Century Guild poets and the loosely formed 'Celtic' group of the Rhymers' Club, whose usual weekly meeting place was the Cheshire Cheese public house in Fleet Steet. The two anthologies of the Rhymers' Club, issued by the Bodley Head in 1892 and 1894, were designed by the contributing poets to satisfy the aesthetic devotion to the book-as-object.

The taste for the book-as-object, and to recent first editions by specific contemporary writers, has been connected by some literary historians to the advance of commodification in the late nineteenth century. Publishers turned educational and literary value to commercial ends. For earlier collectors, books were valued as masterpieces of earlier methods of printing, binding, and illustration. In the eighteenth century collectors tended to think in terms of the eventual public ownership and exhibition of books and manuscripts. The manuscript of Omar Khayyam that Wilde admired at the Bodleian

Library in Oxford is an example of this. By the late nineteenth century, by contrast, the value of the book for the modern collector shifted to criteria of rarity and sentimental association, such as completeness. [19] Entrepreneurial publishers like Mathews and Lane in part catered for, and in part created this vogue in the rare book trade.

Wilde's concern for the book-as-object is evident in his dealings with publishers and book designers. One of the most stylishly eccentric examples of the book-as-object in the 1890s, and a defining moment of English decadence, was John Gray's collection of poems, *Silverpoints* (1893), designed, like *The Picture of Dorian Gray*, by Charles Ricketts. Wilde signed a contract with John Lane agreeing to pay for its production and promotional costs. In the end, the publishers met the expense, either because of a breakdown in Wilde and Gray's friendship, or because of Wilde's increasing disapproval of Lane's methods. In the design and illustration of his own books, he sought commissions for the most innovative young avant-garde artists of the day—Aubrey Beardsley and the francophile partners Ricketts and Shannon, whose Symbolist 'art and lit' magazine, the *Dial*, he admired and praised. Ricketts and Shannon provided the designs and decoration for the cover of *A House of Pomegranates* (1891), with Ricketts also providing the decoration for *The Picture of Dorian Gray*, 'The Sphinx', and the beautiful binding design 'The Seven Trees' for the 1892 Bodley Head reissue of Wilde's *Poems*. These, together with Gray's *Silverpoints*, and Beardsley's drawings for the *Yellow Book* and for *Salome*, both issued in 1894, represent the quintessence of the English *fin de siècle*.

The fact that the vogue for limited editions and collector's items can be identified as a feature of the commodity culture from which it sought to dissociate itself does not diminish the avant-garde aims of Wilde and Morris in the English literary and book market. In writing to Morris, Wilde assigns to his older contemporary an artistic integrity that he himself clearly wished to emulate: 'I have always felt that your work comes from the sheer delight of making beautiful things: that no alien motive ever interests you: that in its singleness of aim, as well as in its perfection of result, it is pure art, everything that you do' (*Letters*, p. 476). Wilde himself generally privileged artistic decisions over financial considerations. When the partnership of Mathews and Lane finally split up over the publication of the *Yellow Book*, Wilde preferred the more business-like and genuinely artistic

Mathews to the venal, commercially go-getting Lane. That he stayed with Lane was probably the result of Mathews's desire to distance himself from the direction given to the spirit of decadence by Lane's commercially driven instincts and Wilde's artistic ones.

The Reaction against Realism

A striking feature of the publishing world in the last two decades of the nineteenth century was the fragmentation and labelling of 'popular literature' into different categories and sub-genres of fiction to appeal to the specialist tastes of different groups of readers. There is no simple explanation for this. Until the 1870s, reading matter tended to be divided into popular classic fiction catering for the 'cultivated' reader, and 'cheap' fiction—sensationalist 'penny dreadfuls' and 'yellowbacks'—for the unsophisticated. Quality novels, which also included the crop of second rank 'sensation novels', were normally first published in expensive three-volume editions (called triple-deckers). Priced uniformly at 31*s.*, these were far beyond the pockets of the majority of readers, who customarily borrowed them from subscription libraries, one volume at a time—hence the description of these subscription libraries as 'circulating libraries'. The largest and most powerful of the circulating libraries in the latter half of the century was Mudie's Select Library, founded in 1842, with W. H. Smith's trailing in second place as the only serious rival. The demise of the three-volume novel, already in decline since 1890, occurred in 1895 after price-fixing by Mudie's and Smith's forced publishers to issue new fiction in the cheaper single-volume form previously held over until reprints. Already by the 1880s, leading publishers of the three-volume format, such as Chapman and Hall, Blackwood, and Macmillan, faced competition from the new breed of entrepreneurial editors and publishers keen to supply the growing demand for cheaply priced, one-volume adventure stories and thrillers. Some of the older, more traditional publishing houses unwittingly contributed to the demise of their lucrative three-volume format by launching their own sanitized, 'improving' version of light, escapist fiction for the young, against the perceived excesses of the penny dreadfuls and yellowbacks. John Cassell, a Victorian temperance missionary turned successful publisher, departed from the staple and profitable format of part issue of 'cheap' fiction to produce bound volumes—notably of the phenomenally successful *Treasure Island* (1883) by Robert Louis Stevenson and Rider Haggard's *King Solomon's Mines* (1885).

In its improving mission, publishing followed the civilizing trend towards regulation and control that affected all areas of late-Victorian social life and leisure. In 1887 the *Edinburgh Review* urged literary reformers to 'Carry the war into the enemy's camp: flood the market with good, wholesome literature instead of the poisonous stuff to which hapless purchasers are now condemned. The battle must be fought out by the purveyors of fiction, and it must be as easy and profitable to provide a dainty, harmless, and well-seasoned repast as a dish of poison.'[20] Children were felt to be particularly at risk. In Gissing's novel *Thyrza*, also published in 1887, the idealistic middle-class hero is inspired to his mission of culture after the shock of hearing that the working-class father had exposed his little girl of 10 to a comic paper burlesquing the Bible. In real life that same year, the pioneering publisher George Hutchinson went into business on his own to provide 'improving' anthologies of stories for boys and girls. Hutchinson had served his apprenticeship with Alexander Strahan, best known as the publisher and editor of the wholesome and popular *Good Words (for the Young)*. From a commercial as well as an artistic point of view 'good' escapist literature, as literary reformers knew, had to mean literary merit and not merely 'goody-goody'.[21] George Newnes, the most pushy and commercially motivated of the new publishers, included an impressive range of works combining literary and commercial value in his list, among them Arthur Conan Doyle's Sherlock Holmes stories.

The proliferation of new categories of adventure tales, scientific fiction, and psychological romances on publishers' lists was in one respect the result of a widespread reaction to realism. The apparent realism of the classic Victorian novel had always been diluted by idealistic elements—by coincidences, unexpected returns, saving legacies, and happy endings—in comparison with its French counterpart. The English novel, as Charlotte Brontë acknowledged, was written for readers with 'sunny imaginations'. By the 1860s, the novel in England had become more distinctly sombre and naturalistic in colour and tone. The change came about in two ways. First, English novelists themselves began to subvert romantic elements in their fiction, partly in response to the weakening of optimism in society as a whole. One needs only to compare Dickens's darker later works to his cheerful early fiction to notice the change. Simultaneously, some younger novelists sought to emulate the experimental objectivity advanced in France by Flaubert and Maupassant and culminating in Zola's naturalistic manifesto *Le Roman expérimental* in 1880. Henry James, in particular, drew fire from English readers for what was felt to be his morbid, French-influenced experiments in pessimism and microscopic analysis of character. A debate ensued in the 1880s on the relative merits of 'the novel of character' and the 'novel of adventure'. In his famous essay 'The Art of Fiction' (1884), James set the frankness and rigour of French fiction against the 'moral timidity' and formal diffusion of the English novel.[22] James was noticeably careful to exempt Robert Louis Stevenson and the new 'novel of adventure' from his general criticism of Victorian fiction. In response, Stevenson's essay 'A Humble Remonstrance' took friendly issue with James's apparent privileging of art over life, but endorsed James's passionate advocacy of geometric form over diffusion in fiction.[23] The short one-volume novel of action and incident flourished in England at the very moment when French naturalistic theories were being most loudly trumpeted. Labelled romance, to distinguish it from realism, the new novel of adventure embraced many categories—historical, philosophical, scientific, and psychical.

As preacher of the new aestheticism, Wilde was a passionate advocate of romance. The principle of the new aestheticism is that 'art never expresses anything but itself'. In 'The Decay of Lying', the character Vivian rejects the imitative spirit among the leading writers of the day. Wilde has him repeat Ruskin's scathing dismissal of George Eliot's characters 'as being like the sweepings of a Pentonville omnibus'. Henry James wastes his 'neat literary style' upon 'mean motives and imperceptible "points of view"'. The French are 'not much better', in Vivian's comprehensive demolition of the 'monstrous worship of facts' in contemporary literature. Maupassant 'strips life of the few poor rags that still cover her, and shows us foul sore and festering wound'. Surprisingly, Vivian also denounces the contemporary 'romancers' whose fiction seems close to Wilde's own. The bar is set high indeed. Thus Stevenson's transformation of Dr Jekyll 'reads dangerously like an experiment out of the *Lancet*'. Rider Haggard gives unnecessary factual corroboration to the 'marvellous'.

Although appearing to enjoy his role as demolisher of reputations, Vivian is capable of discerning judgements. His qualified admiration of the 'almost epic' quality of Zola's *Germinal* might be put down to Wilde's fascination with Zola's compelling portrait of the anarchist Souvarine. *Germinal* was a novel that repelled and appealed to radicals and conservatives alike. Yet Vivian draws a contrast between Zola's 'unimaginative realism' and Balzac's 'imaginative reality'. In praising Balzac's fictions for being as 'deeply coloured as dreams' he takes his cue from Baudelaire. Balzac, he concludes, 'created life, he did not copy it'.

The basis of Wilde's own fiction emerges most clearly in the denunciation of psychological analysis of upper-class characters by his French contemporary, Paul Bourget. Wilde argues that 'what is interesting about people in good society is the mask that each of them wears—not the reality that lies behind the mask'. Behind the mask, he declares, people are depressingly and humiliatingly the same, whatever their place in society. Wilde's aim, then, is not to demythologize or demystify human illusions, but to find in them the truest, most suggestive testimony of the human spirit and imagination. He regarded romance as the form least dependent on fact and personal experience, and therefore the most freely imaginative. In his own writing, he favoured traditional romance forms: the fairy-story; the pre-historicist 'history' ('The Portrait of Mr W. H.'); and the fantasy tale (*The Picture of Dorian Gray*). Even the naturalist settings and treatment of Wilde's social comedies have to be regarded with circumspection. Wilde found in Balzac, and possibly even in James, what he saw lacking in Bourget. The force of his social drama lies not in its sentimental analysis or exposure of hidden lives, but in the energy with which his characters play out their invented selves. His plays are in some respects costume dramas in modern dress.

Interestingly, Thomas Carlyle was one of Wilde's listed favourites among Victorian poetical prose writers. In 'The Decay of Lying', Carlyle's *History of the French Revolution* is praised because 'facts are either kept in their proper subordinate position, or else entirely excluded on the general ground of dullness'. Wilde's admiration for Carlyle's novelistic history is another reminder that the spirit of romance was not totally eclipsed by realism in the nineteenth century. Yet it tended to survive in its shadow, or to survive in the margins of 'literature'. Carlyle's influential *Sartor Resartus* never achieved the commercial success of the classic Victorian novels. Mid-Victorian 'sensation novels' and late-Victorian 'shockers' like Stevenson's *The Strange Case of Dr Jekyll and Mr Hyde* (1886) and Wilde's *The Picture of Dorian Gray* did not win complete literary acceptance. They shared narrative features of the 'gothic' genre that flourished in the age of Romanticism from the 1790s to the 1820s, not least in their psychological interest in mental disturbance, revulsion, and paranoia. Among Wilde's favourite reading as a youth was J. W. Meinhold's *Sidonia the Sorceress*, which his mother had translated, and his great-uncle Charles Maturin's terror novel, *Melmoth the Wanderer* (1820). Yet Wilde's and Stevenson's 'new gothic' differed significantly from the 'old gothic' of Maturin, Mrs Radcliffe, and Mary Shelley, and from the mid-Victorian 'sensation novels' that followed. The setting of the late-Victorian 'new gothic' is the recognizable modern world of consumerism and technology; its theme is invariably the encounter between the scientific or modern and the primitive, and the space that divides these worlds.[24]

The spirit of romance also continued to flourish in the nineteenth century in the growing field of folk-tales and children's literature. The original folk-tales, from which literary fairy-stories evolved, had in fact been rooted in social and historical realities. Traces of this survive in the settings and characters of fairy-tales. Theirs is a late feudal agrarian world of forests and villages, peopled with princes, millers, blacksmiths, and terrifying strangers. In their original form, they are often disturbing and non-didactic. Wilde's interest in fairy-tale was deeply rooted in the Celtic folklorism of his Dublin childhood. His father was a distinguished amateur antiquarian and member of the Royal Irish Academy. He continued the work of the first great name in Irish archaeology, George Petrie, in providing a descriptive catalogue of the collection of antiquities at the Academy in 1863. His volume of *Irish Popular Superstitions* collected in the west of Ireland appeared in 1852. Wilde's mother published more of his father's material in *Ancient Legends, Mystic Charms, and Superstitions of Ireland* (1887), and *Ancient Cures, Charms and Usages of Ireland* (1890), after his father's death. The purpose of the oral narratives of common people was not simply to provide amusement and distraction, but to express the spiritual history of their community, and fear of the incomprehensible. Literary folk-tales and fairy-stories, by contrast, tend to be more sanitized, and more opti-mistic versions of the original. The dreams and superstitions of pre-industrial agrarian society are incorporated into a literature for children. Its purpose is to amuse and instruct. The Brothers Grimm, for instance, eliminated uncomfortable sexual elements in the editing of their tales, and altered them to reinforce contemporary middle-class values.[25]

Dickens's illustrator George Cruikshank's edition of the Brothers Grimm (1824–6) gave fairy-tales an immense and immediate popu-larity that lasted for the rest of the century. The vogue received fresh stimulus with the translation of Hans Christian Andersen's *Danish Fairy-tales and Legends* in 1846. The decades that followed saw the appearance of home-grown products such as John Ruskin's popular *The King of the Golden River* (1851), Charles Kingsley's didactic *The Water-Babies: A Fairy Tale for a Land Baby* (1863), and Lewis Carroll's *Alice's Adventures in Wonderland* (1865). These were major landmarks in the genre. Another important figure in the fairy-tale revival was the anthropologist and belle-lettrist turned writer of fairy-tales, Andrew Lang, whose Scottish tale *The Gold of Fairnilee* (1888) was followed by a series of anthologies beginning with *The Blue Fairy Book* (1889). In an article in the *Contemporary Review* in 1886, Lang argued that contemporary romances and adventure stor-ies were a healthy antidote to the morbid and unmanly tendencies of realism.[26] Arguably, though, the most creative fantasist and writer for children was George MacDonald. His children's books *At the Back of the North Wind* (1871) and *The Princess and the Goblin* (1872), and his adult allegories such as *Lilith* (1895), derive both from the tradi-tions of Celtic religious writing and from German Romanticism. Both traditions re-asserted the value of fantasy and imagination. In this respect, his writing shares the same influences at work on Carlyle, a fellow Scot. Carlyle's 1827 translations introduced the British public to the tales of the German romancers, including E. T. A. Hoffmann, whom Wilde greatly admired (*Letters*, p. 393).

It was in this context that Wilde produced his first published volume of fiction in 1888, *The Happy Prince and Other Tales*. Early readers and reviewers of Wilde's fairy-tales compared them favour-ably with Hans Andersen's wholesome 'authored' versions of Scan-dinavian folk-tales. The actress Ellen Terry wrote to congratulate him: 'They are quite beautiful dear Oscar, and I thank you for them from the best bit of my heart. I think I love "The Nightingale and the Rose" the best . . . I should like to read one of them some day to NICE people—or even NOT nice people, and MAKE 'em nice.'[27] Certainly on one level Wilde's fairy-tales operate as rebukes to selfishness and narcissism. Beauty and spiritual awakening are invariably the reward that comes from suffering and sacrifice. The Selfish Giant learns to share his garden with the children and is rewarded with paradise. Little Hans nobly sacrifices himself to the egotistical, self-deceiving Miller in 'The Devoted Friend'. Both the Happy Prince and the Swallow achieve perfect beauty in the sacrifice of themselves for others. The New Testament ethic is even more insistent in Wilde's second collection *A House of Pomegranates* (1891). The Young King awakes from an inward aestheticism to a consciousness of the miseries of the world, and is transformed miraculously into a Christ figure. The Fisherman in 'The Fisherman and his Soul' acts out Christ's temptation in the desert, and in oblique and paradoxical conformity to the Christian message chooses love over the refinements and specialization of the 'soul'.

Yet Wilde's method also involves a destabilizing of the genre by sometimes amplifying and sometimes burlesquing the conventions. Burlesque was of course a hallmark of the period. In literary and artistic terms, it gave the reaction to realism a playful, self-conscious edge. The heightened histrionics of Wilde's plays—their shift from analysis to surface—was a feature of the London theatre in the 1880s and 1890s, notably in the plays of J. M. Barrie and G. B. Shaw. Farce is also a prominent feature of Wilde's collection of stories, *Lord Arthur Savile's Crime and Other Stories* (1891), which first appeared in magazines in 1887. The title story is a spoof Victorian melodrama in which the hero learns from a professional chiromantist that he will commit a murder, and feels duty-bound to get the deed out of the way before marrying his fiancée. 'The Canterville Ghost' is both a farcical ghost story and a satire on the theme of the American in Europe popularized by Henry James. These tales have a serious side, but their happy, tongue-in-cheek endings pander to the expectations of magazine readers who read for amusement only. Wilde's fairy-tales are potentially more unsettling. The subtitle to *The Happy Prince and Other Tales*—'for children from eight to eighty'—erases the division between children and adults on which the sweet and wholesome basis of the fairy-tale generally depended.

Wilde was not the first to subvert the conventions of the fairy-tale. Hans Andersen also used self-deflationary techniques. The burlesque is also a feature of Thackeray's *The Rose and the Ring* (1855). Yet among earlier writers, self-reflective devices tended to serve as endearing reinforcements of the moral certainties of their tales. Wilde, by contrast, resists unqualified conclusions or enduring 'happy ever afters'. Wilde's estranging techniques can be seen to have something in common with the techniques of the German romantic fairy-tales (*Kunstmärchen*), in their adoption of similar multi-dimensional rather than unitary reality. Wilde's tales are not so nightmarish as Hoffmann's, but as in Hoffmann, reconciliation of the warring sides of man's nature—desire and reality, the flesh and the spirit—is not imagined or realized in this world.

Looked at within a broad cultural perspective, the attachment to romance and fantasy by Wilde and other nineteenth-century Irish writers has been explained in terms of the instability of Irish national and political identity. Realism, according to this argument, flourished in a world of bourgeois settlement and social stability. The uncanny and primitive, the formally diffuse and elaborately self-conscious, by contrast, reveal an excess of reality. This would certainly explain the flowering of fantasy and the gothic in the undeveloped nationhood of eighteenth- and nineteenth-century Germany, and in other recent periods of cultural and political upheaval. On the Celtic fringes of British society, where national identities remained historically more ambivalent and divided, the reaction to realism was liable to be transformed into the quaint and picturesque regionalism of Mrs Oliphant and William Black, or the Scottish 'Kailyard' school of J. M. Barrie and S. R. Crockett. Although Hardy was initially admired as a chronicler of rural life, readers in the end reacted against the thematic ambivalence and formal excesses of his novels of rural decline and social transition.

Little that Wilde is reported to have said about Hardy is reliable. While in prison, he asked for Hardy's last novel *The Well-Beloved* (1897) which he described as 'pleasant' (*Letters*, p. 790). By contrast, his comments on regional writers who immolated themselves 'upon the altar of local colour' were mordant. In 'The Decay of Lying', Mrs Oliphant is pilloried for prattling 'pleasantly about curates, lawn-tennis parties, domesticity, and other wearisome things', while William Black is wittily dispatched with the comment that on seeing his 'phaeton' approach, 'the peasants take refuge in dialogue'. In identifying himself as part of the Celtic renaissance, Wilde carefully dissociated himself from the quaint and sentimental. In acknowledging Shaw as second only to himself in 'the great Celtic school', he praised not only Shaw's 'superb confidence in the dramatic value of the mere facts of life', but also 'the horrible flesh and blood' of his characters, and his 'trenchant writing and caustic wit' (*Letters*, pp. 563–4). At the same time Wilde, unlike Shaw, also laid claim to the supposedly emotional, keenly imaginative temperament of those born with Celtic blood. In *De Profundis*, he uses this defensively to justify his past improvidence: 'Prudence and thrift were not in my nature or race'. It serves both as a confession of weakness and an assertion of superiority over the more practical and prosaic English temperament. He believed 'lack of imagination' to be characteristic of the 'Anglo-Saxon race', while 'every Celt' had 'inborn imagination'.

Wilde's thinking owes much to Matthew Arnold's thesis of the natural, spontaneous, essentially feminine Celt as a necessary corrective to masculine, Anglo-Saxon pragmatism.[28] Although they are a plea for integration, Arnold's claims for distinct but complementary Celtic and Anglo-Saxon qualities only reinforced racial constants which ignored social and economic influences, and denied individual identity. In turning to the fairy-tale in particular, Wilde, according to one commentator, lays himself open to the charge that he 'internalized the child-like qualities projected on the Irish by a Celticism as much in the service of the imperial masters as of the cultural nationalists'.[29] Wilde's statements about nationality certainly seem rooted in the narrowly racial and hereditary assumptions of his time. Yet his artistic insights and quick play of ideas always worked against the accepted, seemingly natural view of things. Wilde's writings show his understanding that Celtic reaction 'against the despotism of fact' is founded not upon fixed temperament, but upon historical relations of power. The political basis of his anti-realist aesthetics can be seen clearly in his unconcealed contempt for the English historian J. A. Froude's picture of eighteenth-century Irish-English relations in his novel, *The Two Chiefs of Dunboy* (1889). Froude's characterization of English self-control in his Cromwellian hero, Colonel Goring, and Irish recklessness, in Goring's Celtic enemy, Monty Sullivan, is denounced as 'false' and 'exaggerated'.[30] Wilde recognized that Froude's appeal to the 'facts' of experience was simply a justification for English rule in Ireland. From an Irish perspective, 'the facts of life' consisted of 'race hatred and religious prejudice'. In reviewing W. B. Yeats's *Folk-tales of the Irish Peasantry* in 1889, he quoted Yeats's praise of his mother's *Ancient Legends* approvingly, yet also knowingly. Yeats had written: 'The humour has all given way to pathos and tenderness. We have here the innermost heart of the Celt in the moments he has grown to love through years of persecution, when, cushioning himself about with dreams, and hearing fairy songs in the twilight, he ponders on the soul and on the dead. Here is the Celt, only it is the Celt dreaming.'[31] Neither Wilde nor Yeats was blind to the undreaming Celt, nor to the historical and political realities that fed those dreams. Yeats's own schematic prose romances of the 1890s were attempts to bridge the perceived gap between truth and reality. Yeats's characters Owen Aherne and Michael Robartes are allegorical embodiments of the antithesis of dream and action, reason and imagination. Yet Yeats in the late 1880s and 1890s remained, for his contemporaries at least, the Celt as dreamer. It was Wilde who led the way artistically in England, not by means of pathos, but daringly by paradox, insincerity, and the self-conscious artifice of the mask. For Wilde, the mask was an ironic, self-cancelling device through which he was able to inhabit and at the same time self-consciously distance himself from different states of being. Art and life were alike performance. The aims of the artist were dramatic. His role was to inhabit different selves and realities at will, and so discredit the tendency to see the world in terms of a unitary reality and truth.

Other Victorians adopted masks and personae. The most notable wearer of masks was the poet Robert Browning, who claimed that the force of his poetry lay in letting other men and women speak. Yet whereas Browning took on the identity of other personalities, Wilde wore what he identified as the mask of 'the modern spirit'. The phrase, as used by Wilde, Walter Pater, and the French Symbolists, is associated with the spirit of restlessness, inner division, paradox, and shifting moods. Wilde's literary strategy was to graft the 'modern spirit' to traditional, non-realistic forms—the fairy-tale, the gothic romance, the prose dialogue. He first recognized the potential for this method in the productions of Shakespeare he attended at Coombe House in 1884 and at Oxford in 1885. Reviewing 'Henry the

Fourth at Oxford' for the *Dramatic Review*, he observed that 'when we have the modern spirit given to us in an antique form, the very remoteness of that form can be made a method of increased realism'.[32] 'Increased realism' in this context suggests a many-sidedness of representation that is an inherent feature of Shakespeare's unique mixture of dramatic styles and moods. In his writings, Wilde aimed at ironic complexity, layering, and inconclusive conclusions. The dandy figures in his plays might be seen as embodiments of his idea of the 'modern spirit'. So too might Lord Henry Wotton in *The Picture of Dorian Gray*. Announcing his hatred of 'vulgar realism in literature', Wotton is named 'Prince Paradox' by Dorian (ch. XVII). Wilde believed that Wotton was 'what the world thinks me' (*Letters*, p. 585).

In turning his back on realism, Wilde turned away from a form that characteristically disguised its fictional artifice to forms whose artificiality and unreality were all on display. In realism, as Wilde recognized in his review of *The Two Chiefs of Dunboy*, the seemingly accurate presentation of characters and relationships could be manipulated to promote a single social-political version of history. In fairy-tale and fantasy, the significance of the action might be more elusive. One tends towards a single meaning or truth; the other to interpretation in which meaning might be many-layered. Wilde recognized the pitfalls lining the path of symbolic literature, not least the temptation to see the work of art as a secondary activity and as a mere reflection of a hidden religious, or philosophical, or social meaning. Yet he accepted the fact that his stories would not be understood or interpreted in the same way by all readers. He consoled a bewildered William Henley with the following when Henley faced a barrage of conflicting reviews of *A Book of Verses* in 1888: 'The richer the work of art the more diverse are the true interpretations. There is not one answer only, but many answers. I pity that book on which critics are agreed. It must be a very obvious and shallow production. Congratulate yourself on the diversity of *contemporary* tongues. The worst of posterity is that it has but one voice' (*Letters*, p. 373). He wrote in similar terms to an admirer about the diverse interpretations of his story 'The Nightingale and the Rose': 'I like to fancy that there may be many meanings in the tale, for in writing it, I did not start with an idea and clothe it in form, but began with a form and strove to make it beautiful enough to have many secrets, and many answers' (*Letters*, p. 354). Diversity of effect was for Wilde a sign of literary value and a guarantee of the continuing survival of a work.

Although Wilde intended that his writings should challenge the reader, he did not write for the few, as the later modernists were to do. Like other British writers of the late-Victorian period, he still aimed to appeal to the general reading public in the way that earlier Victorian writers had done. The marketing of his fiction is revealing in this respect. In approaching Macmillan with his first collection of fairy-tales, Wilde clearly hoped that they would be popular and sell well. Macmillan and Sons was one of the largest and most successful of Victorian publishing houses. Always responsive to new markets, the firm had established a juvenile department in the late 1860s. Disappointingly for Wilde, Alexander Macmillan rejected the manuscript on the advice of his reader who felt that that the tales were unlikely to enjoy immediate popularity. Wilde turned to Alfred Trübner Nutt, who had taken over the publishing firm of David Nutt from his father. Alfred Nutt had founded the *Folk-Lore Journal* in 1883 and specialized in folklore and antiquities, as well as Celtic and German scholarship. *The Happy Prince and Other Stories*, with illustrations by Walter Crane and Jacomb Hood, was issued by Nutt in May 1888 in an initial print run of 1,000 copies at 5*s.* a copy. Nutt brought out a cheaper second edition at 3*s.* 6*d.* the following January, but the average yearly sale settled down at about 150 copies, a figure that a frustrated Wilde found 'really absurd' (*Letters*, p. 617). Wilde went to the new transatlantic book-trading publisher, Osgood, McIlvaine and Co., with his second collection of fairy-tales, for which he received an advance of £120 and royalties of 20 per cent on the retail price. But this collection too achieved little popular or financial success, perhaps unsurprisingly so—at 21*s.* a copy with lavish design and decoration by Ricketts and Shannon, it was clearly aimed at the expensive book market. Ward, Lock and Co.'s 6*s.* book version of *The Picture of Dorian Gray* also achieved only moderate sales, in spite of the six chapters added to the periodical version. The lack of demand can be explained by the fact that cheaper 1*s.* copies of the periodical version had been in wide circulation, but modest sales may also have been the effect of critical hostility. Macmillan rejected *Dorian Gray*; Alexander Macmillan considered it 'weird' and 'rather repelling'.[33] The conservative press responded similarly. Although

Dorian Gray belonged within the popular genre of 'romance', its substitution of aesthetic for manly adventures meant its association with the morbid and unmanly tendencies of French realism. General acclaim for Wilde's stories and tales came posthumously. *The Happy Prince and Other Stories* went through five editions in the United States alone in the decade following Wilde's death. Since then, Wilde's stories and tales have been translated into nearly every language, and sell in millions around the world.

Wilde and Censorship

Wilde's battle with the censors began with his first play. *Vera: or The Nihilists* was cancelled three weeks before its performance at the Adelphi Theatre, London, in December 1881. It has been suggested that the play was cancelled for financial reasons,[34] but the evidence points to political interference. The assassination of Tsar Alexander II in March that year had caused a wave of alarm among the royal families of Europe. The wife of the new emperor, Alexander III, was a sister of the Princess of Wales. In London, establishment fears centred on republican groups and foreign workers' clubs. Johann Most, a prominent revolutionary member of the Rose Street Club, received a sixteen-month prison sentence for praising the assassination of the Tsar in his anarchist journal *Die Freiheit*. As late as 1887, the censors in France responded to Zola's novel about an anarchist workers' uprising, *Germinal*, by forbidding the inclusion of insulting references to the Tsar. In Wilde's Russian costume drama, a secret cell of Moscow nihilists plots the assassination of the Tsar as the first step in the establishment of a republic. In ringing speeches, the conspirators lay the blame for revolution at the door of tyranny and injustice. Wilde sent a copy of the play to Edward Smyth-Pigott, the Chief Examiner of Plays at the office of the Lord Chamberlain. In his 1895 obituary of Pigott, Shaw was to describe him as 'a noodle' and 'walking compendium of vulgar insular prejudice'.[35] Of the plays applying for licences during Pigott's twenty-year term of office, only fifty or so applications were denied, but this figure disguises the many instances in which plays were only licensed after modifications to meet objections, or in which official application for a licence was quietly dropped. Wilde's *Vera* seems to belong within the latter category. Wilde applied to meet Pigott privately in

November 1881, and later wrote to the American actress Clara Morris: 'On account of its avowedly republican sentiments I have not been able to get permission to have it brought out here' (*Letters*, p. 97).

The law governing stage censorship in England had been introduced in 1737 by Robert Walpole, Britain's first 'Prime Minister'. Walpole's purpose was to clamp down on the political and personal satires against himself and his notoriously corrupt administration then prevalent on stage. Previously, the Lord Chamberlain had put pressure on playwrights and theatre managers in an unsystematic, non-statutory way. Subsequently, legislative control of the stage tightened even further. Under the Theatres Act of 1843, every new play and every addition to an old play had to be sent to the Lord Chamberlain. The Lord Chamberlain's Examiner of Plays had the authority to ban any play that in his opinion was contrary to 'good manners, decorum, and the preservation of the public peace'.

The argument against stage censorship in the Victorian age tended to be passionate but largely ineffectual in the face of general public approval of the work of the Examiner of Plays. In the years between 1870 and 1890, the English public and press could take comfort from the fact that they had safeguards against poisonous foreign influences. The attack on censorship received fresh impetus from three main directions towards the end of that period. Generally, the growing challenge to British paternalism and conservatism resulted in the establishment of pressure groups such as the Fabian Society (1884) and the Independent Labour Party (1893), whose programmes of reform were sympathetic towards the liberty of the stage. At the same time, the success of André Antoine's avant-garde Théâtre Libre in Paris in 1887 encouraged the establishment of a succession of independent theatres in Europe. This prompted the novelist George Moore, a strong opponent of censorship, to demand to know, 'Why have we not a *Théâtre Libre* in England?'[36] His demand was answered when Jacob T. Grein, an Anglo-Dutch theatrical agent and critic, opened the Independent Theatre in London in 1891. The first production of the Independent Theatre was a private performance of *Ghosts*, Ibsen's daringly controversial play about syphilis. A third influence was the desire for a new, more adult drama by the growing status of the writer in the late nineteenth century as a serious artist and critic of society. With some notable exceptions, serious literary men and women effectively abandoned the theatre after 1737 for fiction, poetry, and the non-theatrical verse drama. During the nineteenth century the playwright generally played second fiddle to the actors and actor-managers, translating foreign plays, adapting Shakespeare, or producing original pieces that played to the actor-managers' strengths and the time-honoured formulas that the old-fashioned play-going public expected.

The challenge to stage censorship in England found its most powerful and persuasive champion in George Bernard Shaw. Shaw's propagandist essay, 'The Quintessence of Ibsenism' (1891) loudly proclaimed Ibsen's 'higher drama' as a new force sweeping through the English theatre. It also expressed Shaw's exasperation with the unfettered power of veto of the licenser of plays who 'has the London theatres at his mercy', as well as with the more subtle but equally suppressive resistance of actors and critics whose livelihood often depended on conformity. Shaw's central argument against servility to 'public opinion' is that it resulted in the ridiculous suppression of the most serious plays by modern dramatists while blatantly scurrilous and indecent farces flourished unchecked.[37]

Wilde saw a mirror of himself in Shaw's portrait of Ibsen as a courageous artist struggling to give people new forms of truth. He wrote to Shaw praising 'The Quintessence of Ibsenism': 'You have written well and wisely and with sound wit on the ridiculous institution of stage-censorship: your little book on Ibsenism and Ibsen is such a delight to me that I constantly take it up, and always find it stimulating and refreshing: England is a land of intellectual fogs and you have done much to clear the air' (*Letters*, p. 554). In 'The Soul of Man under Socialism' which appeared the same year, Wilde expressed his own belief that the advances made in serious drama 'in the last ten or fifteen years' were 'entirely due to a few individuals refusing . . . to regard Art as a mere matter of supply and demand'. Wilde's career followed the trajectory advocated in Shaw's account of the changing function of the playwright. In correcting the belief that he had written *Salome* for Sarah Bernhardt, Wilde stated: 'I have never written a play for any actor or actress, nor shall I ever do so' (*Letters*, p. 559). From the first, his letters to actresses and actor-managers about the performance of his plays are model examples of a playwright's effort to win their sympathy to his artistic aims. He did not always succeed. As he became more popular and powerful, he quarrelled with actor-managers such as George Alexander and Herbert Beerbohm Tree over changes to his plays. But for Wilde as for other serious playwrights, the actor-manager was only a small part of the problem: the main battle was with the Censor.

Wilde's quarrel with the Chief Examiner of Plays came to a head with Pigott's refusal to grant a licence to *Salome*. Wilde had been impressed by the poetic sensuousness of the Théâtre d'Art, founded by the French poet Paul Fort in Paris in 1890, and had written his *Salome* in French as a poetical, Symbolist exercise without interference from actors or actor-managers. The great French actress Sarah Bernhardt agreed to play the leading role. Rehearsals were already in progress at the Palace Theatre, London in June 1892, when Pigott decided to ban the performance. He invoked an old law forbidding the representation of biblical characters on the stage. In a series of interviews in English and French periodicals, a furious Wilde developed the arguments of Shaw's 'The Quintessence of Ibsenism'. Wilde objected to the hypocrisy of the Examiner in 'licensing every low force and vulgar melodrama' while at the same time prohibiting superb biblical dramas by foreign playwrights from the English stage (*Letters*, pp. 531–3). He questioned why the restraints imposed on drama should be greater than the common laws of libel and obscenity that applied to the other arts. He was also dismayed at the lack of protest from actors and drama critics, many of whom sided with the pro-censorship lobby. In 'The Soul of Man under Socialism', Wilde had singled out Henry Irving, actor-manager of the Lyceum Theatre, as a model of one whose aim was not simply 'to give the public what they wanted' but 'to realise his own perfection as an artist'. Now he faced the fact that 'not one single actor has protested against this insult to the stage—not even Irving' (*Letters*, p. 532). For Wilde, this was disappointing proof of 'how few actors are artists'. The reality was that actors were generally unwilling to offend the public, while the leading dramatic critics usually wrote for magazines that depended financially on advertising by the theatrical establishment. Acquiescence had already been in evidence at the meetings of the Select Committee of the House of Commons on Theatres and Plays that had convened earlier that year to inquire into the censorship of the drama. The one exception was William Archer, dramatic critic of the *World* and Ibsen's translator, who argued decisively for abolition when he went before the Committee in May that year. Two months later, his was again to be the lone voice raised in protest against the banning of Wilde's play by the Censor. Archer knew that the Censor would be as unshakable as the Select Committee had been by his arguments and concluded that: 'The Censor is the official mouthpiece of Philistinism, and Philistinism would doubtless have been outraged had *Salome* been represented on the stage.'[38] For Archer, the banning of *Salome* was 'perfectly ridiculous and absolutely inevitable'.

Salome was finally produced by the French actor-manager Aurélien Lugné-Poë, at the Théâtre de l'Œuvre in Paris in 1896, with Lina Munte in the leading role; but in England, the ban on *Salome* was not lifted until 1927. By the 1920s, continuous lobbying and campaigning by Shaw and the abolitionists had discredited the role of the Censor and brought about a relaxation of restrictions in some areas. But stage censorship continued in England until 1968 when the authority of the Lord Chamberlain's Office was finally abolished. By then it had become clear that the notoriety achieved by a banned play gave it a greater publicity than it would have normally received.

The furore surrounding *Salome* had matched Wilde's earlier quarrel with the critics over the publication of *The Picture of Dorian Gray*. In fiction there was no Lord Chamberlain, but in challenging restraint and fixed belief, particularly those touching on sex, writers met strong resistance. The legislation controlling censorship was the strict puritanical Obscene Publications Act (Lord Campbell's Act) of 1857 which ruled against 'works written for the single purpose of corrupting the morals of youth, and of a nature calculated to shock the common feelings of decency in any well regulated mind'. Lord Campbell's target was not works of serious literature or artistic merit, but the assumption that books in themselves might deprave and corrupt made life difficult for serious writers. This became increasingly so in the closing decades of the nineteenth century. The campaign for 'realism' in fiction, for instance—for the need, if necessary, to expose unpalatable truths—was in full cry in the 1880s. The censorship debate to which many of the younger writers contributed their views reflected a widespread impatience with artistic insincerity—with the sentimental, the self-satisfied, and the unreal. More specifically, it marked their protest against the reticent treatment of sexuality in fiction.

Among the leading advocates of a new frankness in fiction were Thomas Hardy, George Gissing, and George Moore. Gissing looked back in admiration to the example of 'true realism' in eighteenth-century literature and art. In his contribution to the debate on censorship in the *Pall Mall Gazette* in 1884, he turned against the whole course of the English novel from the time of Fielding.[39] In this he took his cue from Thackeray's review of Thomas Roscoe's single-volume edition of Fielding's *Works* of 1840, where Thackeray wrote: 'The world does not tolerate now such satire as that of Hogarth and Fielding . . . Fielding's men and Hogarth's are Dickens's and Cruikshank's, drawn with ten times more skill and force, only the latter humorists dare not talk of what the elder discussed honestly.'[40] Honesty to nature distinguishes Gissing's intentions as a novelist. One finds little trace in his work of the Richardsonian cult of sensibility that shaped Victorian fiction and culture.

Hardy also argued for maturity and truth, particularly in the representation of relations between the sexes. In a symposium on 'Candour in Fiction' in the *New Review* in 1890, Hardy compared the restraints on sexual frankness in fiction to Bottom's farcical fears in Shakespeare's *A Midsummer Night's Dream* that his play might frighten the ladies. Hardy drew strength from the natural candour of rural life. Yet he also acknowledged the potentially disastrous consequences of integrity for the artist in bringing down 'the thunders of respectability upon his head, not to say ruin his editor, his publisher, and himself'.[41] Both Hardy and Gissing found acceptable compromises with editors and publishers for 'bread and butter' reasons. Hardy's frustrations, and eventual abandonment of fiction for poetry, have been well documented. For Gissing, popularity and financial success came only in the last years of his life, with his return to a more light-hearted treatment of contemporary themes.

George Moore looked uncompromisingly to Zola and French naturalism, and as a result his first three novels—*A Modern Lover* (1883), *A Mummer's Wife* (1884), and *A Drama in Muslim* (1886)—were banned by Mudie's and Smith's. Moore declared war on the circulating libraries. His provocative pamphlet 'Literature at Nurse, or, Circulating Morals' (1884) echoed some of the arguments of the abolitionists against the hypocrisy and inconsistency of stage censorship. Moore tried to show that the circulating libraries refused to stock serious realistic fiction while profiting from the salacious trivia of popular novels. His campaign against the circulating libraries drew attention to his publicity-conscious publisher, Henry Vizetelly, who after 1884 specialized in cheap 'unabridged' translations of 'realistic' French novels for the mass market. It was a lucrative business that threatened the commercial as well as moral stranglehold of the circulating libraries. With friends in high places, the circulating libraries hit back. In May 1888 concerns were expressed in the House of Commons about 'the rapid spread of demoralizing literature in this country', and the need for the law on obscenity to be vigorously implemented. This was a signal for the moral lobbyists and campaigners of the National Vigilance Association to bring a private action of 'obscene libel' against Vizetelly for publishing a translation of Zola's *La Terre* (*The Earth*). At the subsequent trial, Vizetelly was ordered by the Solicitor General 'at once to withdraw all those translations of M. Zola's work from circulation'. Following a second action by the National Vigilance Association a year later over his failure to comply, the 70-year-old salesman publisher was sentenced to three months' imprisonment, becoming, to general embarrassment, an unlikely martyr to the literary cause.[42]

Wilde made his views on the Zola débâcle clear in 'The Decay of Lying' which appeared in the *Fortnightly Review* in January 1889. He objected to Zola's dreary, documentary realism on artistic grounds, but felt no sympathy at all with 'the moral indignation of our time against M. Zola'. He compared the moral lobby to 'the indignation of Tartuffe on being exposed'. He himself was to become a target of censorship when the original version of *The Picture of Dorian Gray* appeared in *Lippincott's Monthly Magazine* in July 1890. The reaction of the press was almost unanimously hostile. Wilde was accused of immorality, cynicism, and prurience. The review in the *Daily Chronicle* described 'dullness and dirt' to be 'the chief features' of the story, condemned as 'a tale spawned from the leprous literature of the French *Décadents*—a poisonous book, the atmosphere of which is heavy with the mephitic odours of moral and spiritual putrefaction'.[43] The *St James's Gazette* wondered whether the Vigilance Society would think it worth while to prosecute Wilde or the publisher.[44] William Henley's *Scots Observer* stigmatized Wilde 'for having written for none but outlawed noblemen and perverted telegraph boys',[45] a dangerous reference to the notorious homosexual scandal involving Lord Arthur Somerset and telegraph boys at a homosexual brothel in Cleveland Street the previous year.

Although incensed by the reviews, Wilde responded to the press in a series of letters that aimed to be rational and carefully measured in tone. His stance was consistently that books are not directly answerable to morality, and indeed might be weakened, as he believed *Dorian Gray* was, if a moral design became too obvious or insistent. He answered the review of the *St James's Gazette* with: 'The sphere of art and the sphere of ethics are absolutely distinct and separate; and it is to the confusion between the two that we owe the appearance of Mrs Grundy' (*Letters*, p. 428). ('Mrs Grundy' was a character in the play *Speed the Plough* (1798) who had become the proverbial symbol of rigidly conventional values.) In a subsequent letter, he reminded his critics of the obvious fact, often overlooked by the moralists that 'Bad people are, from the point of view of art, fascinating studies. They represent colour, variety and strangeness' (*Letters*, p. 430).

Wilde developed his attack on literary censorship in his essay 'The Soul of Man under Socialism', and in a series of epigrams that became the Preface to the revised book version of *The Picture of Dorian Gray*. In 'The Soul of Man under Socialism', Wilde condemns any attempt by the public, the church, or the government, to interfere with the process of creative imagination as 'aggressive, offensive, and brutalising'. He targeted the language of moralistic critics who condemned works as 'immoral', 'unhealthy', and 'morbid', as inappropriate when applied to art and literature: 'To call an artist morbid because he deals with morbidity as his subject matter is as silly as if one called Shakespeare mad because he wrote *King Lear*.' In his Preface to *Dorian Gray*, Wilde wittily and provocatively compressed his thoughts and responses to the moral backlash that had greeted the periodical version of the story. His aphorism— 'There is no such thing as a moral or an immoral book. Books are well written, or badly written. That is all'—openly mocked the law of the time. With the aphorisms, 'It is the spectator, and not life, that art really reflects', and 'Those who find ugly meanings in beautiful things are corrupt without being charming', Wilde's Preface restated his aesthetic conviction that evil is in the eye of the beholder.

Wilde's aphorisms first appeared in the *Fortnightly Review* in March 1891, a month before the reissue of *Dorian Gray* in book form in an attempt to silence his critics in advance. Wilde indicated his intention in a letter to the ex-secretary of the Society of Authors: 'I am curious to see whether these wretched journalists will assail it so ignorantly and pruriently as they did before. My preface should teach them to mend their wicked ways' (*Letters*, p. 475). Wilde's hopes for a quieter reception for the book version of *Dorian Gray* were satisfied. There was an appreciative review from Walter Pater. [46] Pater's understanding of Wilde's aesthetic intentions was unsurprising given the echoes and influences of Pater's own writings in the novel. There were some comparisons with Stevenson's *Dr Jekyll and Mr Hyde*. Yet adjectives such as 'unmanly', 'sickening', and 'vicious' continued to be applied to the book, indicating the gulf that separated Wilde and his critics. Wilde's critics saw *Dorian Gray* as a disgusting, disguised confession of homosexuality. Wilde considered such literal readings to be reductive and revealing of the minds of his accusers. Of Dorian, we are told that, 'There were moments when he looked on evil simply as a mode through which he could realise his conception of the beautiful' (ch. XI). Wilde's summary of the novel's message—'All excess, as well as all renunciation, brings its own punishment' (*Letters*, p. 430)—is not an acknowledgement of the folly of sensuous indulgence, as is sometimes supposed, but a cancellation of the conventional moral distinction between hedonism and self-denial. Responding to the request to name the 'poisonous book' that enflames Dorian Gray's imagination, Wilde sidestepped the literal in saying that 'it is a fantastic variation on Huysmans's over-realistic study of the artistic temperament in our inartistic age' (*Letters*, p. 524). 'Over-realistic' and 'inartistic' to Wilde's way of thinking are practically synonymous. Both indicate the obvious and the commonplace. Wilde thought Huysmans's anti-bourgeois romance, *A Rebours* (*Against Nature*) tried but failed to avoid these things. In particular, Huysmans's hero Des Esseintes recalls explicit sexual and homosexual exploits. With the exception of *Salome* and his social comedies with their conventions rooted in the battle of the sexes, Wilde, contrary to popular assumptions, generally avoided sexual candour, in contrast, say, to New Woman fiction, with its obsessive preoccupation with and discussion of sexual matters.

Wilde shared a resistance to blatant sexuality with Henry James. James was a much more frank and sexually courageous writer than is generally supposed, but James believed that the intimate treatment of passion or physical sex would produce a distorted, falsifying report of human relations. Sex, in his view, would drive everything else out. Wilde, though identified with sexual daring, was equally resistant to 'the crude brutality of plain realism' in the treatment of sex. Wilde took pains to dissociate himself from the sensation-seeking methods of George Moore and the 'realists'. He objected strongly to the *St James's Gazette* review of the periodical version of *Dorian Gray* under the headline, 'Mr. Wilde's Latest Advertisement', and its identification of his work with the sensation-mongering techniques of the New Journalism. The style of the New Journalism was, for Wilde, the review itself:

I am afraid, sir, that the real advertisement is your cleverly written article. The English public, as a mass, takes no interest in a work of art until it is told that the work in question is immoral, and your *réclame* will, I have no doubt, largely increase the sale of the magazine; in which sale, I may mention, with some regret, I have no pecuniary interest. (*Letters*, p. 429)

He was to react even more angrily to John Lane's sensational promotional advertisement for *Salome*: 'This is the play the Lord Chamberlain refused to license.' Wilde reminded Lane that it was its 'tragic beauty' that made his play of interest and value 'not a gross act of ignorance and impertinence on the part of the censor' (*Letters*, p. 547).

A threat to artistic integrity, Wilde recognized, lurked in the space of tolerance and freedom for the artist in the choice of daringly sexual themes. The 1890s craze for works with sensational subject matter fed on the same prurience that underpinned the sensational New Journalism. Wilde was conscious that the success of his social comedies was due in part to the puritanism and hypocrisy of his largely middle-class audiences. Hence perhaps his defensive response to those who found fault with his condescending curtain speeches: 'The artist cannot be degraded into the servant of the public.'[47]

The undermining effect on the antagonistic artist of the ending of reticence was to be acknowledged by the modernists who followed Wilde. Virginia Woolf, for instance, accused D. H. Lawrence and James Joyce of spoiling their books by 'their display of self-conscious virility'.[48] Lawrence and Joyce, in turn, accused each other of the same sin against art that was the basis of Woolf's disapproval of her male contemporaries. Joyce dismissed *Lady Chatterley's Lover* as 'a piece of propaganda in favour of something which, outside of D. H. Lawrence's country, makes all the propaganda for itself'.[49] Lawrence had an equally low opinion of Joyce, describing the last part of *Ulysses* as 'the dirtiest, most indecent, obscene thing ever written'.[50] Yet all these writers shared the contempt of artists for counterfeit sentimentality and prurience in the portrayal of sexual relations, which separated them from the common run of contemporary novelists and critics.

A similar divide between the writer and prevailing critical taste is evident not only in the reception of *The Picture of Dorian Gray*, but in the response to Wilde's most daring and least classifiable essay-story, 'The Portrait of Mr W. H.' For Wilde's critics, 'The Portrait of Mr W. H.', like *Dorian Gray*, flirted with the revelation of Wilde's own homosexuality at a time when sexual acts between men were severely punishable by law. The *Fortnightly Review* rejected the story on the grounds that the subject was 'too dangerous', and rudely advised Wilde 'not to print it lest it should corrupt our English homes'. The response is understandable. The cult of personality had given fresh critical credence to the idea of literature as self-expression. One of the literary preoccupations of the period engaged the question of the degree to which even realistic and dramatic literature revealed the life and personality of the writer. Hugh Crackenthorpe declared famously in the *Yellow Book* in 1894 that all art was subjective. Shakespeare in particular became a test case in the debate. The interpretation of Shakespeare as a fellow pessimist by German scholars in the age of Romanticism had influenced Coleridge's arrangement of the plays according to the poet's life and moods. The tradition was passed on to Arthur Hallam, Tennyson's friend and critic, and to Ernest Dowden, the poet, and found widest currency in the 1890s. The sonnets in particular became the focus of autobiographical interest. Wilde's 'The Portrait of Mr W. H.' emerged in the context of a series of articles in *Blackwood's Magazine* bent on solving the riddle of the sonnets, which explains why the highly respectable family monthly accepted it for publication after its rejection by the *Fortnightly*. Wilde's part-story, part-essay is on one level a playful satire on the way scholars created Shakespeare in their own image. In doing so, it also appeared to expose Wilde's own secret life. Yet the story's elusiveness and indeterminacy of conclusion have also been understood in terms not of a cautious fear or coy flaunting of Victorian reticence, but as a strategic resistance to vulgar, grossly physical readings of love between men.[51] Wilde, in twenty-first-century parlance, refused 'to come out' not because it was dangerous, but because it would falsify.

Such contested readings, and stratagems of evasion, were to be played out under cross-examination during Wilde's libel action against the Marquess of Queensberry. *The Picture of Dorian Gray* and 'The Portrait of Mr W. H.' were used as evidence against him by the defence. Edward Carson, Queenberry's counsel, read out extract after extract from *Dorian Gray* in court and attempted to corner Wilde into admitting that his writings were suggestive of unnatural tendencies. Wilde pleaded ignorance with regard to the terms 'perverted' and 'unnatural'. In the minds of his prosecutors, a 'good' book from a literary point of view' might also be a 'perverted' and 'corrupting' book. Wilde's argument—that it was meaningless to discuss a work of art in this way—did not become acceptable in British law until the collapse of the Crown prosecution of Penguin Books over *Lady Chatterley's Lover* more than sixty years later.[52]

CHAPTER 4

WILDE AND SOCIAL ISSUES

OSCAR WILDE is still widely considered to be a writer of clever but ultimately superficial works whose genius lay in his personality and conversation. This view of Wilde as a gifted raconteur whose writings are a pale and mediocre version of his witty conversation was already current in his lifetime. 'Mr. Wilde had wonderful cleverness, but no substantiality', the *Pall Mall Gazette* obituarist wrote on the announcement of his death.[1] Richard Le Gallienne, one of Wilde's peotégés and usually a generous critic, described the works in his introduction to the one-volume New York edition of 1909 as 'the marginalia . . . of a striking fantastic personality'.[2] Wilde himself is reported by André Gide to have said: 'I've put my genius into my life; I've put only my talent into my works.'[3] Yet the record of Wilde's reasoned arguments with his critics provides evidence of a committed writer deeply concerned with the literary and social controversies of his day. Wilde's claims for consideration as a serious artist and intellectual received a boost with the publication of Rupert Hart-Davis's edition of Wilde's letters in 1962. Since the 1960s there has been a significant revaluation of Wilde's life and work. In particular, Wilde's writings have been recognized as deeply resonant with the main social questions of the day—anarchy and socialism, poverty and privilege, feminism and gender, imperialism, and prison reform. The extension in literary studies of the category of 'literature' to include a various mix of popular, non-canonical, non-fictional forms of writing has allowed the rehabilitation of Wilde as a major all-round writer and intellectual. In some of his writings, Wilde addressed social issues directly. He outlined a programme of individualistic socialism in 'The Soul of Man under Socialism', for example. He exposed the inhumane conditions of prison life in his letters to the *Daily Chronicle*, and in the didactic *Ballad of Reading Gaol*. Wilde even introduced an incongruous emotional plea on behalf of battered wives in his verse play, *The Duchess of Padua*, at a time of matrimonial legislation in the early 1880s. More characteristically,

though, Wilde's approach to social issues was a more oblique unsettling of existing attitudes and conventions. Earlier disquiet about
the insincerity and derivativeness of Wilde's work has gradually
been replaced by an appreciation of his playful annexing of literary
convention and genre. In his continuing adherence to traditional
forms, Wilde would seem to follow the example of other late-
Victorian writers, especially Pater and Morris; but in one respect at
least he is strikingly different. Both Pater and Morris use tradition
and myth to give authority to their radical views. Wilde by contrast
drains tradition of all authority.

Politics and Political Writings

Wilde's political radicalism might easily be dismissed as an artistic
pose, as a romantic and emotional rather than a genuinely political
commitment. His politics were unquestionably complex and contradictory. Republican in sympathy, Wilde, like his mother, was politically conservative by instinct. A critic of empire, he never seriously
considered separation from England, and remained attached to the
monarchy. In the first stage of his career, his missionary aestheticism,
like Arnold's idea of 'culture', held out the promise of spiritual
transformation, while conveniently ignoring political realities. His
part in the decorative revival was regarded in England and America,
not as revolutionary, but humorously picturesque. He appeared to
conform to Matthew Arnold's idea of the poetical as opposed to
political character of Irish identity.[4] Significantly, Wilde's most out-
spoken statements in support of militant nationalism were made
during his American tour in an emotional atmosphere of Irish
nationalist feeling in expatriates. It was an expression of affinity, one
could argue, rather than of political commitment.

Wilde himself was uneasily conscious of the contradictions and
inconsistency of his social and political convictions. Some of the
poems he wrote in the period before his tour of America give frank
expression to his perplexity. In 'Libertatis Sacra Fames' (which
translated from the Latin means 'The Sacred Hunger for Freedom'),
his love of freedom leads him, paradoxically, to denounce the violence and destructive anarchy that alone might bring about a new
social order. The clash between republican sympathies and fear of
violence return him to a conservative resolution:

> Better the rule of One, whom all obey,
> Than to let clamorous demagogues betray
> Our freedom with the kiss of anarchy.   (ll. 6–8)

In his first play *Vera: or The Nihilists*, written during the same period, the Tsar-elect takes to the stage as a republican sympathizer and would-be citizen-king, thus providing a convenient, if implausible resolution of his contradictory allegiances.

A similar divided loyalty would seem to shape his early and frequently anthologized poem 'Ave Imperatrix' ('Hail to the Empress'). Wilde had only recently gone down from Oxford when news broke of a terrible setback in British fortunes in the Afghan War. Britain had gone to Afghanistan in 1878, after the Afghan ruler entered into rival trade agreements with Russia. In July 1880 the Afghan army defeated British forces at Kandahar and laid siege to the city. 'Ave Imperatrix' is appropriately patriotic, in keeping with the mood of the time. Of the poem's thirty-one verses, the first fourteen consider what the judgement of history will be on England's record of bloodshed and war. England is represented as the light of the world ('the star of . . . chivalry'), dispelling foreign darkness and savagery ('the lords of Night . . . with gaping blackened jaws'). The east is wakened from its Epicurean luxury and self-indulgence by 'the measured roll of English drums'. The intrusive 'tread of armed men' is justified, and English outrage and prejudice stirred in the final verse of this section by the vision of the treacherous Tsar's unholy gift of a young virgin to the Afghan ruler:

> . . . through the narrow straight Bazaar
> A little maid Circassian
> Is led, a present from the Czar,
> Unto some old and bearded khan.   (ll. 53–6)

The justification of war in the first part of the poem is balanced, however, by an equal number of verses that debate the hidden and unacknowledged costs of war—the bereaved widows, orphans, and girl lovers of those who have died abroad. For them, to conquer also involves being conquered; victory also means defeat:

> Wave and wild wind and foreign shore
> Possess the flower of English land—
> Lips that thy lips shall kiss no more,
> Hands that shall never clasp thy hand.   (ll. 97–100)

It is a theme treated more idealistically by Rupert Brooke in his famous poem 'The Soldier' at the outset of the First World War. In Thomas Hardy's poem 'Drummer Hodge', about the death of a British soldier in South Africa during the Anglo–Boer War of 1899, it is turned, as in Wilde, into an ambiguous rebuke to Empire. In verse twenty-four of 'Ave Imperatrix', Wilde commands England to a change of image, from self-glorying victor to suffering Christ, and to a change of tone, from celebration to sorrow:

> Go! crown with thorns thy gold-crowned head,
>   Change thy glad song to song of pain.   (ll. 93–4)

The biblical echoes increase with the repeated 'what profit now' in verses twenty-six and twenty-seven, an allusion to Christ's question in the New Testament: 'What does it profit a man if he gain the whole world, but lose his own soul?' The claims of English glory are mocked by the sense of wasted lives ('O wasted dust! O senseless clay!'), and by the consequences of suffering for the victors and defeated alike. The two closing verses of the poem attempt to silence such doubts and criticisms, and sound a renewed positive note of hope. The poem ends in a mood of reconciliation with the Christ-like image of the British Empire ('childless, and with thorn-crowned head') on its way to sacrifice and future rebirth as a peaceful repub-lic. Yet within the traditions of the debate poem to which 'Ave Imperatrix' belongs, the second voice—the voice of doubt and criticism—tends to carry the greatest weight. Wilde himself was later to associate his poems with the more conservative tendencies of his early manhood, but in this poem at least, there is a profound questioning of the costs of empire.

There would seem to be an obvious connection between the ambivalence of Wilde's early poetry and the creative double-think of his later mature writings. Given a choice of alternatives, as Wilde's biographer Richard Ellmann has noted, Wilde always succeeded in choosing both.[5] This sense of continuity in Wilde's life and personal-ity nevertheless obscures the real development in his cultural politics in the 1880s and 1890s. Following the fanfare of his American tour, his residence in France was politically and artistically formative. In the sphere of political action, Wilde, according to Shaw, was the 'only name' outside of direct socialist circles to sign a petition for the reprieve of four Chicago anarchists sentenced to death in 1886

(Ellmann, pp. 273–4). In his political writings, he established a resistance to dogma and formula in his exposure of the distortions of language itself. In a period of social and political turmoil, when words could be used to persecute people and groups, Wilde turned rhetoric against itself. His satire on the snobbery and exclusivity of high society in his social dramas of the 1890s was an extension of his critique of empire. His famous quip that England was 'the most deeply occupied of British colonies' reveals the connection between British imperialism and British pragmatism and common sense. 'The Critic as Artist' calls for an end to race prejudice and warfare in terms that annul the received logic of cultural difference: 'If we are tempted to make war upon another nation, we shall remember that we are seeking to destroy an element from our own culture and possibly its most important element.'

Wilde's most political work, 'The Soul of Man under Socialism' is a subversive play upon contemporary political labels and debates. His brand of utopian individualism strategically bypasses the practical political programmes of the competing versions of socialism and individualism in his day. Fabian socialists like Shaw, for example, generally favoured the extension of state control and municipal powers. For them, individualism was effectively synonymous with *laissez-faire* liberalism and was therefore the enemy of socialism. The opponents of socialism, on the other hand, the self-styled Individualists of the conservative Liberty and Property Defence League propagated the idea of voluntary association as an alternative to state ownership. In 'The Soul of Man', Wilde argues that true individualism will only evolve as the next and higher stage of socialism, along with the abolition of private property. This idea had already been put forward by Grant Allen in his essay 'Individualism and Socialism', which appeared in the *Contemporary Review* in 1889.[6] Wilde develops Allen's argument, proclaiming the perfection of the self as the proper goal of human life in a way that sets him above the contemporary debate. Wilde's witty, anti-authoritarian version of Individualism grows out of his own ideas about the self, but is supplemented, as critics have noted, by various earlier influences. One hears in 'The Soul of Man' echoes of the New Testament, of William Morris's anarchist socialism, and of the American Transcendentalist Ralph Waldo Emerson's educational and spiritual claims for 'self-reliance'.[7] In opposing all dogma and laws, Wilde's individualism remains logically though paradoxically an evolutionary process whose utopian goal can never be finally realized or reached. Furthermore, by erasing the distinction between culture and anarchy, between moral order and 'Doing as One Likes', as Matthew Arnold has it in *Culture and Anarchy*,[8] Wilde was finally able to resolve his early political anxieties.

Far from being regarded in his day as an aesthete rather than a political thinker, Wilde was accused by one journalist at the time of his trial of being 'the real leader of . . . the revolutionary and anarchist school which has forced itself into such prominence in every domain of art'.[9] Wilde himself summed up his political and literary convictions when he described himself in 1894 as 'rather more than a Socialist. I am something of an Anarchist, I believe' (Ellmann, p. 273). His is the anarchy of the mind and heart, the anarchy, one might argue, of the marginalized Anglo-Irish consciousness, caught between the clashing irreconcilable claims of Protestant and Catholic nationalism, and of Englishness and Irishness.

Wilde identified his own artistic radicalism in terms of his Celtic nature. His claims to Celtic identity may be scattered and infrequent, but they are made with unusual passion and conviction. In 1893 he praised Shaw's play *Widowers' Houses* as 'Op. 2 of the great Celtic school' (*Letters*, pp. 563–4), 'op. 1' being his own *Lady Windermere's Fan* whose humour Shaw had identified the previous year as characteristically Irish.[10] Wilde also warmly endorsed Grant Allen's description of him as an Irishman to the core in Allen's essay in the *Fortnightly Review* on the link between Celticism, the decorative movement, and radicalism (*Letters*, pp. 469–70). With the exception of the boisterously comic 'Lord Arthur Savile's Crime', the figure of the criminal saboteur in Wilde's writings is not the anarchist bomber of popular fiction, but the artist, the critic, the dandy, and the connoisseur.

Sexual Politics: Feminism and Gender

Wilde's development in the 1880s from aesthete to anarchist artist coincided with his editorship of *Woman's World* and the rise of the 'New Woman'. There was little agreement as to what the New Woman was. Grant Allen presents her in his novel *The Woman Who Did*, as a champion of free love; the conservative writer Mrs Eliza

Lynn Linton criticized the New Women as modern man-haters 'unsexed by the atrophy of their instincts'.[11] Conservative feeling fed the anti-petticoat satires and cartoons of the New Woman as affectedly mannish in dress and appetites. The laughter often concealed real fears of the danger posed by advanced or independent womanhood to the *status quo*. The contributions to the *Yellow Book* of New Woman novelists such as Sarah Grand and Menie Muriel Dowie, and New Woman poets such as 'Michael Field' and Constance Naden only served to reinforce the association of the New Woman in the public mind with immorality and decadence. So much so, that at the time of Wilde's trial, the *Speaker* proclaimed that the New Woman, together with the New Criticism and the New Poetry, were all 'more or less the creatures of Mr. Oscar Wilde's fancy'.[12]

Even Oscar Wilde cannot take the credit, or blame, for having invented the New Woman; however, as editor of *Woman's World* in the late 1880s, Wilde provided a platform for women to construct a new image of themselves for themselves. Domesticity and women's fashions still featured prominently: to ignore them would have been commercial suicide. Priority, though, was given to articles of social, intellectual, and artistic interest. Wilde intended the magazine to be 'the organ of women of intellect, culture, and position' (*Letters*, p. 317). The change of the magazine's title from *Lady's World* to *Woman's World* itself signalled a change in its contents. The first article in the first issue was a part-obituary, part-celebration of the designer E. W. Godwin by Lady Archibald Campbell, who had played the male lead in Godwin's famous production of *As You Like It* at Coombe House in Surrey in the summer of 1884. The illustrations of Lady Archibald as Orlando present a defiant, stunningly aesthetic challenge to vulgar caricatures of the mannish woman. As editor of *Woman's World* Wilde encouraged his contributors to disregard conventional ideals of femininity and gender.

Wilde's subversive resistance to taking sides extended to the logic of sexual difference. In 'Pen, Pencil and Poison', his essay portrait of Thomas Griffiths Wainewright, whose forgeries and alleged murders had been a *cause célèbre* in the 1830s and 1840s, Wilde connects Wainewright's 'subtle artistic temperament' with the 'laxity' of the French free-thinkers Baudelaire and Gautier. Like Gautier, Wainewright, we learn, 'was fascinated by that "sweet marble monster" of both sexes that can still be seen at Florence and in the Louvre'. The 'sweet marble monster' is the erotic Greek statue of the Hermaphrodite. Théophile Gautier's novel about cross-dressing, *Mademoiselle de Maupin*, celebrates ambiguous and indeterminate sexuality, illusion over reality, as an extension of the imaginative possibilities of desire. Wilde responded enthusiastically to Gautier. His own 'The Truth of Masks', originally published as 'Shakespeare and Stage Costume' in 1885, is a spirited defence of illusion. A belief in the transformational power of indeterminacy and illusion in art lies at the heart of his major writings.

LADY WINDERMERE'S FAN

Wilde's seemingly innocuous and publicly acceptable social comedies also played a significant role in questioning Victorian attitudes to the sexes. Wilde's audiences laughed, but uncomfortably so. The original title for *Lady Windermere's Fan*—'A Good Woman'—was changed at the request of George Alexander, who felt that it would put audiences off.[13] Its retention in the sub-title, 'A Play about a Good Woman', teasingly signals to the scandal the previous year—1891—concerning Hardy's sub-title for his novel *Tess of the D'Urbervilles: A Pure Woman*. Both novel and play challenged Victorian attitudes to the woman with a past. In Victorian literature, fallen or wayward women are invariably punished or expelled from respectable society. The same might be said of *Tess* and *Lady Windermere's Fan*, except that the endings of both novel and play rebound ironically on society's judgement.

In the first act, Lady Windermere—the 'good' wife—fends off the temptations of Lord Darlington at the point at which her two-year marriage is threatened with her husband's clandestine liaison with the disreputable Mrs Erlynne. The audience quickly discovers that Mrs Erlynne is really Lady Windermere's mother, drawn back by maternal instincts to respectable society and the daughter she had abandoned at birth. In the denouement of the third act, Mrs Erlynne talks her daughter out of a planned elopement with Lord Darlington, and saves her reputation by claiming ownership of the fan left behind in Lord Darlington's rooms. The play concludes with husband and wife reconciled and Mrs Erlynne leaving the country with a wealthy husband in tow. Lady Windermere's ringing declaration that Mrs Erlynne is 'a very good woman' overturns her rigid puritanical conviction in the first act that 'women who have committed what the world calls a fault should never be forgiven'. She has learned the unreliability of language itself in categorizing people, reflecting that 'There is a bitter irony in things, a bitter irony in the way we talk of good and bad women' (Act 4).

The fan itself is the stuff of melodrama, a far from subtle symbol of wayward femininity. The 'saving' of Lady Windermere does not cancel out the uncomfortable spectacle of a possible sexual tit-for-tat. At the same time, Mrs Erlynne's mocking refusal to 'weep on her daughter's neck and tell her who I am, and all that sort of thing' marks a comic rejection of the fictional codes of repentant woman-hood (Act 4). One important influence on Wilde, often noted by critics, was Pierre Leclerq's play, *Illusion*, first produced at the Strand Theatre in London in July 1890. At the end of *Illusion*, Leclerq's wayward mother, La Faneuse, swaps her glamorous ball-gown and jewels for drab mourning costume. Mrs Erlynne, in con-trast, asserts her attractiveness and her right to enjoy herself: 'Repentance is quite out of date. And besides, if a woman really repents, she has to go to a bad dressmaker, otherwise no one believes in her. And nothing in the world would induce me to do that' (Act 4). The audience's laughter undercuts the sanctity of society's codes, but uneasily so.

The 'fallen woman' theme also engaged the question of Victorian class relations. In Victorian literature, one of the principal causes of the heroine's fall was often the desire to become a lady. The downfall of Hetty Sorrel in George Eliot's novel, *Adam Bede*, and to some extent in Hardy's *Tess of the D'Urbervilles*, is linked not to sexual instinct, but to social aspiration. This allows a partial, ambiguous criticism not only of society's double standards, but also of aristo-cratic attitudes. In *Lady Windermere's Fan*, by an odd twist, the questioning of different rules for men and for women, is marked by the adoption of 'aristocratic' values. Mrs Erlynne's final choice of brazen independence over motherly duty transforms her into a female version of the aristocratic dandy, Lord Darlington. This is what most shocked conservative critics at the time. To Clement Scott, Wilde was a cynic who seemed to say: 'I will prove to you by my play that the very instinct of maternity—that holiest and purest instinct with women—is deadened in the breasts of our English mothers.'[14]

Clearly Mrs Erlynne falls short of Ruskin's ideal of the self-sacrificial 'good mother' that helped shape the Guardianship of

Infants Act of 1886 in favour of women's rights to custody of children. Yet Wilde reacted against criticism that he had created a heartless mother. He thought that the newspapers failed to understand the psychological truth of the play, which he outlined to an admiring correspondent:

A woman who has had a child, but never known the passion of maternity (there are such women), suddenly sees the child she has abandoned falling over a precipice. There wakes in her the maternal feeling—the most terrible of all emotions—a thing that weak animals and little birds possess. She rushes to the rescue, sacrifices herself, does follies—and the next day she feels 'This passion is too terrible. It wrecks my life. I don't want to know it again. It makes me suffer too much. Let me go away. I don't want to be a mother any more.' And so the fourth act is to me the psychological act, the act that is newest, most true. (*Letters*, pp. 553–4)

For Wilde, the critics who failed to see this lacked artistic instinct. Both Shaw and Henry James sensed heartlessness in Wilde's plays, but in the satirical school of Irish dramatists from Sheridan through to Wilde and Shaw himself, heartlessness is an effective device to expose society's self-deceptions. One of the reasons Wilde initially resisted Alexander's request to reveal Mrs Erlynne's real identity in the second rather than the fourth act was that 'if they knew Mrs Erlynne was the mother, there would be no surprise in her sacrifice—it would be expected' (*Letters*, p. 516). Wilde's artistic intention is not to deny noble instincts, but to resist a sentimental and falsifying reading of human motives. That is why perhaps, for all their melodramatic plots and paraphernalia—lost letters, lost fans, and rediscovered parents—his plays continue to ring true.

A WOMAN OF NO IMPORTANCE

Parental responsibility preoccupied Wilde in the early 1890s, at a time when he himself was increasingly neglectful of family duties. The theme is central to his next play, *A Woman of No Importance* (1893) which he wrote while holidaying with Douglas near Cromer in Norfolk. In this play the battle-lines between the virtuous and the vile would appear to be even more sharply drawn. On the side of the good is Mrs Arbuthnot, a fallen woman turned self-sacrificing single mother; on the side of wickedness is the cynical, worldly-wise Lord Illingworth, the seducer who refused to marry her. Her suffering intensifies when Illingworth plans to take her son Gerald under his wing. On discovering the truth, Gerald rejects Illingworth's patronage to return to his mother and to marry Hester Worsley, a pure American girl. Until the Guardianship of Infants Act, the father was legally the sole parent, though the mother could sue for custody of children under 16. Although Gerald is grown up, his choice of his mother is in the spirit of the new legislation. Conveniently Hester—the play's advanced New Woman and the play's most eloquent rebel against the unequal sexual code—has undergone a conversion of her own from a puritanically moral attitude to fallen women to admiration for Mrs Arbuthnot, the wronged woman.

A Woman of No Importance is, on the face of it, the most conventional and cliché-ridden of melodramas. Wilde himself dismissed the plot as being of the wicked seducer and virtuous maiden variety that audiences loved. What makes the play interesting is not its questioning of the double standard—Hester as naïve American outsider is scarcely a representative figure—but its psychological handling of stock characters and situations, together with its treatment of marriage relationships and legislative reform. At the heart of *A Woman of No Importance* is a playful demonstration of a mismatch between abstract ideals and the reality of men and women's lives. The brittle, witty exchanges within Lady Hunstanton's country-house set display an uncertainty of response to political intervention in areas of private and sexual behaviour at the close of the Victorian age, to the attempt to 'banish the beast' of sexual immorality. The play offers a comment on the social purity campaigns of the 1880s and the adoption of a more repressive stance by feminists and reformers. The earnest MP, Mr Kelvil, maintains that the purity of the poorer classes is an issue of 'national importance' (Act 1). While paying lip-service to Kelvil's Ruskinian ideal of womanhood, Wilde's country-house guests voice a range of richly subversive attitudes to marriage and women. Mrs Allonby, Illingworth's female counterpart, wants women to have the freedom enjoyed by men, and not the restriction of male latitude demanded by Hester Worsley. Illingworth points the comic moral: 'Women are a fascinatingly wilful sex. Every woman is a rebel, and usually in wild revolt against herself' (Act 3). The middle-class marriage ideal is mocked as a limitation of freedom and development in the battle of the sexes.

The wit and laughter of the play is all on the side of the rebels and individualists. One could argue that they are merely comic foils to respectability and therefore not to be taken seriously, but in his society comedies Wilde ironically revises the characters and plots of Victorian melodrama in ways that invite comparison with the so-called English 'realists' and 'naturalists'. Their 'reality', like Wilde's, often lies in a subversion of Victorian sentimental themes. Wilde distanced himself from his realist contemporaries, both English and European, including his Norwegian rival Ibsen, whose methods he described as 'analytic' rather than 'dramatic'.[15] Yet William Archer, fresh from his translation of Ibsen, praised Wilde's portrayal of the relation between Mrs Arbuthnot and Lord Illingworth enthusiastically as 'a piece of adult art'.[16] In the play's most predictable set pieces, callous seducer and wronged woman step momentarily out of their stereotypes into a psychological reality. Mrs Arbuthnot's prolonged lament for the woes of motherhood in the fourth act compels not so much audience sympathy as an uneasy recognition of her neurotic attachment to shame and martyrdom. She has already used her suffering as a weapon against Illingworth, and as a means of silencing her son's accusations: 'You have always tried to crush my ambition, mother—haven't you? You have told me that the world is a wicked place, that success is not worth having, that society is shallow, and all that sort of thing—well, I don't believe it, mother' (Act 3). Her maternal sacrifice demands sacrifice and submission as moral payment. At the same time, Illingworth is allowed to step out of his role as villain, to reveal a rational philosophy of life behind the mask of insouciant immorality. Wilde's description of himself applies equally to Illingworth: 'To the world I seem, by intention on my part, a dilettante and dandy merely—it is not wise to show one's heart to the world—and as seriousness of manner is the disguise of the fool, folly in its exquisite modes of triviality and indifference and lack of care is the robe of the wise man. In so vulgar an age as this we all need masks' (*Letters*, p. 586).

Illingworth's philosophy of life is one that resists the tyranny of emotional blackmail and the heart, 'the tyranny of the weak over the strong' (Act 3). According to Illingworth, women have always ruled society, and the play itself sets out to demonstrate this in a

characteristically comic way. There is the henpecked Sir John Ponte-
fract and the Archdeacon's martyrdom to his wife's headaches. The
woman as child exploits her power in reducing men to slaves. In this
Wilde remains true to comic type. Even Gerald's future bondage to a
possessive mother and a pure young wife might appear to bear out
Mrs Allonby's comic description of men as 'married women's property'. She laughingly asserts traditional womanly ways over emanci-
pating entitlements of the Married Women's Property Acts of 1870
and 1882. In Mrs Allonby's history of women, 'we have always been
picturesque protests against the mere existence of common sense'
(Act 2). She remains indifferent both to the middle-class concept of
strong husbands and deferential wives, and to the contemporary
feminist critique of existing marriage relations. Wilde, in the end,
does not take sides, but the final image of the virtuous Hester, Gerald, and Mrs Arbuthnot entering the garden 'with their arms round
each other's waists' is far from appealing or comfortable (Act 4).
True to his anarchist principles, Wilde's progressivism, in this play
at least, would seem to lie as much on the side of reaction and
resistance on the issues of feminist morality and the marriage laws.

SALOME

Between the success of *Lady Windermere's Fan*, and the writing of *A
Woman of No Importance*, Wilde had suffered the humiliating ban of
Salome by the Lord Chamberlain. The chorus of resisting voices to
sexual laws and restrictions in *A Woman of No Importance* may well
have been influenced by his brush with the Censor. It is not difficult
to see why *Salome* was refused a licence. Even had dramatization of
biblical subjects not been forbidden on the English stage, Wilde's
play represented a radical challenge to Victorian concepts of
womanhood and sexuality. In the gospel story of Matthew, Mark,
and Luke, John the Baptist is imprisoned for condemning Queen
Herodias's incestuous marriage to her husband's brother, Herod.
Herod lusts after Herodias's daughter, Salome. During a drunken
feast, he promises to grant her any wish if she will dance before him.
In the gospel accounts, Salome dances for the head of John the
Baptist in obedience to her mother's instructions. In Wilde's version, Salome demands the prophet's head when he refuses to satisfy
her frenzied lust. In creating his Salome, Wilde drew upon the traditions of a thousand years of iconography. He was familiar with the

famous late-medieval and Renaissance portraits of Salome by Titian, Leonardo da Vinci, Bernardino Luini, Rembrandt, Dürer, and Peter Paul Rubens. The subject appealed to nineteenth-century European writers and artists, in a period ruled by otherwise pedestrian subject matter and respectable bourgeois values. Salome became an erotic symbol of daring, transgression, and perversity. Wilde most admired the passionate and decadent Salome of the French Symbolist, Gustave Moreau, which J. K. Huysmans's decadent hero Des Esseintes describes excitedly in *A Rebours* as 'no longer just a dancer', but the symbol of undying lechery and 'the monstrous, indiscriminate, irresponsible, unfeeling Beast'.[17]

Wilde brought his *Salome* to England at a time when the forces of moral vigilance were intent upon 'banishing the beast'. The new morality of the 1880s, and the desired enforcement of sexual conformity were, on one level, a reaction to more general fears about changes within society. It was a point at which moral and political anxieties converged. Paradoxically, the new puritanism was also entangled in more enlightened, scientific attitudes to sexuality and birth prevention (the term 'birth control' did not become common until 1914). Annie Besant's passionate plea for family limitation at her trial for obscenity in 1877 led to the immediate founding of Britain's first campaigning birth prevention organization, the Malthusian League. However, in spite of a commitment to 'voluntary motherhood', on the grounds of women's right to 'rational control', the League and many of its feminist supporters resisted artificial preventatives out of fear that it would lead to uncontrolled sexuality.[18] Fear of women as independent sexual subjects was written large in the social purity movement of the 1880s, and in the spate of pseudo-scientific and psycho-medical accounts of 'unnatural' sexual behaviour—sado-masochism, nymphomania, and inversion— in the 1890s.

In the new science of sexology, descriptions of deviance tended to conform to the general social assumption of women's sexual dependence on men. Gustave Bouchereau's *A Dictionary of Psychological Medicine* (1892) is typical in asserting: 'As a general rule, the man solicits and the woman complies.'[19] Dictionaries and encyclopaedias explained insatiable sexual desire—in men, satyriasis; in women, nymphomania—as a pathological disease that could result in complete insanity. There were also fears that the infection could be transmitted and spread by predatory women. Anxiety about the effects of sexual excess was matched by anxiety about the effects of sexual repression. The latter was often associated in the English Protestant mind with the unnaturalness of Catholic monasticism. Worries about the 'slumbering beast' of female sexuality received a public airing during the controversy surrounding the publication of the verse narrative, 'A Ballad of a Nun', in the first issue of the *Yellow Book* in 1894, shortly after the publication of *Salome* in English with Beardley's illustrations. Based on the Symbolist writer Villiers de l'Isle-Adam's version of a medieval tale, 'A Ballad of a Nun' tells the story of a young nun's abandonment of the convent and her vows to satisfy her sexual longings. W. T. Stead, then editor of the *Review of Reviews* and an earnest puritan, locked horns with the poem's author, John Davidson, over the interpretation of the poem. For the poet, the nun was satisfying natural sexual impulses. For the journalist, her actions pointed to nymphomania, which he describes in textbook fashion, as 'a malady which sometimes affects the most innocent virgin'.[20] In his plea for early release from Reading Gaol, Wilde wrote in almost identical terms about his fears that his disorderly sexual life before his imprisonment—'the most horrible form of erotomania'—might result in his insanity (*Letters*, p. 657). 'Of all modes of insanity . . . the insanity of perverted sexual instinct is the one the most dominant in its action on the brain. It taints the intellectual as well as the emotional energies. It clings like a malaria to soul and body alike' (*Letters*, p. 667). Wilde's sanity lay in overcoming such irrational fears, but it is indicative of the deep-rooted nature of sexual anxieties in the later Victorian period that in the silent loneliness of prison life, such terrors took hold of the defiant creator of *Salome*. *The Times* described *Salome* as 'morbid, bizarre, repulsive and very offensive in its adaptation of scriptural phraseology to situations the reverse of sacred'.[21]

Salome has been the subject of a variety of interpretations and cannot be reduced in any specifically conclusive way to contemporary social and sexual issues. If it could, it would not, for Wilde, be art. One approach has been to read the play in the context of contemporary New Woman dramas. Salome has been described, for instance, as a 'Biblical Hedda Gabler'.[22] Like Ibsen's frustrated, restricted heroine, Salome is perverse, monstrous in her desire to control her own sexuality, and so challenge a repressive patriarchal culture. In the year that Wilde's *Salome* was refused a licence, Hardy caused similar outrage by lifting the veil surrounding female sexuality. His sympathetic portrayal of the fallen and finally murderous Tess was condemned as an attack on Victorian ideals of womanhood. Wilde's heroine was also associated with popular representations of the voluptuous libertine type of New Woman popularized by the novelist Marie Corelli. The identification of Wilde's resolute, untouchable Jokanaan with Ruskin gives an added force to the reading of his heroine as the dark other face of the Victorian 'angel in the house'. Ruskin was the leading Victorian prophet of the spiritualized ideal of woman. His own marriage, annulled on grounds of non-consummation, was common knowledge. Salome's Jewishness also links her, ambivalently, to contemporary anti-Semitic representations of the foreign, the degenerate, the perverse, and the predatory, notably in Bram Stoker's vampire story, *Dracula*. It would be simplistic to reduce the logic of the play to nineteenth-century fears about the dangers of undisciplined sexuality, or to a psychological emphasis on man's fear of women, although such tendencies are not absent. The most paradoxical aspect of the play is Wilde's representation of Salome as both sexually active and naïvely pure, a seemingly contradictory conception that cuts through the rigid dualism of nineteenth-century attitudes to sexuality. The inner life of the play is its mysterious, dream-like quality. In this, it is like Moreau's hallucinatory canvases. The figure of Salome, stripped in the end of her sexual veils, is the symbol of an appalling loss of boundaries. As in many of Wilde's stories, desire ends in death. The final words of the drama, Herod's horrified, remorseful 'Kill that woman!' expresses society's ultimately repressive, conscience-stricken fears.

AN IDEAL HUSBAND

In 1894, the year that *Salome* was finally published, Wilde completed his last two comedies of modern life. Both *An Ideal Husband* and *The Importance of Being Earnest* deal with the disclosure of a double life. In *An Ideal Husband*, Wilde places society's unrealistic ideals of husbands and political leaders under the microscope in an ironic double exposure. Sir Robert Chiltern's marriage and political career are threatened with ruin by the disclosure that he made his fortune dishonestly. He is blackmailed by Mrs Cheveley, a spirited but wayward adventuress in the mould of Thackeray's Becky Sharp in

Vanity Fair. Just as Becky stands in sharp contrast to her former school friend Amelia Sedley, so the cynical Mrs Cheveley occupies the same role in relation to Gertrude Chiltern, the innocent, devoted wife. Amid the usual props and accessories of Wilde's social comedies—misdirected letters, a stolen brooch, overheard conversations—the unlikely saviour turns out to be the morally doubtful dandy and idler, Lord Goring. Goring not only sees off the blackmailer with blackmail; he also converts Lady Chiltern to a proper recognition of the difference between personal and public life. In the play's final ironic twist, the man of masks and surfaces is himself converted to love and marriage to Chiltern's sister, Mabel, an irreverent New Woman posing as *ingénue*. In matching his philosophy of tolerance and forgiveness to action, the perfect dandy is in the end in danger of earning the serious title of 'An Ideal Husband'.

An Ideal Husband has frequently been compared to Ibsen's dramas of idealized men with a secret criminal past. Both playwrights criticize the impossible standards set for public figures, and the puritan witch-hunt that follows any lapse. In Wilde's play, it is the blackmailer, Mrs Cheveley, who spells out the rules to her victim: 'Nowadays, with our modern mania for morality, everyone has to pose as a paragon of purity, incorruptibility, and all the other seven deadly virtues—and what is the result? You all go over like ninepins—one after the other' (Act 1). In Ibsen's *The Pillars of Society*, for example, Consul Bernick's public confession brings about a change of heart within the community. *An Ideal Husband* offers no such hope of a moralized world. There is simply a cover-up. Lady Chiltern has been taught how to turn a blind eye. In confessing his crime to Goring, Chiltern defends it as a heroic act of courage and will. His defensive self-justification echoes claims for the sinner and true individualist in Wilde's other writings, most notably in *The Picture of Dorian Gray* and 'The Soul of Man under Socialism'. Chiltern combines the traditional Victorian male ideal of economic achiever and Christian gentleman with a new Darwinian element of the competitive master-animal.

To what extent *An Ideal Husband* dramatizes a positive acceptance or a subversive exposure of social hypocrisy is thus difficult to determine. The same can also be said of the Don Juan-like view of woman's subservience to heroic male destiny: 'Women are not meant to judge us, but to forgive us when we need forgiveness . . . A man's life is of more value than a woman's. It has larger issues, wider scope, greater ambitions. A woman's life revolves in curves of emotions. It is upon lines of intellect that a man's life progresses' (Act 4).

Part of Goring's resistance in this speech is to the extension of the ideal of womanly purity to men. The idea was one that many feminists and New Woman writers promoted at the time. Shaw's hearty treatment of the subject in *The Philanderer* the previous year had proved too strong for the licenser of plays. *An Ideal Husband* might be said to leave masculine notions of gender differences safely intact. In Act 4, for example, the forgiven Chiltern describes his wife as 'the white image of all good things, and sin can never touch you'. Yet Chiltern's criticism of his wife's naïve adoration at the close of Act 2 recognizes the danger to both sexes: 'Why do women place us on monstrous pedestals? We have all feet of clay, women as well as men.' Wilde's psychological interest in *An Ideal Husband* is on the 'passion . . . for making idols', both of ourselves and of others (Act 2).

It is a passion that Mabel Chiltern resists. Mabel, like Hester Worsley in *A Woman of No Importance*, represents the intellectual type of New Woman. Both provide a contrast to the comic chorus of reactionary society *grandes dames* who believe that education for women is an unfortunate development among the rising commercial classes, and will only result in unhappy marriages. The degree to which Wilde's audiences are encouraged to share the anti-petticoat comedy against the educated New Woman, the 'blue-stocking', is curtailed by the allegiance of some of the more sympathetic characters to women's education. The Chilterns are both 'champions of Higher Education for Woman'. On the opposing side, the prejudices of Mrs Markby, the reactionary *grande dame* of the old school, are made comically ridiculous. Mrs Markby is absurdly convinced that too much intellectual activity enlarges the noses of young women, thus making it difficult for them to find husbands.

Beneath its layers of paradox and contradiction, the play's dramatic appeal is for a correction, as well as an enlargement and transference of gender roles. The spokesman for the traditional gender differences (woman's 'curves of emotion', man's 'lines of intellect') is himself an androgynous figure combining male and female qualities. Consistent with Wilde's representation of ambiguous sexuality in 'Pen, Pencil and Poison' and 'The Portrait of Mr W. H.', the figure of the dandy confronts Victorian values of fixed identity, the masculine and the feminine, the natural and the unnatural. Rather than confirming the Victorian separate spheres for men and women, *An Ideal Husband* displays the stirrings of a contemporary challenge to the cultural division of men and women's world. At the close of the play, we learn that Goring's future career will be 'entirely domestic', while his 'remarkably modern' wife, the intellectual New Woman, renounces the very idea of an ideal husband as sounding 'like something in the next world' (Act 4).

THE IMPORTANCE OF BEING EARNEST

Attempts to interpret *The Importance of Being Earnest* as an attack upon political and social institutions can seem laboured and heavy-handed—the play as a satire on the codes of Victorian social etiquette, for instance, or as a version of Wilde social anarchic politics. The plot itself, by Wilde's own admission, is 'slight'. Jack Worthing and Algernon Moncrieff's invention of alter egos—one as a pretext for visiting the town, the other as a way of escaping to the country—is an ancient plot device that leads to the usual sequence of absurd complications and mistaken identities as the comic net tightens around them. William Archer, who admired Wilde, saw in the play the defeat of criticism itself: 'What can a poor critic do with a play which raises no principle, whether of art or morals, creates its own canons and conventions, and is nothing but an absolutely wilful expression of an irrepressibly witty personality?'[23] With the play's publication a year before his death, Wilde himself referred to it as 'so trivial, so irresponsible a comedy'. Yet he also recalled his 'airy mood and spirit, mocking at morals and defiance of social rules' at the time of writing it (*Letters*, p. 1124). His subtitle for the play, 'A Trivial Comedy for Serious People', makes clear its satirical purpose.

In the 1830s, when the word 'earnest' began to be used approvingly to denote Victorian devotion to moral and civic duty, the name Ernest became fashionable. To Wilde's audience, both his title and his subtitle were recognized as ironically subversive of traditional Victorian attitudes. Wilde had used the name before, calling the younger man Ernest in his dialogue–essay 'The Critic as Artist'. The subtitle of 'The Critic as Artist'—'With some remarks upon the importance of doing nothing'—provides another link between the two works. Both works demonstrate in different ways a critically anti-realistic attitude to the rules and conventions that govern our everyday lives.

Much has been written to suggest that the play contains a homosexual politics and sub-text. There is some evidence to support this. Wilde's collection of aphorisms, 'Phrases and Philosophies for the Use of the Young', appeared in the Oxford undergraduate magazine the *Chameleon* (1894) alongside several homoerotic poems and stories. One of the contributors, John Gambril Nicholson, had published a short collection of Uranian poems, *Love in Earnest*, two years earlier, which contained a ballad 'Of Boys' Names' with the closing lines:

> My little Prince, Love's mystic spell
> Lights all the letters of your name,
> And you, if no one else, can tell
> Why Ernest sets my heart a-flame.

Jack and Algernon both pretend to be Ernest in order to maintain a 'double life'. Algernon's special term for this—'Bunburying'—has also been credited as another coded word for homosexual desire, a play on the slang word 'bun' for 'buttocks'.

If we are seriously to believe that Wilde intended *The Importance of Being Earnest* as a private joke about homosexuality, then the relevance of this still lies in the play's subversion of rigidly conventional Victorian attitudes to gender and sexuality. At the dramatic heart of the play is a high-spirited satire of the rules governing courtship and marriage. Wilde himself in his own life felt keenly the illusions of courtship through which we walk into the reality of marriage. It is also a central theme of Shakespeare's love comedies, particularly of *As You Like It*, in which the heroine Rosalind, dressed as a man, mocks love's dependence on the conventions and fictions of courtship. Wilde's admiration for the Coombe House production of the play in 1884 undoubtedly influenced his conception of the stage possibilities of a reversal and extension of gender roles in playing the love scenes.

'The permanence of personality is a very subtle metaphysical problem, and certainly the English law solves the question in an extremely rough and ready manner,' Wilde wrote in 'Pen, Pencil and Poison'. In *The Importance of Being Earnest*, Wilde has the sophisticated society girl, Gwendolen Fairfax, similarly announce in Act 1 that 'metaphysical speculations' have 'very little reference at all to the actual facts of real life, as we know them'. In her courtship with Jack Worthing, Gwendolen does all the running. Her disregard for the usual rules extends to parental prerogatives in the choice of a partner. Her brazen acceptance of Jack's proposal before it is made gives heightened absurdity to the formidable Lady Bracknell's conventional attempt, pencil and notebook in hand, to establish how much Jack Worthing is worth.

Much of the audience's laughter throughout the play comes from the spectacle of domineering women. The play may be seen in this respect to have a streak of misogyny in it. Jack's worry that Gwendolen might become like her mother, Lady Bracknell, is backed up by Algernon's 'All women become like their mothers. That is their tragedy.' But the anti-petticoat humour is immediately overturned by his added, 'No man does. That's his' (Act 1). In Act 2, Gwendolen turns the Victorian ideal of separate spheres for men and women upside down with her remark, 'The home seems to me to be the proper sphere for the man. And certainly once a man begins to neglect his domestic duties he becomes painfully effeminate, does he not? And I don't like that. It makes men so very attractive.' The remark opens suggestively to a whole brave world of sexual meaning and identity. The play's satire constantly cuts in this way through conventional gender divisions and constrictions. In the final act, Jack's belief that he is the son of the unmarried Miss Prism prompts him to ask: 'Cannot repentance wipe out an act of folly? Why should there be one law for men, and another for women?' (Act 3). This can be read as the challenging question not only of *The Importance of Being Earnest*, but of Wilde's society plays as a whole.

Social Remedies

Wilde's social conscience is strikingly evident in his stories. His 'attempt to mirror modern life in a form remote from reality' (*Letters*, p. 388) marked a reaction against the historical tendencies of his day. History and literary realism were closely allied. Both confidently offered a 'true' record of events. In 'realism', as in history, this seemingly natural presentation of characters in action convinces through the suppression of opinions and predilections shaping and affecting that version of events. The weakness of realism, in Wilde's view, was its tendency towards a single meaning or 'truth'.

That said, Wilde's inscription of more than one meaning in his writings allows a return of history, not as transparent or seamless narrative, but as an expression of apparent contradiction in which perception and reality collide. The encounter with the repressed in Wilde's fiction is not simply a psychological recognition, but a social and historical one. In 'The Birthday of the Infanta', for example, the Dwarf's consciousness of his ugliness is answered by the Infanta's admission of the heartlessness and exploitation underpinning the cultured splendours of the court. The irony at the heart of life, the recognition that leisure and privilege depend inevitably on the toil of others, is also to be found in other writers of the period. One finds it in John Davidson's glorification of 'the offal of the world' in his poem, 'Epilogue to Fleet Street Eclogues',[24] and in Joseph Conrad's critique of imperialism in *Heart of Darkness*. It also emerges in William Morris's Marxist-inspired critique of 'alienated labour',[25] where it serves revolutionary political ends. Wilde's thinking moves towards the same condition of paradox. Behind art, beauty, freedom, culture—at the back of all these—is a hidden and ugly reality.

Wilde's stories contain images of poverty, urban deprivation, hardship, and suffering. Readers have frequently related these to the social realities of Wilde's time. The terrifying vision of the famine in 'The Young King', for example, is seen to allude to Ireland during the Great Hunger. 'The Selfish Giant' has been read as a Christian answer to the question of private property debated by socialists in the 1880s, or alternatively as a personal response to Wilde's privileged childhood behind the walled garden of his Merrion Square house. Such interpretations are valid; but the real social impact of Wilde's tales is arguably to be located, not in their reference to contemporary conditions, but in their ironic uncovering of the costs of civilization. In one of Wilde's earliest and most popular tales, the Happy Prince of the title, having passed his life in the Palace of Sans-Souci ('Without Care'), comes to appreciate the nature of suffering only when he stands as a statue overlooking the ugly and sordid city. With the help of a passing Swallow, the Prince sets out to alleviate suffering and misery by the sacrifice of his jewelled eyes, the ruby of his sword-hilt, and the gold that covers him. Both the Prince and the Swallow are rewarded in the end with entry into heaven, and the story may be read as an allegory of Christian salvation. Yet the Happy Prince's recognition of the paradoxical relation between beauty and human misery seems incomplete. Having lost his earthly value, the Prince is recast in the image of the utilitarian mayor. Society itself remains unchanged, and the world is left an uglier place.

A more complete awareness of the irony of life is represented in the story 'The Young King', in Wilde's second collection of fairy-tales, *A House of Pomegranates*. In this tale, the Young King grows up in a world of beauty and privilege. Then, in a sequence of three dreams, he is shown the realities of toil and human misery that sustain Joyeuse ('Joy' or 'Pleasure'), the name of his delightful Palace of Art. He wakes conscience-stricken from his third and final dream on seeing his own face in a mirror. When he tries to renounce his rich coronation robes and jewels, he is opposed at every level of society. The courtiers ridicule him for acting upon dreams ('not real things'). With a stroke of irony, Wilde has the oppressed justify their oppression. A representative of the people declares that the luxury of the rich keeps the poor in pocket: 'By your pomp we are nurtured, and your vices give us bread.' Finally, the Bishop, the Church's representative, urges acquiescence in the suffering and misery of the world on the grounds that God made the world the way it is. The transformation of the Young King at the end into a triumphant Christ figure would again appear to offer a religious solution to the problems of social inequality; but it is one in which the cruel political and economic effects of culture and civilization stand fully revealed.

In their appeal to sacrifice and selflessness, Wilde's tales are usually seen to support charity and benevolence. They appear to belong within the sentimental reforming tradition of nineteenth-century literature. In Dickens and Charles Kingsley at mid-century, philanthropy and sympathy are offered as remedies for social misery and political unrest. The evil effects of hands-off liberalism are alleviated by idealist-interventionist solutions from above—personal reformation, the giving of charity, and contact between the classes. Victorian literature is a literature of the heart. The wave of benevolence and reforming optimism also inspired the cultural and political theories and movements of the day, from F. D. Maurice's Christian Socialist action groups at mid-century to the colonization of the East End by the well-to-do in the Settlement Movements in the 1880s. These

were a response to social conscience, but that conscience was over-
shadowed by anxieties that socialism might become revolutionary.
The active socialist spirit of the 1840s was rekindled in the run-up to
the Third Reform Act of 1884 by Hyndman's Social Democratic
Federation, and the American lecturer Henry George's call for the
abolition of private ownership of land. At the same time, belief in
organized charity as a sufficient remedy for social evil and unrest was
breaking down. The problem of urban deprivation had swelled
beyond the powers of voluntary intervention. Attitudes to almsgiving also changed. To those who gave, the distinction between the
'deserving' and the 'undeserving' poor proved unworkable. To the
poor, charity was humiliating; it reinforced the segregation of rich
and poor. Charity belonged to an age of paternalism and face-to-
face relations that had passed. There was an insistent call for state
intervention and the incorporation of the working classes into the
political system.

Criticism of philanthropy was already an element in mid-
Victorian literature. Mrs Gaskell incurred her old friend W. R.
Greg's disapproval in 1849 in the *Edinburgh Review* for her sceptical
attitude towards kindly masters in *Mary Barton*, her novel of
working-class unrest.[26] To Walter Bagehot, reviewing Dickens's
works in the late 1850s, the appeal to benevolence and sentiment
already seemed dated.[27] Among Wilde's contemporaries, George
Gissing was the blatant critic of charity. His anti-Dickensian novels
poured scorn on philanthropy as a social remedy or as a healing
bridge between rich and poor.

The other-worldly endings of Wilde's fairy-tales also take the
reader beyond available economic and political solutions to poverty
and inequality. Altruism is exposed as a servant of the capitalist
system it purports to remedy. In 'The Devoted Friend', Wilde
reveals the devotion of master for man—the Miller for Little Hans—
for the exploitative, self-serving thing that it is. His use of a frame
narrative, in which the Green Linnet hopes to correct the Water-
rat's equally self-deceiving sentimentality, reinforces the irony. Like
the Miller, the Water-rat is all talk and beautiful sentiment: 'I like the
Miller immensely. I have all kinds of beautiful sentiments myself,
so there is a great sympathy between us.' The Water-rat remains
impervious to the real moral that the Green Linnet's tale urges. In
'The Happy Prince' Wilde employs another favourite device of the

skilled raconteur—the double ending or take—to equal effect. In the first ending, before the final invocation of paradise, the statue of the Happy Prince is melted down by the town counsellors and recast as the mayor. The Happy Prince's sacrifices have merely served society's inexorable ends. To read these stories as ironic exposures of delusory panaceas to social ill is to place Wilde within the tradition of Marx and Morris, and of contemporary anti-idealists like Gissing, rather than within the reforming traditions of Dickens and Kingsley, or of Wilde's contemporary Walter Besant. In 'The Critic as Artist', Wilde dismissed Besant's picturesque novels of East End life for being 'all for the far-fetched and unnatural'. His view of Besant is also revealed in his witty comment on Besant's practical organizational abilities as President of the Society of Authors: 'It would perhaps be too much to expect that the universal benevolence of Besant should condescend to details. For philanthropy so wide as his, fiction is the proper place' (*Letters*, p. 356).

This interpretation of Wilde's anti-philanthropic stance may seem exaggerated. Yet Wilde's rejection of the sentiment of reform is quite explicit in 'The Soul of Man under Socialism' and in *De Profundis*. In 'The Soul of Man', he denounces altruism bluntly as admirable but misdirected. It is a remedy that merely prolongs rather than cures the disease. In fact, he identifies it as 'part of the disease'. Wilde does not spare his readers of the *Fortnightly Review* in which the essay first appeared. The best of the poor, he informs them, 'are never grateful' for their charity:

Charity they feel to be a ridiculously inadequate mode of partial restitution, or a sentimental dole, usually accompanied by some impertinent attempt on the part of the sentimentalist to tyrannize over their private lives. Why should they be grateful for the crumbs that fall from the rich man's table? They should be seated at the board, and are beginning to know it.

Wilde himself had come to expect no sentimental gratitude for the dinners and gifts he lavished on his company of young working-class male companions. With savage satire, in *De Profundis* he turned Christ's mockery at the 'whited sepulchres' of respectability against 'the cold philosophs, the ostentatious public charities' of the middle-class philistines of his own day. Christ was neither the philanthropist nor the altruist of the nineteenth-century middle-class imagination.

Accumulation of wealth tempered with do-gooding was 'a thing to be absolutely despised'.

In the social comedies, the amoral characters—Illingworth in *A Woman of No Importance*, Goring and Mrs Cheveley in *An Ideal Husband*—ridicule philanthropy as a social remedy. Illingworth's amusement at Mr Kelvil's mission to London's East End is less callous than clear-eyed. For Illingworth, middle-class sympathy for hardship and poverty shows an ignorance of the joys, palliatives, and fierce independence of lower-class life. Illingworth's assessment of middle-class intervention echoes the protest and rebellion of working-class radicalism itself in the 1870s and 1880s. Illingworth rejects the kind missionary optimism found, for instance, in Besant's philanthropic novel, *All Sorts and Conditions of Men*, and the establishment of the East End Institute, known as the People's Palace, in Mile End Road, which was one of its direct results. For Illingworth, the problem of the East End is 'the public slavery' that cannot be solved 'by amusing the slaves' (Act 1). In *An Ideal Husband*, irritation with exaggerated sympathy unites the aristocratic Lord Caversham and the morally lax Mrs Cheveley and Lord Goring. In this play on the theme of double standards in public and private life, their resistance is to a rectitude that requires reverence. In 'The Soul of Man under Socialism', Wilde himself wrote: 'All sympathy . . . is tainted with egotism.' For Mrs Cheveley, who prefers life's colour to Blue Books, 'philanthropy seems to have become simply the refuge of people who wish to annoy their fellow creatures' (Act 1). Goring too denounces the demoralizing effects of self-sacrifice 'on those for whom one sacrifices oneself', and calls for it to be 'put down by law' (Act 3).

To Wilde's audiences, such expressions would have sounded cynical, and even pessimistic. Indeed, a characteristic labelling of attitudes as optimistic or pessimistic at the time is reflected in Robert Chiltern's caustic comment in *An Ideal Husband* that optimism and pessimism 'seem to be the only two fashionable religions left us nowadays' (Act 1). In the same play, Lord Goring denies that he is a pessimist on the grounds that pessimism rests upon a frustrated and impossible ideal of human perfection (Act 2). Wilde's plays, in effect, react equally against the fatalism of hard-headed realism of the grimly deterministic, 'truth-telling' sort, as against the middle-class panacea of philanthropic idealism. As a response to society and its failings, optimism and pessimism, according to Wilde, were simply two sides of the same coin: optimism, self-deceiving; pessimism, crippling and defeatist. Both left the existing social system exactly as it was.

In their selfish pursuits, Wilde's dandies accept human imperfection and failure as an encouragement to charity of the forgiving, loving sort. Yet there is no idealistic back-pedalling in Wilde to the pretence that society as a whole can be reformed by this means. In the plays, as in 'The Soul of Man under Socialism', Wilde rejects charity as a cheap form of emotional tyranny that perpetuates poverty and social inequality. His remedy in 'The Soul of Man' is neither the spiritualized capitalism of liberal reformers nor is it in any narrow sense the limited redistribution of wealth advocated by their socialist opponents. Wilde argues for the extension of ample, aristocratic leisure and freedom for all individuals.

Wilde's sympathy of intellect as opposed to sympathy of feeling is an attempt to outflank socialists and conservatives alike. In 1890 the Fabian socialist and feminist Annie Besant lined up against Frederick Miller, the representative for the conservative Liberty and Property Defence League in a public debate on the opposing claims of 'Socialism and Individualism'.[28] In 'The Soul of Man', a year later, Wilde out-Fabians the Fabians by embracing gradualism as simply an evolutionary stage on the road to true Individualism. At the same time, by playing up the anti-authoritarian rhetoric of Individualism, he turned Liberal opposition to state interference against itself. In Wilde's aesthetic paradise, the poor are delivered from poverty, and the propertied from responsibility.

Wilde's aestheticism—in particular his emphasis on contemplation over accumulation—owes much to Matthew Arnold. Arnold's idea of culture indicated a critical attitude of mind—the development of a 'best self'—that set itself above a material and mechanical civilization. Wilde, in 'The Soul of Man under Socialism', argues that culture depends upon material accumulation. Both were devoted Hellenes. Both based their ideal of a cultured civilization on ancient Greek society. Yet Wilde's Hellenism was more historically and archaeologically rooted. He did not lose sight of the fact that Greek civilization had depended upon slaves 'to do the ugly, horrible, uninteresting work'. Civilization, Wilde knew, required slaves. Wilde's answer was that under future arrangements, modern machines would take the place of slaves. His unexpected solution set him apart not only from Arnold, but also from William Morris, whose utopia is founded upon co-operation and community. In Morris' utopia, men share the rougher work; in Wilde's, machinery leaves every man 'quite free to choose his own work'. In 'The Critic as Artist', Wilde wrote: '[Men] rage against materialism, as they call it, forgetting that there has been no material improvement that has not spiritualized the world.' The socialist critic Raymond Williams, writing in the 1950s, recognized in this passage that Wilde had shown what the tradition of nineteenth-century English social criticism 'had still to learn'.[29]

In Arnold's writings, as has been noted, culture is a spiritual antidote to the political consequences of anarchy, or 'doing as one likes'. In Wilde, the two are practically synonymous. Contemporary readers did not miss the anarchist force of Wilde's redefinition of individualism. 'The sort of individuality to which Oscar attaches great moment is one which recognises no law or authority. He wants the world to be all Oscar Wilde,' wrote one.[30] In 'The Soul of Man under Socialism', the aristocratic ideal of the dandy attains a paradoxical, sharply democratic edge. Since anarchy thrives only in relation to the social laws and foundational consciousness that it seeks to eliminate, Wilde imagines a process of unending opposition. His description of utopia as 'the one country at which Humanity is always landing' sounds conceptual and benign. Yet Wilde's anticonformist argument transforms crime, rebellion, and civil disobedience into virtues: 'Disobedience, in the eyes of any one who has read history, is man's original virtue. It is through disobedience that progress is made, through disobedience and through rebellion.' And in another passage quoting the Taoist philosopher Chuang Tzu: 'He who would be free must not conform.' There is a recognition in this that labels and meanings change depending on which side one is. To those with plenty, theft is a crime; to those who are hungry, the crime is starvation.

Prison and Prison Writings

Wilde's strongest hostility was reserved for those who inflicted punishment. He welcomed legislation that made it its task to eliminate the barbarism and brutality of the penal system. At the time of writing 'The Soul of Man under Socialism', he was aware of the failure of the prison system to reform offenders, although he had no real knowledge of prison procedures. In response to Herbert Spencer's observation that 'severe laws do not decrease crime', he noted in his Commonplace Notebook while a student at Oxford that 'nothing speaks so well for the noble nature of man as his showy indifference to any system of rewards and punishments either heavenly or terrestial.'[31] In 'The Critic as Artist', he denounced moral reformation wittily as 'a much more painful process than punishment'. In fact the prison regime introduced by the Prison Commission under Sir Edmund Du Cane in 1878 applied harsh punishments such as solitary confinement, hard labour, and disciplinary floggings, as necessary elements of moral reformation. By the 1860s public punishments were no longer considered appropriate to a civilized society, but brutality and executions continued out of sight behind the high walls of the Victorian prison. In January 1894, a series of articles in the *Daily Chronicle* sought to raise public concern about the harmful dehumanizing effects of the English prison system. The call was for a more scientific approach to criminal pathology, and for the separation of juvenile offenders. There was a growing literature on criminal anthropology—a new science pioneered by an Italian professor of forensic medicine, Cesare Lombroso, who claimed to be able to classify criminals according to observable physical and psychical abnormalities.

Wilde's early attitude to criminals was a typically Victorian view that they formed a distinct and separate class. Visiting Lincoln State Penitentiary, Nebraska, in 1882, he was relieved that the prisoners were all sad, mean-looking types. 'I should hate to see a criminal with a noble face,' he remarked (*Letters*, p. 166). Visiting Kansas just two weeks after the killing of the notorious train robber and outlaw, Jesse James, he was amused that Americans should take their heroes 'from the criminal classes' (*Letters*, p. 164), forgetting that he himself tended to idealize the rebel and outcast. At this stage, his attitude to crime was formed largely through literature. As a boy, one of his favourite characters was Julien Sorel in Stendhal's novel, *Le Rouge et le noir* (*The Red and the Black*), who dies on the scaffold. His great-uncle Charles Maturin's *Melmoth the Wanderer*, another tale of transgression, was among his earliest reading. He also admired the Russian novelists Turgenev and Dostoevsky, believing that real-life

Nihilists were largely their invention. He praised Dostoevsky's *Crime and Punishment* in 'The Decay of Lying' as a psychological masterpiece, and thrilled to the hero Raskolnikov's declaration that 'crime, though it is punishable in ordinary men and woman, is permitted to extraordinary beings'.[32]

Wilde's earliest revolutionary sympathies were also influenced by the communal memory of his mother's role in the Young Ireland movement in the 1840s. His first play, *Vera: or The Nihilists*, has been identified by Sos Eltis as the only play in the popular genre of 'Russian' plays in the 1880s and 1890s to include a woman among its conspirators.[33] Yet Vera remains a theoretical and self-consciously poetic production. It was only during the 1880s that Wilde developed a more mature understanding of the connection between crime and free will, and between literary representations and real-life anarchists. In Paris in the early 1880s he met writers and artists of the French Symbolist movement, such as Felix Fénéon and Adolphe Retté, for whom poetry and politics were indistinguishable. In his own life, he departed more and more from conventional paths in the 1880s. In his sexual adventures, he became, technically at least, a criminal under the law.

All these factors appear to have intensified his anti-authoritarian position. Wilde's first homage to the artist as criminal, his essay portrait of the poet and poisoner Thomas Griffiths Wainewright, owes much to Thomas De Quincey's essay 'Of Murder Considered as a Fine Art' and Swinburne's essay on William Blake. Swinburne's insouciant defence of Wainewright's stylish artistry 'with pen, with pencil, or with poison' gave Wilde the title of his essay, 'Pen, Pencil and Poison'. Swinburne's vignette, which appears as an aside in his essay on Blake, is generally interpreted as a satire on the idea that art can be judged according to everyday moral and utilitarian standards. Wilde appears to follow suit, but with an insistence on Wainewright's heroic personality that discomforts any easy laughter at the seemingly ludicrous proposal that there is no essential difference between art and crime. Wilde believed that crime satisfied an imaginative need. To sin was to reassert an irrational freedom of soul against nineteenth-century social and political theories that would limit man's freedom. The final message at the close of 'The Soul of Man under Socialism' is a rejection of any scheme that would 'do away with poverty, and the suffering that it entails', or that 'trusts to

Socialism and to Science as its methods'. Wilde indicates the source of his ideas in Russian writing:

Even now, in some places in the world, the message of Christ is necessary. No one who lived in modern Russia could possibly realise his perfection except by pain . . . A Russian who lives happily under the present system of government in Russia must either believe that man has no soul, or that, if he has, it is not worth developing. A Nihilist who rejects all authority because he knows authority to be evil, and welcomes all pain, because through that he realises his personality, is a real Christian.

The identification of Christ and Christianity with anarchism was common among anarchists and their opponents in Europe in the 1890s. In *De Profundis*, Wilde identified the anarchist Peter Kropotkin as 'a man with the soul of that beautiful white Christ that seems coming out of Russia'. Kropotkin, who had experienced both Russian and French prisons, believed that imprisonment and criminal rehabilitation were blatant forms of political oppression and control. Kropotkin argued against rehabilitation from statistical evidence, and on the grounds that criminals were being reformed for return to a hypocritical society. For Wilde, too, the unjust social order and the legal system that upheld it were the origin of crime. Yet, unlike Kropotkin, Wilde at first viewed imprisonment as a test of integrity. 'Even in prison, a man may be quite free,' he wrote in 'The Soul of Man under Socialism'. Wilde drew his heroic conclusions from the stories of Irish political patriots. Their literature of heroic resistance marked an important point of connection between his background and the wider political stage. He remembered with admiration the prisoner-patriots of the Young Ireland movement he had met at his parents' house in Dublin. Later, he met Wilfrid Scawen Blunt, imprisoned in 1888 for opposing British imperialism during the Balfour regime in Ireland. He praised Blunt's collection of prison poems *In Vinculis* with the observation that imprisonment has 'converted a clever rhymer into an earnest and deep-thinking poet'.[34] Imprisonment seemed to be the inevitable fate of supporters of the Irish cause. Parnell too had emerged from prison in 1882 strengthened in his campaign for Home Rule for Ireland.

Wilde's bitter experiences as a prisoner were to change fundamentally his idealized attitude to prison life. In the shocking immediacy of the real thing, his grim anatomy of demoralization among prisoners in *De Profundis* unconsciously echoes Kropotkin's *In Russian and French Prisons*. Wilde records the deadening effects of sombre environment and iron routine on the sensory life of the prisoner—the cutting-off of social contacts, the demeaning prison uniform aimed at making him look ridiculous, and the contempt for all ordinary human feeling. The triumph of the human spirit is a leitmotif that runs through Wilde's letter of despair, but this hope is a desperate, consolatory expectation that something good may come 'out of the depths' of his suffering: 'I try to say to myself, and sometimes when I am not torturing myself do really and sincerely say, "What a beginning! What a wonderful beginning!" It may really be so. It may be so.'

Wilde's immediate aim on leaving prison was to draw public attention to the terrible cruelties and conditions of prison life, and to speak on behalf of all prisoners. Among the books he ordered in the weeks before his release from Reading Gaol were the Revd William Douglas Morrison's writings on criminology and prison conditions, published as *Crime and its Causes* (1891) and *Juvenile Offenders* (1896). Morrison had been chaplain at Wandsworth Prison during Wilde's time there. With the journalist H. W. Massingham and the trade union leader and Labour MP John Burns, Morrison had co-authored a series of campaigning articles on prison reform in the *Daily Chronicle* in 1894. Wilde's own first article on the cruelties of the prison system appeared as a letter to the *Daily Chronicle* ten days after he left Reading Gaol. It was prompted by news of the dismissal of Thomas Martin, a kindly warden at Reading Gaol, for giving biscuits to a child prisoner he was guarding. Both Kropotkin and Morrison had condemned prisons as schools of crime. Morrison in particular urged the segregation of juvenile offenders. Wilde added his voice to the chorus of protest against the inhumanity of prison conditions. His criticism was directed not only against the justice system, but against the concealment of the unpleasant that accompanied Victorian bureaucratic developments. Victorian ignorance and complacency were his chief targets. The unimaginable cruelties of the prison system were the result not of extraordinary evil, but of a blind and banal obedience to rules. Children were made to endure the psychological terror of 'a lonely and unfamiliar cell', hunger, and the 'badness' of sanitary arrangements. While arguing for segregation, Morrison and other prison reformers generally submitted to economic realities: separate prisons were too expensive. Wilde gave an ex-prisoner's ironic twist to the philanthropists' demand for a separate prison for juveniles. The young, he argued, needed protection not from the prisoners—they were 'extremely kind and sympathetic' to each other—but from the prison system itself. Wilde's letter concluded with a chillingly authentic account of the systematic flogging of a fellow prisoner at Reading Gaol. The man, who was evidently insane, was accused of 'shamming' (*Letters*, p. 853).

Wilde's second letter to the *Daily Chronicle* almost a year later was in response to the recommendations of the Prison Reform Bill for an increase in the number of inspectors and official visitors. Under the headline, 'Don't Read This If You Want To Be Happy', Wilde condemned the instincts of officialdom to check that rules were being carried out, rather then reform 'an inhuman code'. Once again Wilde outlined in graphic detail the 'misery and tortures' of English prison life—weak food resulting in incessant diarrhoea, 'revolting sanitary arrangements', and insomnia caused by a plank-bed. He acknowledged that his letter was a kind of 'trespass' on the sensibilities of his Victorian readers. The word is carefully placed—an allusion to the plea of the sinner who is also sinned against in the Lord's Prayer. Wilde does not spare the prison doctors or the prison chaplains in their perfunctory performance of their duties. His own list of recommended reforms—a prison library, regular visits, letters, and contacts with the outside world—concludes with an appeal to the whole society 'to humanise the governors of prisons, to civilise the warders and to Christianise the chaplains' (*Letters*, p. 1049).

A month earlier Wilde had published *The Ballad of Reading Gaol*. The poem describes the hanging of 'C. T. W.' (Charles Thomas Wooldridge), a trooper of the Royal Horse Guards at Reading Gaol on 7 July 1896, for slitting his wife's throat. Public executions had been abolished over twenty years earlier because of public concerns about the dangerous and degrading spectacle of the drunken crowds that gathered to watch the scaffold drama. The crowds attracted prostitutes, pickpockets, and profiteering street-hawkers. The shift to private executions did not lessen the suffering of the condemned man; it only meant that his death now took place out of sight, behind the walls of the prison. In writing *The Ballad of Reading Gaol*, Wilde sought to bring to public attention the inhuman reality of capital punishment itself. His 'ballad' follows the traditional rhyme schemes and verse patterns of the popular folk-ballad, used from the time of the ancient minstrels through to self-consciously 'literary' imitations like S. T. Coleridge's *The Rime of the Ancient Mariner*. The ballad form enjoyed a popular revival in the 1890s with the growth of new markets for verse that would appeal to a wide audience. Wilde's voice in the poem is not the 'come-ye-all' of the traditional street balladeer, but the anguished voice of the suffering insider and fellow prisoner of the condemned man. At the close of the second canto of the poem, the speaker identifies himself as an equal 'outcast' from society. At the point of execution, he claims special kinship with the murderer:

> And all the woe that moved him so
>   That he gave that bitter cry,
> And the wild regrets, and the bloody sweats,
>   None knew so well as I:
> For he who lives more lives than one
>   More deaths than one must die.   (ll. 391–6)

Wilde worried that the poem was too personal and realistic. He also fretted over the evident tension between its didactic and its purely artistic aims. The poem seemed to betray his philosophy of art. 'It is a new style for me, full of actuality and life in its directness of message and meaning,' he wrote (*Letters*, p. 922). Yet he found the attempt to shape the undignified and unpoetic realities of prison life in verse form an artistic challenge. He delighted when he managed to get in commonplace words like 'latrine', which he thought looked 'beautiful' (*Letters*, p. 930). 'I feel I have made a sonnet out of skilly,' he told Frank Harris (*Letters*, p. 1025; 'skilly' was the gruel given to prisoners). The truth was that the degrading and banal details of prison life—the 'real experiences', as Wilde called them—were as exotic and unfamiliar to his middle-class readership as the strangeness of romance. Wilde himself acknowledged this when he considered having the poem appear in *Reynolds Police News* because it was read by the lower and criminal classes, so ensuring him a sympathetic audience (*Letters*, p. 964). In his descriptions of the sordid, Wilde discovered for the first time in his writing the romance of the 'real'.

It was the realism of the poem that was to receive most praise. Yet, as Wilde feared, many readers felt that the poem's propagandist aims undermined its artistic effect. To the modern mind, propaganda and poetry make an uneasy mix. Robert Ross urged Wilde to finish the poem at the end of the fourth canto with the reconciliatory:

> Yet all is well; he has but passed
>   To Life's appointed bourne:
> And alien tears will fill for him
>   Pity's long-broken urn,
> For his mourners will be outcast men,
>   And outcasts always mourn.   (ll. 529–34)

Yet Wilde wanted more for his poem than to induce or re-enforce fatalistic attitudes to guilt, suffering, and death. The fifth canto gives bitter, poetic force to the protests voiced in Wilde's letters to the *Daily Chronicle* on the conditions of prison life. Again, his purpose is to expose what is hidden from sight and conveniently ignored. Ironically, in the poem, the prison walls are seen as man's attempt to blur and conceal their created Hell from Christ:

> . . . every prison that men build
>   Is built with bricks of shame,
> And bound with bars lest Christ should see
>   How men their brothers maim.   (ll. 549–52)

However the poem does not rest here. The last two verses of the sixth and final canto announce a new recognition:

> And there, till Christ call forth the dead,
>   In silence let him lie:
> No need to waste the foolish tear;
>   Or heave the windy sigh:
> The man had killed the thing he loved,
>   And so he had to die.
>
> And all men kill the thing they love,
>   By all let this be heard,
> Some do it with a bitter look,
>   Some with a flattering word,
> The coward does it with a kiss,
>   The brave man with a sword!   (ll. 643–54)

This is neither reformist nor fatalistic. Rather, understanding lies in a corrective answer to the question raised in Shakespeare's *The Merchant of Venice* by Bassanio, the youthful lover who unintentionally betrays both mistress and friend. In response to the naïve Bassanio's question, 'Do all men kill the thing they do not love?' is Wilde's profound understanding of the paradoxical message of Shakespeare's play that is the theme of his ballad, that 'all men kill the thing they love'. The poem's famous refrain is at once a protest against society's limited view of the guilty man, and a realization that hatred and human cruelty also have their origin in an excess of love. The trooper's crime of passion provides Wilde and his poem with a universal truth about human nature. The acceptance that 'all men kill the thing they love' extends to the justice system itself for the heartless punishment and legalized murder of its subjects in the name of goodness. The shift in the ballad injunction from 'By each let this be heard' in the first canto to 'By all let this be heard' in the last, is a shift from the individual to the community. The appeal, as in *The Merchant of Venice*, is to mercy and, beyond that, to the terrible coming of Christ in final judgement. As in his stories, Wilde looks beyond social remedy and reform to the judgement of another world.

Consumerism: Dorian Gray and Other Collectors

The rise of consumerism is a prominent theme in Wilde's work. The Great Exhibition of 1851 was a ceremonial signal for the beginning of a new age of consumerism. The superabundance of commodities on display at the Crystal Palace promised a future when every individual might be supplied not only with the bare necessities of life, but with a variety of goods and gadgets administering to every human desire and need. The new method of mass advertising made commodities the objects of desire, to be sold by means of myths of national loyalty or social consensus. Consumerism became the justification for the free market, and the new route to the common good.

Wilde's claims for the socially transformational power of decoration and design during his lecture tours of the early 1880s are connected to this cultural development. The new aestheticism and the Arts and Crafts movement, which Wilde evangelized, saw themselves as part of a protest against nineteenth-century industrial society. Wilde, like Morris, promoted the beauty of craftsmanship over the ugliness of the machine-made. At the same time, the appeal to the 'man of taste', the connoisseur, in arranging and decorating one's surroundings, was an advanced version of capitalist consumerism. Wilde's lectures in America—'The House Beautiful' and 'The Decorative Arts'—were seductive 'sells'. The promotion of the virtues and advantages of certain materials; the preference for higher order goods; the contempt for lower quality and aspirations: Wilde's lectures sound like nineteenth-century equivalents of modern-day advertisement voice-overs, weaving a wish for things that would make life richer and more complete. Everything has a value in the service of pleasure and repose: the exquisite gradations of colour; material tones; variety; the arrangement and symmetry of objects; the cut and colour of one's clothes. Wilde's claims for the superiority of Queen Anne-style furniture—'made by refined people for refined people'—would not seem out of place as a modern-day advertising caption or slogan. His stories themselves are commodities—works artfully stylish and artfully constructed to give aesthetic pleasure of a distinct sort.

For Wilde, the highest order in the scale of human pleasure was after all art. According to the new aestheticism, commodities and materials, like works of art, should further sensation, pleasure, and heightened individuality. Wilde's ideal owes much to Walter Pater whose aesthetic doctrine of pleasurable impressions in a world of flux might almost serve as a description of commodity consumerism. In *The Renaissance: Studies in Art and Poetry*, Pater regards all objects 'as powers or forces producing pleasurable sensations'.[35] Wilde was to develop Pater's ideal of the aesthetic consumer in Wainewright in 'Pen, Pencil and Poison', in his dialogues and essays, and in his fictional portraits of the philosophical aesthete as *flâneur*, dandy, and man of fashion. In *De Profundis*, the famous remorseful review of his past life, Wilde tries to distinguish between higher and meaner sensations. Yet here, as in his fictions, the difference threatens to disappear in the claim for experience.

Wilde's narratives provide a critique of the denial upon which the new aestheticism might come to rest. Taste and choice are recognized as forms of consumerism in which things in themselves threaten to invert the relations between subjective and objective worlds. Tales of people turning into things, and inanimate objects coming to life are as old as literature itself. The Latin poet Ovid, in his *Metamorphoses*, brings together stories of this kind. Famous among them is the story of Pygmalion, whose beautiful sculpture of a woman is brought to life by Venus. The Pygmalion story underlies many nineteenth-century fictions, including Prosper Merimée's archaeological ghost story, 'Venus of Ille', Gautier's 'The Mummy's Foot', and Henry James's 'The Last of the Valerii'. In all of these nineteenth-century tales, the erotic animated female threatens to reify or emasculate the hero. Dickens's more general comic deployment of personified objects and reified people has also been widely noted, particularly in *Dombey and Son* and *Our Mutual Friend*, where the transformations are connected to the transformed object world of nineteenth-century industrial urban civilization. The spectacle of malleable or disintegrating selfhood, and of an object world out of control, is also played out in Lewis Carroll's *Alice's Adventures in Wonderland*.

By the turn of the century, the figure of the collector begins to take definite fictional form. The collector's fantasy is invariably to control and domesticate the foreign, the alien, and the fearful through arrangement and manipulation. In a realistic treatment of the theme in Henry James's *The Golden Bowl*, the American Adam Verver's priceless collection includes human specimens. The attempt by Verver's wife, Charlotte Stant, and his daughter's husband, Prince Amerigo, to re-establish previous intimate relations is defeated. The exotic Charlotte is 'put back in her cage', and Prince Amerigo, the tasteful foreign commodity, is repossessed. In Arthur Conan Doyle's fantasy tale 'Lot 249', as in earlier ghost stories, the exotic object takes on a life of its own and threatens to possess the possessor.[36] As is characteristic of such fantasies and fictions in the nineteenth century, control over the object world—the realm of the repressed, the alien, the strange—is in the end reassuringly restored.

In Wilde's comedy ghost story 'The Canterville Ghost', the threat is comically deflected. Wilde pokes fun at the Jamesian theme of the rich American Hiram B. Otis's aesthetic view of England as a museum world of interesting ruins and curiosities. The story ironically inverts the usual relations between animated object and petrified people in the traditional ghost story. Here the unfortunate ghost is mocked and terrorized by the terrible Otis family twins. Domesticated at last, the ghost is reduced to oiling his creaking chains with Rising Sun Lubricator, and wearing slippers to avoid disturbing the new owners of Canterville Chase. The ending marks the triumph of bourgeois materialism and commodity culture over old guilt-ridden relations. The resident ghost is the ultimate commodity, who is released into death in exchange for a box of jewels. The ghostly is contained and repelled. Everything has its exchange value; everything here has its place and its price.

In *The Picture of Dorian Gray*, by contrast, the repressed or ghostly reasserts itself with a vengeance. Dorian and his portrait begin as mirrors of each other—provocatively dandified, feminized images. Both are at once protests against vulgarity, and beautiful commodities. Like Huysmans's decadent hero, Des Esseintes, on whom he is modelled, Dorian is a collector whose refinement and taste are measured by the rarity of the objects he accumulates, and the artistic feelings they create. His luxuriously decorated house is a museum of precious objects and part-objects from every time and place—old brocades, ivory carvings, bronzes, and Renaissance tapestries. Even his water-closet is dignified with the refinement of a silver Louis Quinze toilet-seat. Dorian is economic man freed at last from the demands of production into a life of conspicuous consumption.[37] To Lord Henry Wotton, Dorian's mentor and *âme damnée* in the art of pleasure, 'a cigarette is the perfect type of a perfect pleasure' because it leaves one unsatisfied (ch. VI). Dorian's quest for new sensations leaves him ultimately a prisoner of desire. On one level, nemesis, or punishment, might be read as the result of Dorian's descent into lower or meaner pleasures and sensations. The ugliness of the portrait increases in proportion to his crimes and sinful indulgences. The moral reading is of a piece with Wilde's own regretful recantation of his life of 'senseless and sensual ease' as unworthy of the artist. Yet the change to the picture begins when Dorian cruelly abandons his mistress, the actress Sibyl Vane, for choosing life over art. It is the consequence of an intensified yet limited aestheticism on his part, of a 'new-born feeling of luxury' (ch. VII). Art and indulgence become inseparable under the sign of the commodity. The attempt to suspend time and history and to transcend human relationships fails at last. In *Dorian Gray*, these return in fury, first in the form of Sibyl Vane's would-be avenger, James Vane, and finally in the repressed, guilt-ridden vision of the corporeal life mirrored in the painting. The ending offers no reassuring fantasy of control. Written when, in Wilde's words, 'unnecessary things are our only necessity' (ch. VIII), *Dorian Gray* is not so much a moral tragedy, as a paradoxical commentary on the aesthetic tendencies of its time that would conceal and repress the true relations between people and things.

CHAPTER 5

WILDE AND INTELLECTUAL ISSUES

Philosophy and Science

ON meeting Wilde, many of his contemporaries recognized that, far from being the effete aesthete of popular caricature and lampoon, Wilde was a scholar and intellectual. Not only was he a prize-winning classicist; he was equally at home with much of the leading philosophical and scientific thought of the day. His position with regard to science was ambivalent. As prophet of the new aestheticism and self-professed leader of the Celtic school of literature, Wilde advocated a symbolic reaction against the rationalism and materialism of the age, living up to Arnold's notion of the imaginative Celt, always 'ready to react against the despotism of fact'.[1] He accepted Arnold's definition, and made frequent allusions to it in his writings. Yet unlike Arnold and exponents of the 'Two Cultures', who identified science as the enemy of art and imagination, Wilde took pleasure and interest in the scientific aspects of contemporary life and thought.

To some extent this was a consequence of his Irish education. Although it was common, particularly among those concerned with the revival of native Irish culture, to stress the claims of imagination over reason, Ireland boasted an impressive and influential scientific community that reached back to the eighteenth century. That tradition eventually went into partial decline after 1880, as a consequence arguably of the political troubles and emigration to England and the United States. But it was still flourishing when Wilde was growing up. Wilde admired poets such as Goethe and Shelley who valued a scientific approach to life. His enthusiasm for the link between science and poetry received fresh inspiration from his reading of John Addington Symonds's *Studies of the Greek Poets*. The second volume of Symonds's work argued that the effort to establish morality on a scientific basis united both the ancient Greek world and nineteenth-century evolutionary theory.[2] Wilde attributed the charming, dispassionate cheerfulness in Goethe and the Greeks to the same scientific view of life.[3] He believed that the exercise of the poetic or imaginative faculty so intimately blended with scientific worship in the early Greeks, in Goethe, and in Shelley, anticipated nearly all modern scientific truths.[4]

Wilde sought confirmation for the link between ancient and modern thought in his reading of contemporary scientists and philosophers. In this he followed the example of his contemporaries. It was a mark of the 'modern spirit', strikingly evident in the ninth edition of the *Encyclopaedia Britannica* published between 1875 and 1889, and including for the first time articles on biblical criticism, comparative religion, psychology, and evolution.[5] Wilde reviewed volumes X and XI of the *Britannica* for the *Athenaeum* in 1880, promoting the modern or romantic elements of Graeco-Roman literature and thought against the received Victorian view of its serenity and balance.[6] The two notebooks he kept at Oxford also reflect his keen interest in the connection between ancient and modern thought. He was especially interested in Herbert Spencer's evolutionary theory of society in *The Study of Sociology* (1873), which seemed to give scientific support for Plato's metaphor of the state as 'man writ large'.[7] In Aristotle too, he recognized an anticipation of two maxims of contemporary evolutionary theory. The first is that man and society are to be understood in terms of a general law of growth from simpler to more complex life. The second is that progress and the 'survival of the fittest' (Spencer's phrase, not Darwin's) depend upon organic diversity. The more simple and unified an organism the more vulnerable it was to instability and threat. For Wilde, Spencer's law of 'differentiation' (that is, the need for variety, complexity, and freedom) was only Aristotle's law of organic development by a different name.

EVOLUTIONARY STORIES

The Spencerian formula runs like a scarcely visible figure in the carpet through Wilde's writings. *The Picture of Dorian Gray* is, on an important level, an experiment in creative evolution gone wrong. In applying the spirit of natural science to society, Lord Henry Wotton preaches a doctrine of selfish individualism over the bankruptcy of Victorian earnestness and altruism. According to Wotton's modern scientific view, the aim of life is self-development, and the age demanded a new hedonism unbounded by the maladies of medieval and puritanical conscience. It required not only openness to every experience, but the breaking of taboos since 'it is only the sacred things that are worth touching' (ch. IV). Wotton's linking of conscience and cowardice is a characteristic one in Wilde's work. In *An Ideal Husband*, Robert Chiltern sacrifices conscience for an immoral but profitable transaction with the wicked Lord Arnheim. In *The Picture of Dorian Gray*, Dorian becomes the guinea-pig for Wotton's evolutionary experiment. The road to complete self-realization involves a rejection of the standards of the age, and freedom from all creeds and systems. To Wotton, sin, remorse, and degradation are outmoded medieval concepts.

Wotton's philosophy of pleasure would seem, on the face of it, to combine the subjective hedonism of Pater's *The Renaissance* with the decadence of Huysmans's Parisian hero in *A Rebours*. Yet Wotton's scientific conviction that 'no life is spoiled but one whose growth is arrested' is Spencerian in formula (ch. VI). His goal of development from medievalism to 'something finer, richer, than the Hellenic ideal' is dialectical in force (ch. II). His dismissal of love and art as 'simply forms of imitation' marks him as a full-bloodied rational evolutionist (ch. VII). It can be argued that Wilde intended *Dorian Gray* neither as a celebration of decadence, nor as a moral rebuke to its excesses, but as a philosophical-scientific romance on the theme of evolutionary failure. Following Spencer, Wilde noted down in his Oxford Commonplace Book: 'Progress in thought is the assertion of individualism against authority, and progress in matter is differentiation and specialization of function: those organisms which are entirely subject to external influences do not progress any more than a mind entirely subject to authority.'[8] He also jotted down the following thought: 'Mankind has been continually entering the prisons of Puritanism, Philistinism, Sensualism, Fanaticism, and turning the key on its own spirit: but after a time there is an enormous desire for higher freedom—for self-preservation.'[9] Spencer's influential belief in 'the survival of the fittest' introduced a secular moral dimension to evolutionism (those energetic enough to survive did so by right of nature).

Another important element in Wilde's treatment of Dorian's temptation and ruin is the Victorian psychology of influence. Victorian writers were fascinated by the theory of 'animal magnetism' propounded by the eighteenth-century Austrian doctor, Franz Anton Mesmer, to account for his power to 'magnetize' his patients during treatment. Mesmer's theory proposed a mysterious fluid that could be stored and transferred to others. Dickens was an enthusiastic believer. By the 1880s the crude physiological theory of animal magnetism known as 'mesmerism' was being replaced by the more psychological theory of hypnosis. In France, for example, one school of thought argued that the power of suggestion was pathological in origin, and occurred only in sufferers of hysteria.

In his earlier story, 'The Portrait of Mr W. H.', books and personalities are alike capable of exercising seductive, hypnotic influence over the receptive, impressionable mind. 'The Portrait of Mr W. H.' is a tale of transmission in which the charm of stories and of the makers of stories is indistinguishable. Yet whether these serve pathological instincts or creative imagination, degeneracy or evolution, is initially in question. Erskine's story of his charming effeminate friend Cyril Graham's theory that Shakespeare's dramatic genius found inspiration in a boy-actor of great beauty and personality, the player of his noble heroines, is itself an act of seduction on the theme of artistic suggestion. Erskine's account of Graham's forgery of the portrait of the boy-actor, Willie Hughes, and suicidal martyrdom to prove the truth of his theory inspires in turn the story's first-person narrator. Reading and rereading Shakespeare's sonnets under the spell of Graham's theory, he feels himself awaken for the first time to the secrets of his own soul: 'A book of Sonnets . . . had suddenly explained to me the whole story of my soul's romance.' Graham's influence on the more practical-minded Erskine turns out to be less positive. In forging his suicide, Erskine shows himself to be a mere imitator of his dead friend. The narrator, by contrast, is led on to elaborate an evolutionary aesthetic based on the influence of love between men that connects the spirit of the Renaissance with the classical ideal of male friendship expounded in Plato's poetic dialogue, the *Symposium*. It is one that opposes the stern Hebraism of English life with a new Hellenism. 'The Portrait of Mr W. H.' itself aims to transmit Wilde's neo-Hegelian aesthetic of art as the incarnation of spirit in beautiful and living form.

The Picture of Dorian Gray reproduces a similar pattern of influence and self-realization. The painter Basil Hallward is mesmerized by the beauty of Dorian's face and form, and inspired to a new style and theory of art. Dorian in turn falls under the spell, first of Wotton's beautiful seductive voice and *carpe diem* philosophy, and then of the hypnotic, 'poisonous' yellow book that Wotton sends him. Like the narrator of 'The Portrait of Mr W. H.', Dorian discovers in the book 'the story of his own life, written before he had lived it' (ch. XI). The effect of his reading is narcotic. As he passes from chapter to chapter, the cadence of the sentences produces hypnotically 'a form of reverie, a malady of dreaming, that made him unconscious of the falling day and creeping shadows' (ch. X). Wotton himself alludes to the theory of animal magnetism to account for the supreme joy of projecting one's soul into another 'as though it were a subtle fluid or a strange perfume' (ch. III). As in 'The Portrait of Mr W. H.', the aims of the psychology of influence are aesthetic, anti-philistine, spiritually transforming. But in this case, it runs to seed, merely feeding the pathology and corruption of Dorian's soul.

Wilde's record of Dorian's descent and ruin is in accord with contemporary hereditary theories. Before leaving Oxford, Wilde read the philosopher and psychologist William Kingdom Clifford's posthumously published *Lectures and Essays* (1879). Clifford accepted the racialist theory of the inheritance of acquired characteristics. According to this theory, evolution was the result of adaptive responses to environment transmitted to future generations. A keystone of Clifford's philosophy of mind was that evolution by means of inherited characteristics included mental as well as physical processes. Wilde was already familiar with the idea of inherited characteristics from other sources, including non-scientific ones. His initial response to Clifford was the following entry in his Commonplace Book: 'Religion tells us that the father has eaten sour grapes and the children's teeth shall be set on edge.'[10] Yet he was struck by Clifford's view that conscience was not personal or individual, but had its earliest evolutionary origins in the preservation and survival of the tribe. This is the basis of Gilbert's assertion in 'The Critic as Artist' that 'we are never less free than when we try to act'. He puts this more bluntly with the statement: 'When man acts he is a puppet.' By revealing to us that conscience is the mere mechanism of a conservative 'tribal self' or 'tribal instinct', the scientific principle of heredity finally freed Wilde's new individual from the 'self-imposed and trammelling burden of moral responsibility'. The existence of

conscience is 'a sign of our imperfect development'. This has two
logical consequences for Wilde. In the sphere of action and practical
life, it justifies sin. Sin 'increases the experience of the race'. It
prevents stagnation and degeneracy, and furthers progress. Gilbert
characterizes the nineteenth century as a turning-point in history in
this respect on account of Charles Darwin and Ernest Renan—
Darwin as critic of the book of nature; Renan as critic of the book of
God. In *The Picture of Dorian Gray*, Wotton similarly locates progress in overcoming hereditary fears: 'Courage has gone out of our
race ... The terror of society, which is the basis of morals, the
terror of God, which is the secret of religion—these are the two
things that govern us' (ch. II). His call to youth is a call to courage, as
in age 'we degenerate into hideous puppets, haunted by the memory
of the passions of which we were too much afraid, and the exquisite
temptations that we had not the courage to yield to' (ch. II).

As a second logical step, the recognition that the man of action is
under more illusion than the dreamer becomes, for Wilde, 'the warrant for the contemplative life'. Although the subjective, imaginative
life is also the product of heredity—it is, says Gilbert, 'simply concentrated race experience'—it also provides the possibility for
instincts to become self-conscious. Released from the sphere of
action and experience, the free, disinterested spirit is able to create
and recreate itself while mysteriously woven into the nets of the
dead. Wilde's ideal of cultured disinterestedness, of the life of contemplation would seem to derive from Arnold's idea of culture, yet it
is Arnold stripped of its liberal-humanist morality and given a more
subversive hereditary and evolutionary twist.

Dorian Gray is the bearer of flawed hereditary instincts rather
than a victim of evil influences. From his dead mother (who bears the
French name Devereux) he has inherited both extraordinary beauty
and a wayward passionate nature. It is his male forebears who have
appeared weak and spoiled. For Basil Hallward, Dorian's handsome
physiognomy is proof enough against the suggestion of tainted
genealogy, while for Lord Henry Wotton, Dorian's strange origins
make him an interesting specimen for his evolutionary experiment.
In seeking to multiply his personality, Dorian multiplies his sins. He
experiences the 'strange legacies of thought and passion'; his very
flesh feels 'tainted with the monstrous maladies of the dead' (ch. XI).
Dorian fails, not because he sins, but because of his incapacity to

achieve the high tower of contemplative disinterestedness regarding himself and the world. He remains a weak slave to conscience and regressive, degenerative hereditary instincts.

Wilde was taken aback by the moral outrage that greeted *Dorian Gray*. In giving new form to the old story of a young man selling his soul in exchange for eternal youth, he claimed that his difficulty had been in keeping the obvious moral subordinate to the artistic and dramatic effect. The moral, in his reading, was that 'all excess, as well as all renunciation, brings its own punishment' (*Letters*, p. 435). Yet in objecting to criticism of the novel for vamping the moral while promoting immorality, Wilde pointed out that Dorian's weakness and limitations were not ones of consciencelessness and excess, but slavery to 'an exaggerated sense of conscience which mars his pleasures for him' (*Letters*, p. 436). Conscience is linked to sympathy, and sympathy, to Wotton's modern evolutionary way of thinking, is an obstacle to developing instincts. An antipathy to sympathy is found elsewhere in Wilde's work. In 'The Critic as Artist', for example, Gilbert objects to 'Humanitarian Sympathy' on the scientific grounds that it serves 'the survival of the failure'.

In his cruel rejection of Sibyl Vane, Dorian would appear to follow to the letter Lord Henry Wotton's rejection of sympathy. It is a significant turning-point in the story. In his revulsion from the real woman out of preference for aesthetic womanhood, Dorian kills the thing he loves. He turns from the old idea of the Ego as 'simple, permanent, reliable, and of one essence' to a conception of the individual as 'a complex multiform creature' (ch. XI). He believes that by multiplying his personalities, he is developing into a new, more complex being. There is nothing philistine, nothing conventional in Dorian's commitment to sensations. Yet in reality he remains a prisoner to 'medieval emotions' and to the logic of an essential soul or selfhood to which the body is morally answerable. He believes conscience to be the 'divinest thing in us', and can't 'bear the idea' of his soul being 'hideous'. He conceives the hideous picture as 'the visible emblem of conscience' (ch. VII). Yet it is not his crimes that bring about the changes in the painting, or cause the final disintegration of his body into a mound of corrupt atoms, but his effort to conceal and deny his experiences. He remains a prisoner of fear and remorse. He longs to shake free of Wotton's 'subtle, poisonous theories', and to lead an earnest, dutiful life. Later he thinks of praying for an end to the 'horrible sympathy' between himself and the portrait (ch. VIII). Finally, he tries to get rid of the source of his morbid self-loathing, and in his attempt to kill conscience, as Wilde explained simply, 'Dorian Gray kills himself' (*Letters*, p. 436)

A similar treatment of suppressed instincts can be found in Wilde's fairy-tales, for example 'The Birthday of the Infanta', in which an ugly, large-headed Dwarf dies on seeing himself in a mirror. Wilde drew inspiration for his story from the seventeenth-century old master Velásquez's paintings of the Spanish court depicting scenes of royal families and their children accompanied by jesters and dwarfs. Notably, Velásquez's excessively tall King Philip IV and diminutive and tragic 'Dwarf sitting on the floor' both seem awkward and ill at ease in their bodies. Wilde too may have felt awkward in his tall, large physique. 'The Birthday of the Infanta' can also be read in the context of contemporary anthropological theory. In 1888 the armchair anthropologist R. G. Haliburton theorized that modern tribes of pygmies were the 'missing link' between aboriginal dwarfs and Homo sapiens. Like the pygmies described by explorers, as Carol Silver has pointed out, Wilde's dwarf is discovered 'running in the forest'.[11] The narrative describes the lavish birthday entertainment for the 12-year-old princess, the Infanta, who is amused by the deformed Dwarf's dance, and orders that he be retained at the palace to dance for her again. Following the conventions of the genre, 'The Birthday of the Infanta' would appear to contrast the insincere and artificial world of the palace with the simple, more natural world of the Dwarf's forest home. The way is thus prepared for the Dwarf's inevitable disappointment and the ironic rebuke to heartlessness implicit in the Infanta's dismissive final command: 'For the future let those who come to play with me have no heart.' However, the palace and the forest are noticeably creations of the Dwarf's fantasies and desires; they are both aesthetically constructed worlds. In the dramatic climax of the story, the Dwarf comes to a slow and horrified recognition of his own ugly, unpleasant reflection. His death can be read as the inevitable extinction of a lower race of beings ill fitted to survive.

'The Fisherman and his Soul' is even more consistent with *The Picture of Dorian Gray*. In this tale the young Fisherman must sacrifice his soul in order to marry the mermaid with whom he has fallen in love. The theme of mermaid brides was a vogue in Victorian popular and literary culture. In its literary version, it generally expressed a conflict between developing instincts and social and religious restrictions. Like Matthew Arnold's poem 'The Forsaken Merman', Wilde's story might be read as a condemnation of repressive Christian ideals, or alternatively as a tragic expression of the impossibility of a genuine unified self. Yet there is a deviant and highly individual reversal in Wilde's presentation of the heartless corrupted tempter to the world's ways. The Fisherman's pursuit of ideal love turns out to involve a refusal of other instincts. The final union of body and soul in death would seem to suggest that the complete life can be reached only in man's acceptance of all sides of his nature.

Wilde was himself to voice the conviction that 'there is nothing wrong in what one does' in his apology for his own life in *De Profundis*. The passage is worth close attention. Wilde considers first that 'To reject one's experiences is to arrest one's own development. To deny one's own experiences is to put a lie into the lip of one's own life. It is no less than a denial of the Soul.' His appeal is to the freedom of vital self-consciousness against the unselfconscious instincts of nature and necessity. He then turns, with striking aptness, to the relation between the unclean visceral regions of the body and the fair outward physique as analogous to the process by which the seemingly baser passions provide nourishment and food for the development of the soul:

For just as the body absorbs things of all kinds, things common and unclean no less than those that the priest or a vision has cleansed, and converts them into swiftness or strength, into the play of beautiful muscles and the moulding of fair flesh, into the curves and colours of the hair, the lips, the eye: so the Soul, in its turn, has its nutritive functions also, and can transform into noble moods of thought, and passions of high import, what in itself is base, cruel, and degrading: nay more, may find in these its most august modes of assertion, and can often reveal itself most perfectly through what was intended to desecrate or destroy.

Wilde's extended biological metaphor has a distinguished history from Plato through to Shakespeare, but it gained new currency as science's optimistic response to late-nineteenth-century fears of retrogression and degeneration.

Wilde's firm conviction in *De Profundis* that 'whatever is realised is right' has to be reconciled with equally playful expressions of remorse with regard to his life of dissipation before prison, and the shame he had brought upon his family. It would perhaps be too easy simply to argue that Wilde's doctrine of self-realization admits every emotion. Yet the consistency of *De Profundis* is to be located in two aspects of Wilde's philosophy of evolutionary individualism. First, Wilde's regrets concerning his friendship with Douglas are really regrets for having allowed himself to become obsessively in love with one thing. Love is simply a form of imitation, according to Lord Henry Wotton in *The Picture of Dorian Gray*. Wilde's letter goes to some lengths to show how his imitation of the prince of Philistia resulted in a creative loss of will and spirit. 'Indeed my ruin came not from too much individualism, but from too little,' he concludes. Secondly, it was only in the ultimate humiliation of prison, and in the act of writing *De Profundis* itself that Wilde again made the intellectual and emotional journey through morbid self-loathing to an affirmative state of accepting self-consciousness. A year before his trial and imprisonment, he told an admirer that Dorian Gray was what he would like to be 'in other ages, perhaps' (*Letters*, p. 585). The qualification shows Wilde's guardedness in identifying himself too closely with his criminal hero to someone he did not know. His secret life at the time was after all technically that of a criminal. Like his hero, Wilde before prison was still a slave to secrecy and guilty conscience. In prison and after, he saw the lines of his development in 'accepting all that has happened to me'.

Some contemporary readers recognized in *De Profundis* those fictive, rhetorical aspects that the text itself ostensibly denounces. Max Beerbohm, for instance, saw in its author the defiantly proud constructor of identities they had known in the pre-prison days.[12] The controlling narrative of *De Profundis* is not one of penitential remorse but of defiant self-justification that brings Wilde's life and work into line with his earliest philosophical and scientific conclusions. Its evolutionary message has in this context a noticeable political and cultural dimension. From the opening pages of the letter, Wilde casts himself in the role of the imaginative, many-sided Irishman to Douglas's coarse English aristocrat. He mocks Douglas's vanity of his 'little title' while proudly recalling his own inheritance of a noble and honoured name in the arts and sciences, and in the historical evolution of Irish nationhood. He ridicules Douglas's adopted persona of 'Prince Fleur de Lys'—the King's son who changes clothes with a shepherd boy in Douglas's ballad, 'Jonquil and Fleur-de-Lys'. Douglas's poetic aspirations are ironically dismissed as the delusions of a nonentity, without talent or imagination, in contrast to his own achievement as an artist and 'man of world-wide reputation'. At one point he refers contemptuously to Douglas's 'low stature and inferior strength', and quotes from a letter from Douglas's own mother admitting that her son is 'the one of my children who has inherited the fatal Douglas temperament'. Wilde sees Douglas's reigning vice as that of shallowness—the result of flawed heredity, the 'terrible legacy' of 'the mad, bad line' of the Douglas clan. Within this framework of racial psychology, the freedom and self-realization of the creative imagination which only some individuals like Wilde himself achieve is simply 'concentrated race-experience', and the result of England's national degeneracy in Douglas's personal spiritual and pathological ruin.

For Wilde, as for many of his contemporaries, pathology (the study of bodily diseases) and the fledgling science of psychology were virtually synonymous. Pathology suggested to their minds the study of criminality and other states of abnormality by novelists and scientists. In petitioning the Home Secretary for early release from Reading Gaol, Wilde cited the Italian criminologist Cesare Lombroso, and the Hungarian-born sociologist Max Nordau to account for his 'criminal' sexual behaviour as temporary and curable madness (*Letters*, p. 656). Lombroso's positivist study of criminals, *Criminal Man* (*L'Uomo deliquente*, 1875), published when Wilde was at Oxford, took its cue from the medical-philosophical tradition established by the late-eighteenth-century French physician and psychiatrist Philippe Pinel.[13] Pinel's belief that mental illness was the consequence of emotional stress that was to some extent hereditary, particularly interested Wilde, as it was premised on the Aristotelian doctrine of the need to balance the emotions. In his enlightened treatment of the mentally ill, Pinel favoured friendly therapy and personal contact with the patient. Lombroso regarded criminality as the result of similar genetic, neurological malfunctions. Although he is usually remembered for his discredited cranial and skeletal classification of born criminal 'types', he also helped to introduce the idea that criminal behaviour was shaped by environmental factors, including upbringing, and could therefore be countered by preventative and rehabilitative measures. His study of genius as another 'abnormal' condition was similarly pathological in emphasis, and gave scientific credence to the popular view that genius was next to madness. Max Nordau, a Jewish nationalist, extended Lombroso's hereditary and environmental principles into a controversial and vitriolic attack on the ills of contemporary civilization. In a chapter devoted to 'Decadents and Aesthetes' in his treatise on *Degeneration*, dedicated to Lombroso, he attacked Wilde at length as an example of the neurotic artist, responsible for the spread of the decadent disease through modern Europe.'[4] Whether Wilde was sincere or opportunistic in citing Lombroso and Nordau in his petition for rehabilitation remains uncertain. What is clear is that in Wilde's pre-prison works and in his letter to Douglas following the failure of his petition, reformist solutions are discredited. Miss Prism in *The Importance of Being Earnest* is not in favour of 'this modern mania for turning bad people into good people' (Act 2). Rather, personal balance and the advancement of personality are located in Wilde's work in non-conformity and hereditary destiny.

In the Victorian version of the nature versus nurture debate, Wilde would appear to be firmly on the side of nature. Wotton's nurturing of Dorian—his application of the 'scientific experiment'—is unable to compete with his subject's atavistic nature. In his stories and plays, Wilde subverts the liberal humanist version of individualism characteristic of his age by restaging the recurrent Victorian motifs of self-realization such as lost parentage and rediscovered origins in ways that display a predestined or innatist rather than a moral-environmentalist view of individual destiny. It is revealing to contrast the hidden unconscious logic of heredity and nature in earlier Victorian literature, including, say, the Newgate novels, Dickens's *Oliver Twist*, Charlotte Brontë's *Jane Eyre*, or Disraeli's *Sybil*, with its conscious, post-Darwinian treatment in Wilde and other late-Victorian writers. Both Oliver Twist and Jane Eyre win through to a condition of personal and social fulfilment in the face of hostile circumstances, yet as in other early Victorian narratives the novels continue to connect personal achievement with a hereditary 'right of nature'. Oliver, brought up in the workhouse, discovers that he is a gentlewoman's child; Jane Eyre, a lowly governess, that she is really a wealthy heiress. Sybil, Disraeli's 'daughter of the people' conveniently turns out to be also a 'daughter of the aristocracy'. The narrative contradictions are the effect of ideological ones in which progressive middle-class values come into conflict with the aristocratic assumptions underpinning romantic motifs. Yet the imaginative thrust of early Victorian fictions usually sponsors individual determination and self-worth. In later writers such as Hardy and Gissing, by contrast, heredity and circumstance are absolute, and individual energies are exhausted in the relentless struggle for existence.

Wilde presents a different case. In adapting the changeling motif common to fairy-tale and romance, Wilde appears inadvertently to reinforce traditional values and attitudes. The proud Star-Child who learns humility discovers in the end that he is the son of a King and Queen. On a comic level, Jack Worthing in *The Importance of Being Earnest* discovers that he really is Ernest. Cecily Cardew and Miss Prism's earnest faith in the effect of nurture and self-nurture is gently ridiculed. *The Importance of Being Earnest* proves the importance of pedigree. Yet although self-realization in Wilde is the consequence of heredity, it involves a spiritual and aesthetic transformation that neither shores up nor submits to socially constructed notions of nature and identity. In the 'delicate bubble of fancy' (Wilde's description of *The Importance of Being Earnest*),[15] the fictions the characters have of themselves in the end become facts.

Wilde himself maintained that *The Importance of Being Earnest* had 'its philosophy'. That philosophy—'That we should treat all the trivial things of life very seriously, and all the serious things with sincere and studied triviality'[16]—not only flies in the face of the whole Victorian ethos of earnest duty and rectitude, but announces the central importance of that apparently most trivial of all human activities—art itself—in man's creation and re-creation of himself and his world. In treating 'Art as the supreme reality, and life as a mere mode of fiction', Wilde believed he had awoken 'the imagination of my century' and 'altered the minds of men and the colour of things', had 'made art a philosophy, and philosophy an art'.

SCIENCE AND IMAGINATION: THE MAJOR ESSAYS

Wilde's first attempt to advance a coherent system of thought, in particular to establish the relationship between scientific reason and creative imagination is to be found in his university essay, 'The Rise of Historical Criticism'. In his approach to history, he relied upon the nineteenth-century rationalist historians William Lecky and H. T. Buckle. Both ruled out divine intervention in human affairs and rejected free will and randomness in favour of the discovery of uniform laws. The aim of history was to explain the past and predict the future according to these general laws. Their combination of inductive and deductive reasoning could be seen as continuing Aristotle's healthy fusion of the speculative and the empirical. Wilde's essay takes a wide perspective on the rise of a rationalist history of human events that unites the Greek and the modern spirit. In his 'College Notebook', Wilde quotes Aristotle approvingly: 'Nature is not full of incoherent episodes like a bad tragedy'.[17]

Wilde detected another important parallel between nineteenth-century developments and the final scientific achievement of Greek thought in the third century BC. In the ancient world, the school of Euhemerus rationalized ancient Greek myths and legends as glamorized and exaggerated versions of ordinary human characters and events. The hypothesis was an ancient-world version of Victorian 'Higher Criticism'. Such tendencies also had their counterpart in Victorian philologists and anthropologists who sought the origins of myths in actual historical events. While not rejecting the possibility of some substratum of historical fact, Wilde followed his tutors Mahaffy at Trinity College and Friedrich Max Müller at Oxford in attributing the origin of myths to the analogizing tendency of man's language and imagination—to what he identified as 'the workings of the mythopoetic [or 'myth-making'] spirit'. For Wilde the creative-critical or scientific spirit of the Greeks had turned against the false mythology and dualistic thinking of our common Aryan-speaking ancestors, before the mystifying clouds of Eastern religion had again descended over mankind. In the closing section of his essay, Wilde argues that the spirit of progressive thought and sceptical enquiry had been buried with the Greeks, only to rise up again with the revival of Greek learning in the Renaissance. The fulfilment of that spirit was, for Wilde, a new renaissance in the nineteenth century.

The connection between the scientific rationalism of 'The Rise of Historical Criticism' and the iconoclastic aestheticism of Wilde's subsequent writings is a problematical one. 'The Rise' appears to play down the fictitious, the fanciful, and the artificial; the later essays to elevate them. In 'The Rise', nature constitutes a self-determining organism subject to long periods of stagnation and inaction, but evolving through scientific laws towards higher free-dom and perfection. In 'The Decay of Lying' and 'The Critic as Artist', mind and matter are at war, with nature requiring the active stimulation of creative conscious mind to wake it from the sleep of unconscious instinct. Indeed, in 'The Decay of Lying' Spencer and the 'scientific historians' are ridiculed, with Vivian arguing that: 'Nature has good intentions, of course, but, as Aristotle once said, she cannot carry them out.' In these essays, symbolic or imaginative perception is reinstated to a pre-eminent role in the evolution of nature and society.

Previously, much emphasis has been placed on Wilde's annexation and adaptation of the ideas of English cultural critics who promoted art as the basis of personal perfectibility and resistance to a material age. In Wilde's version, 'It is through Art, and through Art only, that we realise our perfection, through Art, and through Art only, that we can shield ourselves from the sordid perils of actual existence.' Matthew Arnold's ideal of art or 'Culture' as disinterested, contem-plative, untouched by the rigidities of politics or dogma, claimed to temper the puritan rigidity of English life, its Hebraism, with the 'sweetness and light' of the Greek spirit, a new Hellenism. Indeed, Arnold's appeal for a fusion of Celtic and Anglo-Saxon tempera-ment, often invoked by Wilde, was simply a variation of this. In John Ruskin's more orthodox evangelizing of Pre-Raphaelitism and the Gothic Revival, the Renaissance and its long aftermath represents a fall from the spiritual balance of the Middle Ages into rampant individualism and the life of the body. Wilde's conscience was stirred by Ruskin's anti-materialist creed, but he was equally attracted to the Renaissance ideal of Ruskin's former disciple, Walter Pater. Pater's *The Renaissance* marked a defection from Arnold's and Ruskin's spir-itualized ideal of art. In the 'Conclusion' to *The Renaissance*, Pater's appeal is to individualism, the worship of physical beauty, and the timeless pleasures of decadence in which the primitive and the sophisticated combine. In following Pater, Wilde goes further by collapsing the distinction between the sensuous and the spiritual life. His theoretical change of emphasis was rooted in the German ideal-ist philosopher Hegel and in the theory and practice of the French Symbolists.

Like other Oxford men of his generation, Wilde was attracted to Hegel. Hegel, who died in 1831, argued that true reality existed only

in ideas in the mind of man, and that history was a continual unfolding of these ideas towards a far distant state of complete understanding. To Oxford Hegelians, such as William Wallace and Benjamin
Jowett, Hegel provided a way of reconciling evolutionary thinking
with traditional religious beliefs about man's divine soul or spirit.
Wilde read and took notes from William Wallace's *'Prolegomena' to
The Logic of Hegel* (1874), which presented Hegel's philosophy as a
corrective to the idea of a purposeless universe encouraged by
nineteenth-century scientific thought.

In 'The Decay of Lying', Vivian's account of the artistic struggle
between the West's 'imitative spirit' and 'Orientalism, with its frank
rejection of imitation' is a playful annexation and adaptation of
Hegel's aesthetics. Hegel distinguished three successive periods of
art: the Symbolic or Oriental, which he associated with the sprawl-
ing, overwhelming forms of Eastern art; the Classical, in which idea
and form are in harmony; and finally the Romantic, also called Modern, in which form is no longer adequate to express the roving,
insatiable longings of the human spirit. For Hegel, Romantic or
Modern art signalled the end of art's reign as the highest activity of
the spirit. He predicted the descent of art into anarchy, individualism, and decadence. For Hegel, the future progress of the world
spirit lay with religion, and at its most advanced and self-conscious,
with philosophy and criticism. In 'The Decay of Lying', and
'The Artist as Critic', Wilde departs from Hegel in rejecting the idea
that art has ceased to satisfy the supreme needs of the spirit, and in
claiming the transformational force of modern art in the realization
of the human spirit. In doing so he followed Baudelaire and the
Symbolists in claiming that criticism itself was poetry and poetry
criticism. In his critical essay 'The Salon of 1846', Baudelaire wrote:
'Since a beautiful picture is nature reflected by the artist—the best
criticism will be a reflection of that picture by an intelligent and
sensitive mind. Thus the best criticism may well be a sonnet or an
elegy.' In 'The Critic as Artist', Gilbert advocates that art should
direct itself not to life but to the creation of further works of art. In
so far as the reader or 'spectator' might stop short of creation, his
goal nevertheless should be contemplation. The 'primary aim' for
both artist and critic—in Wilde, the two are indistinguishable—'is to
see the object as in itself it really is not'. Reflecting on Pater's criticism of Leonardo's portrait of Monna Lisa, Gilbert concludes that

'criticism of the highest kind ... treats the work of art simply as a starting-point for a new creation.'

For Wilde, the function of art remained the revelation of the spirit in sensuous form. Art spoke for both sense and soul. In the relativistic modern world of extended sensations and tightening controls, Wilde's critic as artist provides the antithetical ideas necessary for progress. His aims are transformational, not imitative. In his adoption of the dialogue form over direct expositional style in 'The Decay of Lying' and 'The Critic as Artist', Wilde enacts a witty and dialectical subversion of unity and fixed truth. 'What is Nature?' Vivian asks in 'The Decay of Lying'. 'Nature is no great mother who has borne us. She is our creation. It is our brain that she quickens to life. Things are because we see them, and what we see, and how we see it, depends on the Arts that have influenced us.'

Yet consistent both to 'The Rise of Historical Criticism' and the seemingly divergent essays that came after is the Spencerian formula that healthy development depends upon the un-arrested evolution from simple to more complex forms. The main difference is that, after 'The Rise', Wilde moved away from the rational devaluation of myth and imagination to a view that the complexity of the modern mind is to be located precisely in the coexistence of primitive fancy and modern sophistication. He found the modern spirit in the art of all ages. In his essay-dialogues, art and the myth-making faculty provide a subversive antidote to conscience and custom. Nature and imitation threaten to arrest development even in the highly complex organism that contemporary society has become. Rather than serving as a model for degeneration or the retrogressive, as Max Nordau and others were to argue, Wilde's decadent allegiances constituted a resistance to the threat of stagnation posed by the habitual, the conventional, and the given. 'Poets are the original historians as well as the original men of science,' Wilde noted in his Commonplace Book. The reaction against positivist reassurances in Wilde owed much to Pater's subjective, hedonistic aestheticism, as does his idea of the modern mind as a compound of all ages. Yet it is Pater resting upon a creative adaptation of Hegel and a logical extension of the scientific principles of Herbert Spencer.

Ethics and Religion

THE HIGHER ETHICS

Like other leading Victorian writers and intellectuals, Wilde was concerned with the place for morality and the future of the church in an age of advancing science and materialism. His early *Poems* of 1881 revisit the solemn questions addressed by the major Victorian poets. They explore themes of bereavement and wavering faith (Tennyson), the choice of Protestant England or Catholic Rome (Arnold), the sensual versus the spiritual (Browning and the Pre-Raphaelites), and the divide between paganism and Christianity (Swinburne). The response of contemporary critics to Wilde's treatment of these already familiar themes was generally hostile. The attack on the volume in the Oxford Union was typical: 'It is not that these Poems are thin—and they *are* thin: it is not that they are immoral—and they *are* immoral . . . it is that they are for the most part not by their putative father at all, but by a number of better-known and more deservedly reputed authors' (Ellmann, p. 140). In defending Wilde against the charge of literary larceny, some later apologists have argued that Wilde's borrowings are in fact deliberate, sophisticated acts of ironic transformation of his original sources. This may be so; but underlying the accusation of plagiarism, there was among Wilde's contemporaries a more general dissatisfaction with the lack of logical and emotional consistency in the verses. The *Athenaeum* wrote: 'Worship of beauty, whatever shape it may take, is not likely to be a thing of which to be ashamed, and those by whom it is derided may well be chargeable with offences far more mischievous than a little false aestheticism. We fail to see, however, that the apostle of the new worship has any distinct message.'[18] The frustrated reviewer in *The Spectator* wondered why he had perpetuated violently conflicting states of opinion in the same volume and concluded that 'Probably he has not changed his mind, but only his mood, and thinks one mood as good as the other.'[19]

Overriding the arguments of opponents and apologists, the reality would seem to be that Wilde's early verse displayed an openly Paterian aesthetic, in responding to the varying moods and emotions of existing verse. 'A counted number of pulses only is given to us of a variegated, dramatic life,' Pater had written in the conclusion to *The Renaissance*.[20] Beauty and truth, in Wilde's early poems, exist in an expanded variety of contradictory, sometimes unorthodox forms.

Like other Victorian 'cultural apostates', as one historian has termed them,[21] Wilde rebelled from Anglican intellectual culture; yet, significantly, in finally departing from the familiar 'crisis of faith' narrative, Wilde also rebelled from the variant versions of the secularized religion of humanity characteristic of his day. Wilde was generally impatient with the scenario of religious latitude and moral reformism found in popular 'loss of faith' narratives such as William Hale White's *The Autobiography of Mark Rutherford* (1881) and Mrs Humphry Ward's theological romance *Robert Elsmere* (1888). Wilde first voiced his objections to the 'semi-theological novel' in 'The Decay of Lying' in 1889, at a time when *Robert Elsmere* was enjoying best-seller status. Mrs Ward was Mary Augusta Arnold by birth, granddaughter of Dr Thomas Arnold of Rugby, and Matthew Arnold's niece. Her 'purpose' in *Robert Elsmere*—to show that Christianity could be revitalized by discarding its miraculous element and emphasizing its social mission—was deeply influenced by Matthew Arnold's arguments in *Literature and Dogma* (1873). Wilde's criticism of the novel in 'The Decay of Lying' thus marked a deeper defection from the more pragmatic aspects of Arnold's attempt to recast the religious spirit. 'As a statement of the problems that confront the earnest Christian [*Robert Elsmere*] is ridiculous and antiquated,' Cyril quips:

It is simply Arnold's *Literature and Dogma* with the literature left out. It is as much behind the age as Paley's *Evidences*, or Colenso's method of Biblical exegesis. Nor could anything be less impressive than the unfortunate hero gravely heralding a dawn that rose long ago, and so completely missing its true significance that he proposes to carry on the business of the old firm under the new name.

Cyril's references to Paley and Colenso are a reminder of bygone controversies that shook the Victorian Church. Darwin's theory of natural selection had destroyed the central pillar of William Paley's argument in *Natural Theology* (1802) that the purposeful design of the universe offered proof of God's existence and a cure for atheism. Bishop Colenso's literal demolition of the plausibility of certain passages of the Bible in his *The Pentateuch, and Book of Joshua Critically Examined* (1862) had been the starting-point of Matthew Arnold's attempt to recast the religious spirit as the gospel of 'Culture', beginning with his first series of *Essays in Criticism* (1865). The 'true significance' of Arnold's cultural crusade lay for Wilde in the claims for the 'poetry' and grandeur of religion. He was impatient with the reduction of Arnold's *Literature and Dogma* to a restatement of the religious latitude and moral reformist tendencies of Dr Arnold in the 1830s. This, as Cyril wryly notes, simple carries on 'the business of the old firm' (Dr Arnold's moral earnestness) under a new name.

Wilde's response to religious adjustments of this sort to the growth of historical and scientific knowledge was generally one of derision. In a letter written in the year of 'The Decay of Lying' he dismissed the theologically agnostic John Stuart Mill's defence of the religion of humanity on the grounds of its moral utility as showing 'astounding silliness . . . and sentimentality'. For Wilde, who had amused his fellow schoolboys at Portora by contorting himself into the weird shapes of the saints on the stained-glass windows, the efforts of the new ethical societies to contort their rational beliefs into age-old religious forms and rituals seemed equally weird and preposterous.

In 'The Critic as Artist', the following year, Gilbert is also dismissive of the Browning Society, founded in 1881 to promote Browning as a Christian optimist. Gilbert prefers instead to admire the dramatic incompleteness with which Browning's poetry puts forth contemporary religious problems. The aims of both religious rationalists and sentimental idealists are rejected in Wilde's writings as narrowly this-worldly reforming ones whose purpose is simply to provide affectionate collective goals and altruistic ideals.

Wilde's impatience with the spiritual temper of the times is further demonstrated in 'The Decay of Lying' in Vivian's scathing dismissal of the activities of Frederic Myers's Society for Psychical Research as 'commonplace, sordid and tedious'. The Society was founded by Myers in 1882 to search for empirical proof of the 'survival of bodily death' through séances and telepathic experiments. As for the Church, Vivian contrasts the mythical force of the primitive Church and the prosaic English Church of his day. The passage merits close attention:

As for the Church, I cannot conceive anything better for the culture of a country than the presence in it of a body of men whose duty it is to believe in the supernatural, to perform daily miracles, and to keep alive that mythopoeic faculty which is so essential for the imagination. But in the English Church a man succeeds, not through his capacity for belief, but through his capacity for disbelief. . . . it is sufficient for some shallow uneducated passman out of either University to get up in his pulpit and express his doubts about Noah's ark, or Balaam's ass, or Jonah and the whale, for half of London to flock to hear him, and to sit open-mouthed in rapt admiration at his superb intellect. The growth of common sense in the English Church is a thing very much to be regretted. It is really a degrading concession to a low form of realism. It is silly, too. It springs from an entire ignorance of psychology. Man can believe the impossible, but man can never believe the improbable.

The passage owes a great deal to Matthew Arnold—the claims for the imaginative grandeur of religion independent of dogma; the enduring basis of religion in psychological needs; and its enriching contribution to 'the culture of a country'. Yet Wilde parts company from Arnold's narrowly Victorian identification of the religious instinct with the instinct for morality and right conduct. In Arnold's writings, ethical-aesthetic instincts come close to being synonymous with natural instincts. In Wilde's claims for art's imaginative reach over life's necessity, and for a fully aestheticized ethics, the two are opposed. Arnold's spirit of 'Culture' served universal moral values and preconceptions. Wilde's sought to transform them. Man 'can believe the impossible', Vivian maintains as he prepares to recite his protest essay against the decay of the artistic spirit, 'the decay of lying'. In Wilde's higher ethics, belief in the impossible fills life 'with new forms, and gives it progress', transforming and enlarging what is thought moral and permissible into an ethics allowing greater scope for beauty and non-conformity.

Using the language of science in *Literature and Dogma*, Arnold called for experiment in facing up to the findings of nineteenth-century history and science.[22] In *Dorian Gray*, Lord Henry Wotton's new gospel of self-realization surpasses in controversy and 'experiment' the 'semi-theological' responses of Mrs Ward and the emerging ethical societies of the 1880s and 1890s to Arnold's injunction. The humanists and secular moralists remained attached to an ethics based on a medieval Christian iconography of suffering, self-denial, sympathy, and duty to others. Wotton, by contrast, preaches a Hellenistic aesthetic based on the beauty and goodness of pleasure and self-gratification: 'People . . . have forgotten the highest of all duties, the duty one owes to one's self' (ch. II). Wotton stands the medieval Christian doctrine of sin and punishment on its head in support of his new aesthetic creed of fearless self-development. According to Wotton, self-denial, not self-gratification, breeds guilt and remorse; and sin, not asceticism, becomes 'a mode of purification'. Wotton's famous formulation follows closely the Romantic poet William Blake's perception of the sickness of repressed or forbidden desire: 'The only way to get rid of a temptation is to yield to it. Resist it, and your soul grows sick with longing for the things it has forbidden to itself, with desire for what its monstrous laws have made monstrous and unlawful' (ch. II).

Dorian Gray goes further than Wilde's early poems in its appeal for the maximizing of sense impressions as a fitting response to the transience of all things. The critics condemned its hedonistic doc- trine as antithetical to ethics. In response to the charge that his characters were immoral, Wilde pointed to their artistic and psycho- logical interest, singling out Lord Henry Wotton as 'an excellent corrective of the tedious ideal shadowed forth in the semi-theological novels of our age' (*Letters*, p. 429). The goals Wotton sets Dorian— to regard pleasure as the chief good and proper end of action, and to become a spectator of his own life—fly in the face of preconceived standards of morality. To critics, then as now, the new aestheticism appeared to involve an evasion of moral responsibility. Dorian him- self seems to concede as much, when he tells Basil Hallward that, 'To become a spectator of one's own life, as Harry says, is to escape the suffering of life' (ch. IX). In the controversy that followed its publi- cation, the critics were not deflected by Wilde's explanation of the story's moral, that 'all excess, as well as all renunciation, brings its own punishment' (*Letters*, p. 430), in that Dorian's failure and Wot- ton's disappointment merely concede that their ideal has failed, not that the ideal itself is flawed.

In formulating a final reply to his critics, Wilde held to the convic- tion derived from Plato's *Laws* that 'the whole problem of life turns on pleasure' (Ellmann, p. 289). For Wilde, the problem of life was how to bear its pleasures as well as its pains; and his answer was to live life like a work of art. To a female correspondent, he wrote:

The Saint and the artistic Hedonist certainly meet—touch in many points. Right and wrong are not qualities of actions, they are mental attitudes relative to the incompleteness of the ordinary social organism. When one contemplates, all things are good.

For myself, I look forward to the time when aesthetics will take the place of ethics, when the sense of beauty will be the dominant law of life: it will never be so, and so I look forward to it. (*Letters*, p. 437)

There is a decisive shift of emphasis in Wilde's thought after *Dorian Gray* from action to mental attitudes, from indulgent to 'perfected' or 'artistic' hedonism'. In 'The Soul of Man under Socialism', which appeared in February 1891, six months ahead of the revised book version of *Dorian Gray*—the chronology is significant— Wilde revises Wotton's hedonistic rejection of pain and self-martyrdom by putting greater emphasis on 'contemplation'. Crucially, 'contemplation' for Wilde meant a refusal of 'vulgar standards of goodness' and virtue, and an acceptance of what was considered ugly or dirty, evil or wrong. The relative spirit extends in effect the domain of the beautiful and the good. Wilde's enlarged scope for beauty included the repressed in all its forms—sexual, social, racial—those things that provoke revulsion and a sense of difference. This acceptance of the ugly and the unpleasant can be found in Wilde's fairy-tales, 'The Star-Child' in particular, and is of course a symbolic and psychological element in the fairy-tale form generally.

Yet, as the letter quoted above makes clear, Wilde also recognized the inevitable repressions of reality and civilization that prevented 'the sense of beauty' becoming 'the dominant law of life'. In his reformulation of the new aestheticism in 'The Critic as Artist' during the summer that followed the publication of *Dorian Gray* in its original magazine version, Wilde has Gilbert argue an absolute distinction between 'the sphere of Art and the sphere of Ethics', while maintaining that art transforms and transcends ethics. By keeping ethics at arm's length, art paradoxically furthers our ethical development and discovery. True art reaches beyond received ideas of morality or virtue. That is why 'Society often forgives the criminal; it never forgives the dreamer'. By Gilbert's admission about all art and creative criticism there is something radically 'immoral' as well as 'dangerous', not because it offers a criticism of life, but because it disregards conventional ethical judgments.

Wilde's higher ethics are strikingly visible in his society dramas, all of which followed the writing of 'The Critic as Artist' and 'The

Soul of Man under Socialism'. While some condemned his plays as cynical and perverted, audiences and critics were generally won over by his extraordinary warmth and good humour, a quality that still attracts audiences today. 'The dialogue is exquisitely funny, is satirical without being aggravating to the audience. It is biting, and at the same time genial and good-humoured,' wrote the *Westminster Gazette* of *Lady Windermere's Fan*.[23] Wilde himself on the publication of *The Importance of Being Earnest* in book form recalled how the public had welcomed him 'in airy mood and spirit, mocking at morals and defiance of social rules' (*Letters*, p. 1124).

Today, the plays are generally seen as corrective comedies aimed at ridiculing society's complacency, hypocrisy, and double standards. Yet Wilde's satire is directed in the end against the spirit of correction and reform itself. His dismissal of the gospel of social and moral improvement in his day is not diminished by being voiced by the haughty, the aristocratic, and the worldly. Lord Goring's seemingly flippant regret that Lady Chiltern's society guest list has 'been crowded out by the County Council, or the Lambeth Conference, or something equally boring' (Act 2) is a sly denunciation of practical social and religious zeal in an age of puritanical anxiety about intemperance, purity, and the spread of socialism—leading topics at the 3rd Lambeth Conference of Anglican bishops in 1888 which provides the background to the joke. In serving the world and its ways, such matters of urgent and practical interest, were indeed, as Lady Markby would have it, 'most irreligious', particularly in the context of Goring's hedonistic but generously tolerant version of 'practical life'.

Wilde's satire against the alliance of religious and social aims is at its most exuberant in *The Importance of Being Earnest*. The play's prosaic representative of the pulpit is the benign, this-worldly country rector, Canon Chasuble, happy to adapt his sermon 'on the meaning of the manna in the wilderness . . . as a charity sermon on behalf of the Society for the Prevention of Discontent among the Upper Orders' (Act 2). The joke turns on the Established Church's anxious crusade to counteract too much idealism of the experimental sort, including contemporary moral objections to making personal profit from others. The practical response of the Lambeth Conference in 1888 was to admit the ideal set before men 'by the Divine Master' while upholding existing society on the grounds that there was 'no surer cause of failure in practical affairs than to act on an ideal which has not yet been realised'.[24] Yet in *The Importance of Being Earnest*, this is precisely what all the younger characters do. Gwendolen's ideal 'Ernest'; Cecily's imaginary engagement; Jack Worthing's assumed identity: their triumph in the end is the triumph of the impossible. It is against this backdrop that the final pairing of the pontificating clergyman and the seemingly prim and dutiful Miss Prism marks the defeat of moral earnestness by earnest imagination.

Wilde's intended effect is contemplative, which means the artistic rejection of those serio-comic elements associated with guilt. In *Lady Windermere's Fan*, Mrs Erlynne renounces her role as erring, penitential mother. 'I thought I had no heart. I find I have, and a heart doesn't suit me,' she tells Lord Windermere (Act 4). *A Woman of No Importance* turns in the end on a sin of no importance, asking, in Lord Illingworth's words, 'What sort of love is that which needs to have hate as its brother?' (Act 4). In *An Ideal Husband*, Lord Goring similarly calls for an end to the cycle of guilt and retribution in an already imperfect world. *The Importance of Being Earnest* is Wilde's supreme comic vision of a world irresponsibly free of guilt and shame. Here, secrecy and deception are not covers for past sins or misdemeanours, but endearingly childlike strategies to escape social obligations and to get one's own way. One of the play's central images, as one commentator has pointed out,[25] is baptism—the symbolic reminder of man's guilt and spiritual rebirth, here comically overturned by characters who, reclaiming the past, are allowed effectively to baptize and rename themselves.

THE INDIVIDUALIST AND THE COMMUNITY

Although criticized for promoting the pursuit of isolated aesthetic pleasure, Wilde's instincts and attitudes were essentially social and communal in spirit. Indeed, the same might be claimed for the new aestheticism generally. Arnold envisaged the creation of a freemasonry of individual 'preachers' of culture whose literary evangelism would unify people through a common language and culture.[26] Pater's inward-looking and relativistic cultivation of temperament is balanced, in *Marius the Epicurean*, by the hero's attraction to Christianity, not for its beliefs, but for its spirit of poetry and community in a worn-out pagan world. In 'Winckelmann', the concluding essay of *The Renaissance*, Pater appeals to the Greek ideal of male beauty worship and fraternity. Personal cultivation and mystical community are similarly brought together in Wilde's writings. The declaration of art's indifference to society in 'The Critic as Artist'—'The artistic critic, like the mystic, is antinomian always'—assumes as its goal the creation of a new spiritual community. In Wilde's most artistic and powerful stories, the theme of transgression is associated with the need for transmission. In 'The Portrait of Mr W. H.', the theory that Shakespeare's genius was inspired by his love of a boy-actor is framed within a narrative of seduction and conversion whose goal is the creation of a community of sensitive, knowing souls. *The Picture of Dorian Gray* is dominated by male associations and secret spheres of influence and initiation.

In 'The Critic as Artist', Wilde extends the collective implications of beauty worship beyond the homoerotic. In his acknowledged invocation of a controversial passage from 'Winckelmann', which claims that 'supreme beauty is rather male than female' since 'the beauty of art demands a higher sensibility than the beauty of nature, because the beauty of art, like the tears shed at a play, gives no pain, is without life',[27] Gilbert suppresses all allusion to the Greek ideal of male beauty and fraternity which forms the basis of Winckelmann's art criticism. Gilbert's version is simply: 'The tears that we shed at a play are a type of the exquisite sterile emotions that it is the function of Art to awaken. We weep, but we are not wounded. We grieve, but our grief is not bitter . . . It is through Art, and through Art only, that we can realize our perfection.' Gilbert goes on to express a more general ideal 'that with the development of the creative spirit we shall be able to realize, not merely our own lives, but the collective life of the race'. ('Race' in this instance refers to the human species.) It is not for his sharp and witty style alone that Wilde enjoys an international reputation. 'Criticism will annihilate race-prejudices,' Gilbert predicts. For all his ironic anti-philistine rhetoric, Wilde looked beyond narrower national and moral attitudes that the Arnoldian ideal of criticism was sometimes made to serve. By the same token, his collective aestheticism reached beyond Pater's lonely isolated consciousness and compensatory communal affections. In 'The Critic as Artist' Gilbert insists on 'the unity of the human mind in the variety of its forms'. To miss this, he maintains, 'is to miss the meaning of one of the most important eras in the progress of the world.'

Progress in this context would seem to involve spiritual rather than social change; but Wilde develops further Arnold's sense that spiritual growth and the transformation of actual social relations are complementary. 'Perfection', according to Arnold in *Culture and Anarchy*, is not possible while the individual remains isolated. In 'The Soul of Man under Socialism', Wilde invokes the disturbing and disintegrating force of individualism against the domination of nineteenth-century humanitarianism and socialism. 'The true personality of man . . . will not always be meddling with others, or asking them to be like itself. It will love them because they will be different.' Wilde's attempt in the end was to meet the twin demands of individuality and community with an ethical ideal of a community made up of supreme individuals like himself.

THE CHRIST FIGURE

In 'The Soul of Man under Socialism', Christ emerges as the supreme individual in his absolute resistance to the world and its ways. Wilde's antinomian Christ has nothing to do with laws or institutions either of Church or State. His message, according to Wilde, is neither revolt nor reform, but a gospel of pain 'as a model of self-realization'. At its close, 'The Soul of Man' looks beyond the suffering face of the medieval Christ, and his abandonment of society, to the coming of a new collective individualism in which man will be 'in harmony with himself and his environment'. However, in *De Profundis*, Wilde's perspective changes, and he embraces suffering as the ultimate realization of his artistic self that until prison had followed the 'primrose path of pleasure'. Pain as a mode of self-realization is reinstated, not on the grounds of remorse for excessive hedonism, but as the basis of aesthetic extension and artistic self-development.

The spirit here would seem to owe much to Pater. 'Humility in the artist is his frank acceptance of all experiences,' Wilde writes with evident indebtedness to the author of *The Renaissance*. Yet in his recognition of the intimate connection between the 'true life' of the suffering Christ and the life of the true artist, Wilde believed he saw deeper into the truth of things than Pater when he writes:

In *Marius the Epicurean* Pater seeks to reconcile the artistic life with the life of religion in the deep, sweet and austere sense of the word. But

Marius is little more than a spectator: an ideal spectator indeed . . . yet a spectator merely, and perhaps a little too much occupied with the comeliness of the vessels of the Sanctuary to notice that it is the Sanctuary of Sorrow that he is gazing at.

In contrast to Marius, the Young King in Wilde's story of that title sees in the beauties of the sanctuary a terrible vision of the sufferings of the poor and oppressed. In Wilde's fairy-tales, suffering as a means of self-realization is the dark other side of aesthetic pleasure and freedom. Both the Happy Prince and the Young King seek to atone for the human misery on which the wealth and privilege of the few are seen to depend, while in 'The Soul of Man under Socialism', pain as a means of perfection was, in Wilde's words, 'written down simply and in letters too easy to read'.

Looking back over his writings, Wilde was astonished to find how much they unconsciously foreshadowed and prefigured his mature artistic understanding of the darker side of life's garden. In *De Profundis*, Christ is not only 'the most supreme of Individualists'. He is also 'the true precursor of the romantic movement' whose individualism and 'imaginative sympathy' place him as a type of the Artist. Christ's utopianism is collective in the broadest sense. Christ, Wilde declares in *De Profundis*,

was the first to conceive the divided races as a unity. Before his time there had been gods and men. He alone saw that on the hills of life there were but God and Man, and, feeling through the mysticism of sympathy that in himself each had been made incarnate, he calls himself the Son of the One or the son of the other, according to his mood.

In Wilde's rereading of the New Testament, Christ overcomes limited human perception by means of a supreme artistic personality that refuses the divisions and differences—self and the other, beauty and ugliness, the human and the divine—that narrow and imprison the minds of men. To his eulogy of the Christ figure, Wilde yokes Baudelaire's cry to God in his poem, 'Un voyage à Cythère': 'O Lord, give me the strength and courage to look upon my soul and my body without loathing' ('Ah! Seigneur, donnez-moi la force et le courage | De contempler mon cœur et mon corps sans dégoût!').

Wilde's identification of Christ's war against the philistines as an exact counterpart to his own struggles against the philistines of his age—'their ridiculous estimate of themselves and their importance'—has sometimes been viewed with embarrassment or as simply another example of his whimsical invention and exaggerated, self-aggrandizing imagination. It is in effect not to be taken seriously. Others have been intrigued. 'Oscar Wilde was not a philosopher,' wrote the satirist of the Decadents, George Slythe Street, in a partly repentant appreciation of *De Profundis* when it first appeared in 1905.

In his fashion he was a prophet, and prophets to be of any use in the world must be extreme. The interesting thing is that this one had preached one extreme, and was on his way to preach the opposite. Had his intellect and energy endured he might have ended by seeing some way for the hedonist and the mystic to walk together; then, indeed, he would have been a philosopher at last.[28]

Like many of Wilde's critics, Street recognizes the philosophical significance of Wilde's work while apparently failing to see that its logic lies ultimately in his refusal of a single, fixed, linear, centralizing frame of mind. In his resistance to the separation of opposite or contradictory terms, Wilde would again appear to have much in common with the radical Romantic poet, William Blake, for whom, significantly, Christ was also a spiritual antinomian hero. According to Blake's famous axiom, 'Without Contraries is no progression'.[29] Wilde's provocative declaration at the close of 'The Truth of Masks' is that 'in art there is no such thing as a universal truth. A Truth in art is that whose contradictory is also true.' In Wilde's case, the opposition to settled, antithetical thinking, his double vision, as it were, arguably also has an Irish side to it. The choice of a multiple, fluid, heterogeneous identity might be interpreted in terms of a resistance to what one critic has called the 'colonial calibanisation' of the Irish, an attitude perhaps best epitomized in Benjamin Disraeli's categorization of the Irish as 'a wild, reckless, indolent, uncertain and superstitious race'.[30] Wilde's religious philosophy, in this context, can be seen to be rooted in a utopian resistance to colonial and racial stereotypes and, beyond that, to the limited consciousness that what appears other to man is in reality alien or hostile to himself.

CHAPTER 6

RECONTEXTUALIZING WILDE

DURING his last years of exile in France, lacking concentration for anything but writing letters to his closest friends, Wilde gave thought to his future place in history. He attached a kind of honour to being a pariah. 'The greatest men fail, or seem to have failed,' he wrote (Ellmann, p. 553). He knew that history would make its own judgement. Of one thing he was confident—that his works would survive. 'Fifty years or a hundred years hence . . . my comedies and my stories and *The Ballad of Reading Gaol* will be read by millions,' he told Frank Harris.[1]

At the time of Wilde's arrest and trial his name was removed from the theatre placards for *An Ideal Husband* and *The Importance of Being Earnest*, and both plays closed soon after. Within a year of his death, *The Importance of Being Earnest* and *Lady Windermere's Fan* were successfully revived by George Alexander. There were to be other revivals of Wilde's plays during the Edwardian period, notably Herbert Beerbohm Tree's reprise of his role as Lord Illingworth in *A Woman of No Importance* in 1907. That year came to mark an important turning-point in twentieth-century literature. J. M. Synge's *The Playboy of the Western World* injected a shock of reality into the theatre with its use of peasant characters and setting and strong language. In fiction, Joseph Conrad's *The Secret Agent* struck a new note of ironic modernity. In this atmosphere, Wilde's glittering world of epigram and repartee seemed to playgoers to belong to a different age. To one nostalgic reviewer of *Lady Windermere's Fan* in 1911, Wilde's paradoxes called up 'pleasant recollections of the days when they were young and fresh and seemed good to hear'.[2]

Nostalgia for the 1890s ensured a continuing interest in Wilde's work. The decade passed into folklore as a period of colour and style and youthful irreverence towards the earnest, stiff-necked Victorians who had gone before. This image of the 1890s was partly a literary and artistic creation. Max Beerbohm's caricatures of 'the Beardsley Period', Holbrook Jackson's pre-First World War account of *The*

Eighteen Nineties (1913), and Richard Le Gallienne's glamorization of *The Romantic Nineties* (1926) helped create and foster the myth. Even W. B. Yeats's more sombre reassessment of the period served to reinforce rather than dispel the bohemian legend of the 1890s. 'Then in 1900 everyone got down off his stilts; henceforth nobody drank absinthe with his black coffee; nobody went mad; nobody committed suicide; nobody joined the Catholic church,' he wrote.[3] Some who lived through the period disputed the myth. Virginia Woolf, though only 13 at the time of the Wilde trials, was generally amused by overstated accounts of the 'amazing decade'. William Watson, a popular poet during the 1890s and a contributor to the *Yellow Book*, dismissed the characterization of the 'naughty' or 'mauve' or 'yellow' Nineties for confusing the venal, publicity-seeking techniques of John Lane and the *Yellow Book* with the reality.[4]

Unquestionably the rise of mass-circulation newspapers and the popular press created the cult of celebrity and a taste for scandal and sensation. The 1890s was a demonstratively self-conscious, self-dramatizing age in which Wilde and Whistler were flamboyant participants. Yet the image of Wilde and other leading artists and writers of the period as deliberately idiosyncratic figures whose wish was 'to astonish and arrive' ensured the almost automatic dismissal of much of their work as lacking in artistic seriousness. For attempting to appeal to a mass readership, they were labelled populist at a time when 'highbrow' and 'major', 'popular' and 'minor' were becoming virtually synonymous. Such attitudes have gradually but definitely receded with time. The claims for both reader and writer as ironic resistant forces within traditional literary forms have served as the basis for a significant reassessment of the value and importance of Wilde and other writers of the period that used to be defined condescendingly as 'the age of transition'. Popular forms have been similarly reinstated to become the focus of serious literary attention. Romance narratives and melodramas of the kind Wilde adapted are no longer automatically considered to be poor cousins to the higher evolutionary type of psychological realism.

Attitudes to Wilde himself have also changed. In his own day Wilde made himself available for reproduction. His self-promotional images varied from the lily-bearing aesthete guyed in the press, and the character of the witty decadent dandy of his stories and plays, to the suffering Christ-like artist of *De Profundis*. After his trial, he stood in the public mind, as he himself said, somewhere 'between Gilles de Retz and the Marquis de Sade'. In the century following his death, his life has been the subject of numerous films, plays, television documentaries, and even ballets and musicals. In the process the effeminate aesthete and sexual degenerate of the Victorians have given way to a variety of more sympathetic, more complex, and sometimes more earnest Oscar Wildes.

The revaluation of Wilde as a major thinker is reflected in the number of recent full-length studies devoted solely to his critical writings, the most notable being Lawrence Danson's *Wilde's Intentions: The Artist in his Criticism*, and Julia Prewitt Brown's *Cosmopolitan Criticism: Oscar Wilde's Philosophy of Art*, both published in 1997.[5] The latter gives a significant place to *De Profundis* as a philosophical piece rather than an autobiographical confession or a love-letter. Evidence of greater interest in the earnest Wilde is provided by the warm reception given to Corin Redgrave's understated reading of Merlin Holland's edited version of *De Profundis*, also in 1997, at the Chelsea Centre and Moving Theatre, London, and by the website for the 1997 film *Wilde* starring Stephen Fry, which contained audio clips of Fry's reading extracts from 'The Selfish Giant', *De Profundis*, and *The Ballad of Reading Gaol*.

A historical survey of the criticism and performance of Wilde's work reflects this growing appreciation of Wilde as a serious artist. Criticism in this respect falls into three main stages. Before the 1960s Wilde's reputation rested largely on *The Importance of Being Earnest* and *The Picture of Dorian Gray*, with his work as a whole generally considered as a colourful product of the period of the gay, irreverent, superficial 1890s. Rupert Hart-Davis's edition of Wilde's *Collected Letters* in 1962, which presented for the first time the unabridged text of *De Profundis*, did much to change attitudes to Wilde's life and work.[6] Gradually, Wilde has begun to be seen as a serious literary figure, rather than as a dilettante and witty aesthete. This radical reassessment coincided with the liberalizing atmosphere of British culture from the 1960s onwards which transformed Wilde into a cultural icon for those championing alternative values and the claims for the importance of popular culture. Finally, the gay rights movement and the rise of Irish literary studies in the late 1980s and 1990s resulted in new politicized readings and interpretations of Wilde and a greater appreciation of the contemporary relevance of his writings, so that today Wilde's appeal to a wide variety of readers and theatre-goers is greater than at any time since his death.

Reproducing Wilde

THE PICTURE OF DORIAN GRAY AND THE SOCIETY PLAYS

Fascination with Wilde and the 1890s always had its forbidden side. *The Picture of Dorian Gray*, Wilde's most famous story, epitomized for generations of readers and cinema audiences the atmosphere of evil and decadence, and sin. Given its participation in acts of looking and mirroring, the story understandably attracted the early film industry. The Russian director Vsevolod Meyerhold's 1915 version is said to have excelled in atmosphere the spine-chilling silent film, *The Cabinet of Dr Caligari*, made four years later. Bela Lugosi played the part of Lord Henry Wotton in a Hungarian silent film version of Wilde's story. He was the first in a long line of famous actors to play Wilde's suave, frock-coated Satan, among them George Sanders, George C. Scott, and Herbert Lom. In all of these versions, as in Wilde's original story, the perception of evil lay in the unnatural desire to preserve youth and beauty even at the cost of one's own soul. To the traditional mind, in the Victorian age such a bargain with the devil was a bizarre and wicked attempt to deny the natural order. The added ambiguity of Wilde's story was in making the fear of ageing a specifically male phobia. Some productions, including Meyerhold's, cast a woman in the part of Dorian Gray. In introducing his 1975 stage adaptation, John Osborne expressed his belief that it was preferable for an actress to play the part of Dorian Gray to diffuse the camp of the acting style and 'enable it to be played as straightforwardly, if ironically, as possible'.[7] This did not inhibit John Gielgud from playing Lord Henry as a rouged and ageing satyr to Peter Firth's golden youth in a television production of Osborne's play the following year.

Before the abolition of stage censorship, *The Picture of Dorian Gray* was an obvious inspiration for dramatists looking for a clandestine stage and screen image for the homosexual. The dandy as disguised homosexual makes an appearance in Mordaunt Shairp's *The Green Bay Tree* (1933). In a repeat of the unhealthy bond between Dorian and Lord Henry Wotton, Mordaunt's handsome, epicene Julian succumbs to the 'snake like' charm of his diabolical mentor Mr Dulcimer. This is the Wildean story stripped down to a simple morality tale in which Dulcimer's victory is the consequence of a dangerous, life–destroying indulgence in 'luxury' and 'pleasure'.[8]

A more candid and sympathetic treatment of homosexuality in the first half of the twentieth century was Leslie and Sewell Stokes's biographical portrait of Wilde himself in *Oscar Wilde*, which opened as a club performance at the Gate Theatre, London in 1936. The actor Robert Morley achieved fame playing Wilde with a large green scarab on his finger. The stage direction on Wilde's first entrance indicates the Stokeses' view of him: 'Most people dislike him at first, but they are quickly won over by his charm of manner, his exceptionally fine speaking voice, his genial gaiety and vivacity of expression.'[9] Based closely on the court transcripts of Wilde's trials, *Oscar Wilde* provided the first frank, factual presentation of homosexuality on the stage. The Stokeses' Wilde was a challenging iconoclast, bent on offending social and moral convention. 'I like people with no principles better than anyone else in the world' he announces.[10] The Stokeses received advice and approval from Alfred Douglas, who in a travesty of the truth is portrayed as caring, hard-working young poet to Wilde's genial but irresponsible hedonist. This was again the homosexual as effete and effeminate, as the Victorians had seen him, a victim of his own flagrant egotism and weakness, reduced by the end to a pitiable drunkard, living in exile abroad.

Some literary historians insist, in this context, on a clear divide between the conception and recognition of homosexuality in the nineteenth and twentieth centuries.[11] They argue that, before Wilde's trial and conviction, the manifestly camp and effeminate were not inevitably read as masks or signs of homosexuality. Effeminacy and dandyism differentiated the dissolute leisured aristocracy and the earnest, middle-class ideal of manliness. The exposure of Wilde, the aesthete as homosexual, provided a stereotype of queerness that until that time had remained vague and unformed. The Victorians, in other words, did not identify homosexuality in the way the twentieth century came to recognize it, which serves to explain why until his trial and conviction Wilde 'got away with it' for so long. An important warning is thus issued against potentially anachronistic readings of Wilde's stories and plays as coded expressions of homosexuality. In his sustained quarrel with the critics on the magazine publication of *The Picture of Dorian Gray* in 1890, Wilde himself resisted the suggestion of such readings. That he needed to do so might suggest equally that the idea of a clear divide between the unformed Victorian image and the constructed twentieth-century stereotype of gayness, between an age of innocence and an age of recognition, itself needs to be qualified. It is not so much that effeminate mannerisms were already associated with the queer man in the Victorian age, but that flaunted effeminacy continued to signal not sexual orientation but a refined, aristocratic sensibility or else just the outrageous and defiantly anti-conformist. In the second of Anthony Powell's twelve-volume chronicle of twentieth-century English life, *A Dance to the Music of Time*, the boy-worshipping 1890s artist Mr Deacon has a furious row with the entertainer Max Pilgrim over a camp song which, he claims, 'puts a weapon in the hands of the puritans'.[12] One could conclude that this proves the link between camp and queerness in the twentieth century, but the fact is that Deacon is the only one at the crowded Mayfair party to take offence. In 1963, more than ten years ahead of John Osborne, an American reviewer criticized the American cast of a New York dramatization of *The Picture of Dorian Gray* for too often confusing the characters' 'aristocratic English mannerisms . . . with effeminacy'.[13]

In the performance of Wilde's society comedies, style and nostalgia often joined forces as an antidote both to the serious and the darker side of twentieth-century history. The English Players, whom James Joyce helped to form, chose *The Importance of Being Earnest* as their opening production in a morale-boosting display of British insouciance and optimism in neutral Zurich in 1918. Wilde's society comedy was also popular with silent film audiences, who could enjoy while at the same time scoffing at the life of the idle rich. As in the 1890s, part of the appeal of social comedy during the 1920s was its ironic treatment of the heightened, slightly ludicrous situations and devices of melodrama. Among the leading practitioners of the genre was Ernst Lubitsch who directed a scintillating silent screen version of *Lady Windermere's Fan*, voted one of the ten best pictures of the year in 1925, with Ronald Colman in the role of the would-be seducer, Lord Darlington.

Wilde's irreverence towards upper-class life and authority

influenced not only silent film but also contemporary writers and playwrights such as Noel Coward and Evelyn Waugh. John Gielgud was undoubtedly following their example when, on the eve of the Second World War, he unveiled an artistically definitive style of Wildean performance in *The Importance of Being Earnest*. In the summer of 1925, Gielgud had taken over Noel Coward's role as the young Nicky Lancaster, cocaine addict and clandestine homosexual, in Coward's sensational, crowd-pulling drama, *The Vortex*. Gielgud and the cast performed Wilde with the same meticulous, artificial manner that characterized Coward's period society drama. Wilde's injunction that 'we should treat all trivial things of life very seriously, and all the serious things with sincere and studied triviality' struck a chord with audiences in a period clouded by the threat of war. Gielgud's Wilde was Wilde as 'period piece', soothingly and glamorously reconstructed so that the audience was encouraged to laugh at the manners and attitudes of the old brigade. Edith Evans, whose performance defined the role of Lady Bracknell for years to come, said of her character: 'I know those kind of women . . . They were caricatures these people—absolutely assured, arrogant, and that's the way they spoke.'[14] Gielgud also commented on the change that half a century had brought: '[The original audiences] who laughed at it were, many of them, laughing at themselves. Today we laugh at the very idea that such types ever existed.'[15]

In the atmosphere of drab austerity and rationing that followed the Second World War, Cecil Beaton's lavish designs for John Gielgud's *Lady Windermere's Fan* dazzled theatre audiences in London and New York. In 1949 Otto Preminger's Hollywood adaptation of the play, titled simply *The Fan*, competed with Beaton in opulence in a series of flashbacks from the bombed setting of the London Blitz. Two years earlier Alexander Korda's technicolour screen version of *An Ideal Husband* had given cinema audiences the 'Naughty Nineties' as the public liked to imagine it—an era when fashion and pleasure ruled in the dying days of Queen Victoria's long reign. Noel Coward also joined in the Wildean vogue. 'After the Ball', the title of his 1954 musical version of *Lady Windermere's Fan*, may well have been suggested by Korda's film in which the popular 1890s hit song 'After the Ball' played in the background as the opening credits rolled. Coward's attempt to out-Wilde Wilde in gaiety and wit was out of touch with theatre audiences on the threshold of the new kitchen-sink school of realism. The un-Wildean imperialist lyrics of 'Faraway land' ('It's sweet to know that there's English pride | On the other side of the world') foundered on sentimentality, as did the appeal to an imagined demotic, post-war euphoria in Lord Darlington's camped up 'London at Night':

> And by some oversight
> Low class and high class
> Combine to defy class
> And brightly, politely unite
> In London at night.[16]

Much more popular with audiences was Allon Bacon's amusing musical adaptation of *The Importance of Being Earnest*, *Found in a Handbag*, which reinstated for the first time the scene with Gribsby cut by George Alexander from the original production. Bacon's musical delighted holiday audiences in English seaside resorts during the 1950s and 1960s.

The performance of Wilde's plays to suggest a homosexual subtext was a noticeable development of the later twentieth century. In America, New York State legislation outlawing plays that dealt with 'the subject of sex degeneracy or sex perversion' was repealed in 1967.[17] The law had been hastily introduced forty years earlier, in 1927, to close the American actress Mae West's homosexual melodrama, *The Drag*. The change in America coincided with a change in the law on homosexuality in England in 1967, followed by the abolition of the office of Examiner of Plays a year later.

The recontextualizing of works by Wilde and other known homosexuals as covert homosexual texts received encouragement from the growing gay rights movements of the 1980s and 1990s. Nicholas Hytner's 1993 revival of the *Importance of Being Earnest* had Alex Jennings's elegant Jack Worthing and Richard E. Grant's dandified Algernon Moncrieff greet each other with a kiss. A gay subtext was to announce itself more fully in the exotic drapery, the hookah, and silk floor-cushions of Algernon's room in the Albany in Nicholas Wright's English Touring Company production of 1995. In the same year as Hytner's revival, Lynne Parker's Rough Magic troupe brought a version of *Lady Windermere's Fan* from Dublin to London that used cross-dressing and a mix of performance styles to flaunt established notions of class and gender. Celebrations of gayness with

all-male casts and blatant homosexual readings—Algernon's con-
firmed and secret 'Bunburying' as homosexual slang, for example—
have sometimes met critical resistance, even from those sympathetic
to the enthusiasms on display. Such explicit reinterpretations have
often seemed a cavalier distortion of the texts themselves and at odds
with Wilde's own avoidance of obviousness or singleness of meaning.

Audiences as well as critics have generally responded with greater
enthusiasm to efforts to restage Wilde's social comedies in ways that
reveal their theatrical complexity. Theatrical practices and preconceptions have often hindered full appreciation of Wilde's stagecraft. The high estimation of Wilde as a successor to Sheridan and
Goldsmith on the strength of *The Importance of Being Earnest* alone
led some to underestimate his other society plays. For all the enjoy-
able wit and surface sparkle, Wilde's society dramas were felt to be
weakened by the sentimental and melodramatic conventions that he
used as his framework. This was so even in the 1890s. Wilde's name
sold tickets, as it still does today, but the upper-class audiences
flocked to his plays not for moral or artistic edification, but to see a
flattering send-up of themselves. Great care was taken to reproduce
on stage the fashionable world of the smart set, with actresses spectacularly gowned by London's leading ultra-modish couturières.
While Ibsen's 'social problem' drama was being applauded as artistically serious and groundbreaking, Wilde's plays were considered to
be amusing, but ultimately superficial.

A new appreciation of Wilde's intentions and achievements as a
playwright has been largely the result of modern criticism and performance. Almost a century after Wilde travelled to Glasgow to give
a private reading of *A Woman of No Importance* to Beerbohm Tree,
Glasgow Citizens' Theatre staged the play as the first of three
experimental, groundbreaking revivals of Wilde's society dramas.[18]
The Citizens' Theatre had risen from ailing provincial repertory
company to vanguard experimental theatre with the arrival there of
Giles Havergal and fellow director Philip Prowse in 1969. Their
emphasis on the 'theatre-ness' of the theatre, and extension of illusion even to 'realism' was perfectly suited to demonstrate Wilde's
imaginative effects. Before arriving in Glasgow, Havergal and Prowse
had directed and designed an adaptation of *The Picture of Dorian
Gray* at the Palace Theatre, Watford in 1967. In their first season at
Glasgow, Havergal produced *The Importance of Being Earnest* and

followed this in 1977 with the first official production of the original four-act version, prepared by Vyvyan Holland. A combination of symbolic elements and sumptuous period detail became the basis of their successful revivals of Wilde society dramas in the 1980s. Prowse saw Wilde's plays not as exercises in 'studious artificiality' but of 'heightened realism' that 'accurately reflected the structure of Wilde's society'.[19] Produced at two-year intervals between 1984 and 1988, these helped transform preconceptions about the emotional range and technical possibilities of Wilde's plays.

Since Edwardian times, the performance history of *A Woman of No Importance* has been patchy. Few leading actresses have wanted to play Mrs Arbuthnot, the self-flagellating female victim, while there was always the danger that solemn lines like 'Stop, Gerald, stop! He is your own father!' would make audiences laugh. At the beginning of Prowse's *A Woman of No Importance*, a barefoot young man miming an imaginary game of croquet on Hunstanton lawns prepared the audience for a symbolic interplay of opposing styles that evoked the historical pastness of Wilde's leisured and aristocratic country-house setting. Rather than downplay the theatricality, Prowse's production heightened it, as Beerbohm Tree is said to have done in the play's first production with a quirky, ironic, contradictory style of performance as Lord Illingworth. In Prowse's grandly recreated country-house setting with its walled garden and gilded pots, the battle between Lord Illingworth, the ageing aristocratic seducer, and Mrs Arbuthnot, his abandoned mistress, for the soul of their illegitimate son Gerald, became a clash of self-assertive personalities that offered little hope to the future. The weakness of Illingworth's wit and the forced cadences of Mrs Arbuthnot's Old Testament rhetoric provided a picture of doubleness, not difference. As in the original production, Mrs Arbuthnot's black gown intruded a sensuousness that did not so much unsettle as confirm the repression underlying the puritan nay-sayer. With its autumnal setting, and its aimless drifting groups of country-house guests, seeking distraction and direction, Prowe's *A Woman of No Importance* was Wilde reclaimed as England's Chekhov, according to one critic, showing both the charm and the moral bankruptcy of an aristocratic world that was passing away.[20]

The success of the play was helped by the playful addition of witticisms and *bon mots* from *The Picture of Dorian Gray* and Wilde's other writings. If on this occasion the purists were indulgent, they were much less accepting towards Prowse's alterations to *An Ideal Husband*, which opened at the Citizens' two years later in 1986. With its theme of conspiracy and corruption in high places, *An Ideal Husband* has always seemed capable of updating. Even at its first revival by Alexander in 1914, Robert Ross, as Wilde's executor, tried to emphasize the play's contemporary relevance by altering the Argentine Canal Scheme to the Sahara Irrigation Scheme, and by introducing references to eugenics instead of higher education for women. As with *A Woman of No Importance*, Prowse sought the play's contemporary relevance not by bringing it up to date, but by a heightened re-creation of the opulence and ostentation of the 1890s. Prowse's Chilterns were played as insecure *nouveaux riches* in a morally squalid world. What offended some critics was Mrs Cheveley's use of a four-letter word—Wilde's stage direction is simply 'a curse breaks from her lips'—and her ripping of her bodice to show her breasts at the end of Act 3. Equally controversial was the cutting of Lady Chiltern's final 'It is love, Robert. Love, and only love' in response to her husband's question, 'Gertrude, is it love you feel for me, or is it merely pity?' (Act 4). In Prowse's production, Lady Chiltern's silent stare suggested deeper questions beneath the glittering surface of high society. Despite critical protests, such readjustments seem closer to the ambivalent spirit of Wilde's play than a 1969 BBC production that cut short the play at the point at which Chiltern decides to do the honourable thing and resign. This was an attempt perhaps to reassure the audience at a time of increasing cynicism about those in public life.

The staging in 1988 of *Lady Windermere's Fan*, the third of the Glasgow Citizens' trilogy of Wilde revivals, again took liberties with the text, but this time to restore Wilde's original intention of withholding Mrs Erlynne's identity as Lady Windermere's mother until the final act. The result, the critics agreed, was a tougher, less sentimental play. The beautiful costumes and opulent Whistlerian sets provided a compelling visual index of the play's part-celebratory, part-critical display of magnificent surfaces over necessary secrecy and deception.

While the Wilde cycle at Glasgow's Citizens' Theatre resulted in a definite reassessment of Wilde's standing and reputation as a leading stylist of the English and European theatre, the rediscovery of Wilde by means of a Continental theatricalist *mise-en-scène* also went on in parallel elsewhere. *The Importance of Being Earnest* was adapted by the French absurdist Jean Anouilh at the Théâtre Comédie as *Il est important d'être aimé* in 1954. European avant-garde styles of performance increasingly influenced the English stage in the decades that followed. *Travesties* (1974), Tom Stoppard's re-creation of the events surrounding Joyce's production of *The Importance of Being Earnest* in wartime Zurich, revelled in Wilde's celebration of the power of fiction and imagination over conformity and reality. Often described as 'burlesque' or 'parody', Stoppard's play is more accurately 'critically creative' in the Wildean sense of being created out of a critical engagement with other works of art. In this, Wilde with other *fin de siècle* stylists anticipated the literary techniques that today are known as 'metafictional', where the construction and simultaneous laying bare of illusion dissolves the distinction between creation and criticism.

An altogether different treatment of the recognition of illusion was Peter Hall's production of *An Ideal Husband* in 1992. Hall's staging conveyed character and emotional intensity beneath the social mask. Audiences were taken aback by the social relevance of the play which opened at the moment the Matrix Churchill 'arms for Iraq' scandal was threatening to bring down some senior British Tory politicians. The play was to maintain its topicality for the rest of the decade as fresh scandals undermined public confidence in the British political system, including accusations that leading Conservatives had taken 'cash for questions' in Parliament. Two rival film adaptations released in 1999 emphasized the play's contemporary relevance, Oliver Parker's period version by drawing attention to the dominance of commercial interests at the end of both centuries; Bill Cartlidge's updated setting by shifting political corruption to the English home counties in the 1990s.

Following the inevitable rush of popular revivals, exhibitions, and sensational media profiles that marked the centenary of Wilde's death in 2000, attention has remained on Wilde as one of England's leading theatrical stylists. Exactly 110 years after its first production, with Peter Hall directing, *Lady Windermere's Fan* was revived at the Theatre Royal Haymarket in London. As with his highly acclaimed *An Ideal Husband*, Hall assembled a star cast with the real-life mother and daughter, Vanessa Redgrave and Joely Richardson, as

Mrs Erlynne and Lady Windermere. The effect was again to connect the glamour and sophistication of the star system with the
glittering society world of the play. A remarkable feature of Wilde
revivals has been the way reviewers have divided on exactly the same
lines as those who attended the original productions. One reviewer
of Hall's *Lady Windermere's Fan* went so far as to elevate the actors
above the play in what seemed a knowing reversal of Wilde's claims
for the playwright in 'The Poet and the Puppets' at the time of its
first production.[21] Yet for the play's audiences, as for audiences in the
1890s, the appeal remains the playwright as much as the play or the
actors who play it. Reflecting on Wilde's popularity with the public,
Hall locates it in 'the warmth, even more than the wit', adding:
'Beneath the wit there is always an intense emotional reality.'[22]

SALOME

The gradual acceptance of Wilde's society plays as classics of the
English stage has tended to obscure the idea of the theatre that
shaped his social comedies and his Symbolist dramas alike. After the
banning of *Salome* in England, Wilde did not abandon avant-garde
Symbolist theatre in favour of English society drama and farce. He
continued to hope for a Paris premiere with Sarah Bernhardt, and
discussed stage designs with Charles Ricketts in 1894. Even as *An
Ideal Husband* and *The Importance of Being Earnest* were playing to
full houses in 1895, he was also still at work on a sixteenth-century
blank verse drama, 'A Florentine Tragedy', and a Symbolist play in
the style of *Salome* entitled 'La Sainte Courtisane, or The Woman
Covered with Jewels'. The problem has been how to reconcile
Wilde's successful adaptation of English society drama with his continuing ambition to write and stage poetic costume dramas that
appear altogether different in style and tone. One could conclude
that he did not have a single or consistent idea of the theatre, or that
he saw his commercial successes and his artistic drama as two distinct activities. His correspondence gives some support for this view.
'Personally I like comedy to be intensely modern, and I like my
tragedy to walk in purple and to be remote,' he wrote in 1894 (*Letters*, p. 626). Yet Wilde's final appeal in the same letter is to the artist
who serves neither the public nor 'many publics', but only his art.

The key to Wilde's idea of the theatre is to be found in his
response to his critics. Reviewers of his first productions in the 1890s

frequently pointed out his evident indebtedness to the Parisian romantic dramatists, Eugène Scribe and Victorien Sardou. Their formulaic plots, made up of misplaced documents and past secrets, had ensured box-office success for a succession of English playwrights of the second rank from Edward Bulwer-Lytton through to Tom Taylor and T. W. Robertson. Wilde, like Shaw and even Ibsen, adapted the popular conventions of 'la pièce bien faite' (in English, 'the well-made play') with its misdirected letters, mislaid possessions, and other coincidences. Yet Wilde rejected the identification of his works with the Scribean formula, citing instead as his model Victor Hugo.

Wilde's acknowledgement of Hugo was not simply a preference for an original over his lesser imitators—Hugo having fathered the romantic-realistic school of which Scribe and Sardou were part. Wilde's attachment to Hugo was consistent with his considerations of stagecraft from the 1880s on. In his early essay on stagecraft 'The Truth of Masks' (originally 'Shakespeare and Stage Costume') he singled out Hugo as the first great archaeologist of the French theatre, committed to absolute accuracy in his presentation of speech, setting, and costume. For Wilde, Hugo advocated perfect accuracy of detail not as a quality in itself, but as a vital element in producing 'illusionist stage effect'. Wilde was happy to take his subject matter from anywhere, including the sentimental realism of contemporary playwrights like Henry Arthur Jones. For Wilde, the test of art was not in the subject matter, but in the treatment. 'Execution is all,' John Osborne concluded in his analysis of *The Picture of Dorian Gray*, which is an inspired variation of the age-old story of the Mephistophelian bargain with the devil.[23] Wilde's ideal theatre was one of creative and critical illusion. He employed romantic and realistic elements to ends that were neither romantic nor in any narrowly mimetic sense 'realistic'. Like Basil Hallward, his painter-surrogate in *The Picture of Dorian Gray*, he sought to avoid 'a realism that is vulgar' and 'an ideality that is void' (ch. I).

Aurélien Lugné-Poë first staged *Salome* in February 1896 at the Théâtre d'Œuvre, which formed part of the idealist reaction to naturalism. The leading playwright of the reaction was Maurice Maeterlinck. Apart from Hugo, Maeterlinck was the only other contemporary from whom Wilde claimed to have learned about stagecraft. Maeterlinck's use of symbol, colour, and cadenced language to

achieve effect had a direct influence on *Salome*. Although *Salome* has
been charged with pretentiousness and over-elaborate talk, the characters, no less than the characters of Wilde's social comedies, are
strikingly human figures, presented in a form of symbolic, heightened realism. Richard Strauss was among those impressed by Max
Reinhardt's spectacular Berlin production that ran for over two
hundred performances in Berlin between 1903 and 1904. Strauss's
opera, set to a German translation, opened in Dresden in 1905, and
within the next two years was performed in fifty other European
capitals, prompting Robert Ross's remark that *Salome* made Oscar
Wilde a household name wherever English was not spoken.[24]

The success of *Salome* on the Continent only served to confirm
the play in English minds as foreign 'decadent stuff'. In England,
Salome remained banned from public performance. Low budget
productions by progressive stage societies ensured its reputation as
an indecent, underground work. When the dancer Maud Allen
played the title role in J. T. Grein's Independent Theatre production
in 1918, British MP Noel Pemberton-Billing accused her of acting
on behalf of the Germans to undermine the British war effort in
Europe. As with critical revivals of the society plays, a new appreciation of the dramatic possibilities in staging *Salome* emerged in the
1970s and 1980s through more public, theatrically experimental productions. There was appreciation for the originality of Lindsay
Kemp's all-male cabaret *Salome* at London's Round House in 1977,
and Steven Berkoff's decadent 1920s version was performed on both
sides of the Atlantic between 1988 and 1990. Two years later, in 1992
Al Pacino played an overwrought, red-lipped Herod in Robert Allan
Ackerman's production at the Circle in the Square, New York. Yet,
in the English-speaking world at least, *Salome* still awaits the glossy,
grandly Symbolist treatment that Wilde and the designer Charles
Ricketts envisaged back in the 1890s.

Wilde's Changing Image

In 1960, the public attitude to Wilde himself began to change significantly. That year, two British films of Wilde's life went on general
release, with Robert Morley and Peter Finch as rival Oscars. Both
films were 'X-rated' by the British Board of Film Censors, which
meant that they could only be seen by persons over the age of 16.

The newspapers headlined the event 'the battle of the Oscars'. The distributors of the Finch film, co-produced by Albert R. ('Cubby') Broccoli of later James Bond fame, sued their rivals to prevent distribution, alleging infringement of copyright. This prompted Robert Morley to declare: 'I should have thought two films would be better than one.'[25]

Until the 1950s homosexuality tended to be swept under the carpet. The defection to Russia of the Foreign Office agents, Guy Burgess and Donald Maclean, made it an issue of public concern and led to the setting up of the Wolfenden Commission to investigate homosexuality. The Wilde plays coincided with a free discussion in the press, on radio, and on television in the late 1950s on the recommendation of the Wolfenden Report that homosexuality between consenting males over 21 should be decriminalized. The films became a measure of the attitude of the general public. John Trevelyan, then at the British Board of Film Censors, noted that both films did 'good business' which suggested to him that the public accepted them.[26]

In the stark black-and-white version in which he starred, Morley reprised his 1936 role for post-war cinema audiences, playing Wilde as the amiably unconventional man, bubbling with wit and epigrams, but destined to suffer ignominy and expulsion. 'Theirs was a relationship the world could not, *would* not tolerate,' the film placards sensationally announced. But at 35, John Neville, the actor playing Lord Alfred Douglas looked too old, and a rowdy party in a restaurant and shots of stuffy disapproving Victorians, were the only enlightenment as to the nature of their social deviance.

Peter Finch, a matinée idol, won Best British Actor of the Year Award in Ken Hughes's more frank and complex film portrait of Wilde. His script drew upon two books, John Furnell's *The Springed Lute*, and H. Montgomery Hyde's faithful account of the trials in *The Trials of Oscar Wilde*. Hughes took several liberties with the documentary record—Constance for instance, was not in England when Wilde was released from Reading Gaol—but generally the film was historically accurate. Wilde's homosexuality was made more explicit, while the forces driving his life in the 1890s were dramatically highlighted—his pressing money needs, the moral backlash that greeted *The Picture of Dorian Gray*, and the personal crisis of his family life and destructive entanglement with Douglas and the

Poster for the film *Oscar Wilde*, 1960, starring Robert Morley as Wilde.

Peter Finch as Wilde in *The Trials of Oscar Wilde*, 1960.

The release of rival film versions of Wilde's life that year became known as 'The Battle of the Oscars'.

Queensberry clan. In a controversial scene in Hughes's original script, Wilde's counsel, Sir Edward Clarke, is given a speech that challenges the whole British legal system:

The prosecution's key witnesses have, in their depositions, admitted to crimes ranging from larceny and assault to blackmail and gross indecency. Yet the crown appears to have no intention of prosecuting *any* of these men. It would seem that as long as they give evidence against you then they are to be allowed to get off Scot-free. Such a state of affairs has profoundly shaken my inherent faith in the fairness of British justice.

Hughes's film showed Wilde in a variety of roles: brilliant conversationalist and man about town, worried parent, successful playwright, legal scapegoat, and, as the times also demanded, remorseful and guilty husband. As Wilde boards the train for France in the final scene of the film, his last words to Constance are: 'Constance . . . I want you to remember one thing. I've always loved you . . . I always will.'

That same year, the homosexual, Dublin-based actor Michéal Mac Liammóir unveiled his one-man reading and performance as Wilde in Dublin and London, followed by a tour to various corners of the world for most of the 1960s. Mac Liammóir (in reality Alfred Williams, originally from Kensal Green, London) divided his narration into pre- and post-trial Wilde. As in the two films that year, his charismatic performance (also seen on television and recorded on a long-playing record) was an aesthetic rebuke to the law as bastion of homophobia. In the abrasive, irreverently high-spirited decade that followed, Wilde was given a place in the pantheon of those who had defied establishment attitudes and values. In 1967 the Rolling Stones acted out scenes from the Peter Finch movie in their promotional film for their hit record 'We Love You', celebrating Mick Jagger's release from prison on a drugs charge. Keith Richard portrayed the Marquess of Queensberry and Marianne Faithfull was cast as Douglas. Jagger, in the title role, declared: 'We were luckier than Oscar. As for any connection between *his* life and the record—well, it's all there, isn't it?'[27] That same year, the oppressive law that had governed the lives of homosexuals for over eighty years was finally abolished.

The transformation of Wilde to support a variety of radical agendas has been a striking feature of recent critical and theoretical

revaluations of his life and work. The portrait of Wilde as homosexual martyr in the 1960s was brought into sharper focus in the
1980s by the rise of gender criticism and 'queer' theory. Wilde
emerged as a gay icon in Eric Bentley's 1982 play *Lord Alfred's Lover*
in which heterosexual society is the enemy to homosexual love. In
John Hawkesworth's sensitive three-part dramatization of Wilde's
life for BBC television in 1985, based on H. Montgomery Hyde's
1976 biography, Michael Gambon played the older Wilde as a gentle,
sexually complicated man. Increasingly, Wilde's own works were
read as coded expressions of homosexuality. Although Richard
Ellmann's 1988 biography presented Wilde as a protean, many-sided
personality, it also served to legitimate the emerging gospel of Wilde
as iconic gay martyr. The extent of Ellmann's influence can be seen
in Brian Gilbert's popular and widely acclaimed 1997 film with
Stephen Fry as Wilde. A key scene in the film is an incident,
allegedly told by Wilde to Reggie Turner and given a homosexual
meaning by Ellmann, when Wilde saw a group of rent boys while out
shopping with Constance in Piccadilly and felt something 'clutch-
ing' at his heart 'like ice' (Ellmann, p. 258). The film also followed
Ellmann in showing Wilde's initiation into homosexual acts by the
young Robert Ross. In Gilbert's film, Wilde's reading of 'The Selfish
Giant' to his children in a detached and beautifully cadenced voice
suggests his slow self-recognition of his hidden homosexual nature.
The sex scenes in the film were daringly explicit, although the film
went to sentimental lengths to distinguish between Wilde's gentle
caring homosexual passion and Douglas's brutal exploitative taste in
buggery and rough trade. Fry in the dock was heroic; in prison sadly
dignified. The final scene, in which Wilde and Douglas are reunited
in Italy after Wilde's release from prison, appealed to a contemporary approval and tolerance of the love that finally dared to speak its
name.

A similar approval is found in Tom Stoppard's portrait of Wilde
in his play *The Invention of Love* that same year. In an imagined
meeting between the poet A. E. Housman and Oscar Wilde, Wilde's
social and sexual assertiveness is contrasted starkly with the
repressed and cloistered life of Housman as the stereotypically
repressed Victorian. 'Better a fallen rocket than never a burst of
light,' Wilde declares ' . . . the artist is the sexual criminal in our
midst. He is the agent of progress against authority.'[28] The interest

Edith Evans as Lady Bracknell in *The Importance of Being Earnest*, 1952.

Stephen Fry as Wilde with Jude Law as Douglas in *Wilde*, 1997.

here as in other recent plays and performances, such as Corin Red-grave's understated Wilde in the 1998 revival of Moisés Kaufman's *Gross Indecency—The Three Trials of Oscar Wilde*, and Liam Neeson's manly Wilde in David Hare's *The Judas Kiss* (1998), is on Wilde's heroic character and personality.

The rise of post-colonial criticism and consciousness in Irish studies in the 1980s and 1990s also gave birth to the image of 'Wilde the Irishman'. The importance of Wilde's Irishness was in fact recognized by Shaw in his first notices of Wilde's plays in the 1890s. 'To the Irishman (and Mr Wilde is almost as acutely an Irishman as the iron Duke of Wellington) there is nothing in the world quite so exquisitely comic as an Englishman's seriousness,' Shaw wrote of *An Ideal Husband*.[29] Yet Shaw's insights were largely neglected. Even in *The Field Day Anthology of Irish Writing* of 1991, which set out to reclaim Irish writers by placing them in a specifically Irish cultural and historical context, Wilde's profile remained essentially that of expatriate Irish playwright. His radicalism, then as now, was judged crucially compromised by his concession to English taste.[30]

The image of Wilde as a heroic critic and victim of British colonial rule was virtually the creation of the late 1980s and 1990s. The place of Anglo-Irish relations in Wilde's conviction had previously been located in the general hostility of the British press at the time, or in the perceived duel between Wilde and Edward Carson, a fellow Anglo-Irishman, at the first trial. Wilde and Carson had been at Trinity College, Dublin, together, but temperament and politics divided them. Wilde was artistic and Republican; Carson, legalistic and staunchly Unionist. That Carson was at first reluctant to accept the Wilde case because they had been at Trinity College together has not prevented playwrights from vamping up their personal and political differences. The actual politics of the courtroom battle between the two became the focus of Ulick O'Connor's 1988 Abbey Theatre production of *A Trinity of Two*, which set out to examine differing Irish Protestant attitudes towards the British establishment. In the following year, the 'Irish Wilde' received a full-blooded political airing in Terry Eagleton's irreverent avant-garde *Saint Oscar*, directed by Trevor Griffiths, and performed by the Field Day Theatre Company in Dublin in 1989 and again in London and on Channel 4 television the following year. In a high-spirited style of ribaldry and Brechtian alienation, Eagleton's Saint Oscar is both gay martyr and symbol of Irish colonial oppression, in revolt against the clichés of sexual and national identity. Eagleton's Wilde embraces the perverse pleasures of martyrdom, while maintaining his resistance to his own fiction. 'Myths are fictions that have forgotten that they're such,' he tells the nationalistic Lady Wilde, 'whereas I never forget for a moment how ludicrously unreal I am. I suppose that's the real thing about me. We're both illusions, mother; the only difference between us is that I admit it.'[31]

The alignment of the politics of gender and identity with the racial and political ambiguities of Wilde's Anglo-Irish background, contributed to a new image of Wilde in the decade that followed. Attention turned to the formative influences of Wilde's Irish upbringing. Wilde's career coincided with the political and economic decline of the Anglo-Irish Protestant Ascendancy and the emergence of Catholic Ireland in the second half of the nineteenth century. The resulting crisis of Irish Protestant identity, it was argued, provided a specifically Irish context for Wilde's anti-mimetic creed and subversion of fixed identity. Certainly the internal *émigré* would seem to be favourably placed to see through the provisional, socially constructed nature of reality and relationships. In the impossible play-world that is *The Importance of Being Earnest*, the fictions the characters create in the end become facts. There are manifest parallels between Wilde's category of art as the single imaginative principle of the true individual and Shaw's claims for 'Creative Evolution' and the 'Life Force', of the power of mind over matter, notably in his parable-play *Man and Superman*. Yeats's anti-mimetic ideal of a self-begetting art, of art born of art, also owes much to Wilde. In what appear to be attempts to distance themselves from Wilde, both Shaw and Yeats looked back to Blake. Yet the common view that Irish literature only became fully radical and political with Yeats's founding of the Irish Literary Theatre in 1899 has undergone a significant revision. Wilde's anti-realist treatment of fairy-tale, romance, and society drama was recognized as an unequivocally subversive political strategy that pointed forward in significant ways to the creative self-inventions of his younger contemporaries. In Declan Kiberd's account of contemporary Irish literature, *Inventing Ireland* (1995), Wilde's use of lying, deception, guile, and word-play as an element of identity distinguishes him as the first writer of the Irish literary and national revival.

Wilde continues to be identified with progressive causes. The increasing cross-fertilization of highbrow and popular culture in the second half of the twentieth century encouraged surprising and sometimes unlikely comparisons and parallels. By the century's end Wilde had been transformed from the iconoclastic rebel of 1960s iconography into the forerunner of 'attitude' and 'cool'.[32] To those who elevated attitude and style over old-fashioned social and cultural divisions, Wilde the late-Victorian dandy appeared to have shown them the way. At the same time, in the narrative of sell-outs and burn-outs that shaped the history of popular culture in the twentieth century, Wilde was the first who dared to defy the norm. The proximity of Jim Morrison's grave to Wilde's in Père Lachaise cemetery in Paris, Neil Sammells has suggested, has helped reinforce the emotional link.[33] To fashion a pose that rejects the 'sad', 'straight' world is today to become thoroughly 'Wildean'.

Cultural observers continue to question the extent of complicity between counter-cultural values and the mainstream social order. The same question is also asked of Wilde. Touring America in 1882 to promote the D'Oyly Carte production of *Patience*, Wilde was clearly implicated in the very consumerist commodity culture against which his new aestheticism claimed to be a reaction. He himself had a genius for being recognized and talked about. His picture and celebrity sold newspapers and luxury goods. The image of Wilde as commodified personality returned in the latter part of the twentieth century. Restaurants and cafés are named after Wilde, and his image has adorned everything from high-class commodities to record sleeves, T-shirts, calendars, and souvenir mugs.

There is an important difference between the real Wilde and the images of Wilde celebrated by consumerists and by some sexual and political sub-cultures. For them, Wilde's sense of freedom and identity was largely a matter of choice; for Wilde, it was a matter of concealment and negotiation. In his final years of exile, Wilde settled for becoming one thing—in his sexuality, homosexual; in his politics, an imperialist monarchist. Before then, Wilde's individuality generally announced itself in flamboyant theatricality and indeterminacy. His defence of lying had its origin in the dilemma of conflicting loyalties and membership of different 'we's'. This recognition may not in itself seem new. Thus we have had Wilde the avant-garde traditionalist and 'conformist rebel',[34] and the Wilde of Ellmann's biography who, given a choice of alternatives, always managed to choose both. Yet one need not accept the usual account of such a position as being compromising, contradictory, politically disabling, or even playfully post-modern. In this last respect, Wilde today has become a mythical extra-temporal figure, on a par with English-heritage Shakespeare, Dr Johnson with his quill, or the director Alfred Hitchcock playing cameos in his own films. In the 1999 film of *An Ideal Husband*, Oliver Parker had all the characters attend the first night of *The Importance of Being Earnest*. The appearance of Wilde to deliver a curtain-call speech to his own characters prompts Lady Chiltern to ask her husband, 'Is there any secret dishonour or disgrace? Tell me at once.' Wilde himself promoted such fictional images of himself. Yet Wilde's claims for imagination over fact constituted a resistance to forms of reality and myth that had forgotten their provisional nature. The legal and extra-legal forces of society continue to react uncomfortably to the rejection of their view of 'truth' with new or very old and frightening fears and prejudices—sexual, racial, and religious. Groups and individuals continue to be persecuted for being one thing. It is worth remembering that, like them, Wilde in his day suffered moral and finally legal persecution in ways that many present-day 'Wildeans' do not.

To attempt to predict the future relevance and appreciation of a writer and his work is inevitably hazardous. That the period in which Wilde dominated the literary and cultural scene is no longer viewed simply as an 'age of transition' between high Victorianism and twentieth-century modernity would suggest that interest in the period and its leading figure will increase in the future. The 1880s and 1890s saw the emergence of the modern spirit in art and culture. The spotlight now falls not only as before on the conflict of decadence and counter-decadence, but on the cultural and artistic intersections that came with urbanization, technical innovations, and the emergence of mass markets, when literature, painting, and photography borrowed techniques from each other, and the popular and the highbrow converged as never before. Wilde was among the first to recognize the importance of a systematic aesthetic approach to all areas of culture—the arts, dress, food, fashion, and designs for living—one that disregarded existing distinctions between the popular and the highbrow, and between demotic and aristocratic ways of life. Interest in Wilde's aesthetic resistance to prevailing codes and boundaries and ways of living has been accompanied by an important recognition of his cosmopolitan goals. Wilde looked beyond the nationalist, imperialist communities of his day, and the ironic questioning anti-imperialist discourse that this atmosphere inevitably bred. Meeting Henry James in Washington during his American tour, Wilde reportedly responded to his nostalgia for London with the remark, 'You care for places? The world is my home' (Ellmann, p. 170). To the disapproving James, this indicated a regrettable rootlessness. To Wilde, by contrast, it meant the accommodation of seemingly colliding world-views and competing cultural identities. Our present-day global village, where instant images coexist alongside age-old loyalties, will be the likely stage for a new recontextualizing of Wilde's international, cosmopolitan goals.

NOTES

CHAPTER 1. The Life of Oscar Wilde

1. R. F. Foster, *Paddy & Mr Punch* (London: Allen Lane, 1993), 284.
2. Revd William Steele, 'Examination held at the Royal School of Portora, Easter 1859' (Dublin: McGlashan & Gill, 1859).
3. Joy Melville, *Mother of Oscar: The Life of Jane Francesca Wilde* (London: Allison & Busby, 1999), 119.
4. Terence de Vere White, *The Anglo-Irish* (London: Gollancz, 1972), 185.
5. Sheldon Rothblatt, *Tradition and Change in English Liberal Education: An Essay in History and Culture* (London: Faber & Faber, 1976), 124
6. *The Complete Poems of D. H. Lawrence*, ed. Vivian de Sola Pinto and Warren Roberts (2 vols., London: Heinemann, 1964), i. 433–4.
7. Melville, *Mother of Oscar*, 135.
8. Walter Pater, 'Conclusion' to *The Renaissance: Studies in Art and Poetry* (London: Macmillan and Co., Ltd., 1910), 236.
9. 'Confessional Album', repr. in Merlin Holland, *The Wilde Album* (London: Fourth Estate, 1997), 44–5.
10. Melville, *Mother of Oscar*, 149.
11. *Alumni Oxonienses* (Oxford: Park and Co., 1888), iv. 1553.
12. 'Confessional Album'.
13. W. S. Gilbert, *Patience* (1881), quoted Ian Small (ed.), *The Aesthetes: A Sourcebook* (London, Boston, and Henley: Routledge & Kegan Paul, 1979), 180.
14. 'The Aesthetic Monkey', engraved from a painting by W. H. Beard, in *Harper's Weekly* (28 Jan. 1882).
15. Melville, *Mother of Oscar*, 177.
16. Thomas Wemyss Reid, *Memoirs of Sir Wemyss Reid 1842–1885* (London: Cassell and Co., 1905), 327.
17. E. H. Mikhail (ed.), *Oscar Wilde: Interviews and Recollections* (London: Macmillan, 2 vols., 1979), i. 92–3.
18. 'Un referendum artistique et social', *L'Ermitage* (July 1893), 21, where Wilde is quoted as saying, 'Autrefois, j'étais poèt et tyran. Maintenant je suis artiste et anarchiste.' Quoted Paul Richard Gibbard, 'Anarchy in English and French Literature 1885–1914', D.Phil. thesis (University of Oxford, 2001), 167.
19. James Abbott McNeill Whistler, 'Ten O'Clock', in Small (ed.), *The Aesthetes* 26.
20. 'Mr Whistler's Ten O'Clock', *Pall Mall Gazette*, 41 (20 Feb. 1885), 1–2; quoted Richard Ellmann (ed.), *The Artist as Critic: Critical Writings of Oscar Wilde* (New York: Random House, 1968), 15–16.
21. David Lowe, 'John Barlas: Sweet Singer and Socialist' (Cupar, Fife: Craigwood Publishing Co., 1915), 3.

22. Melville, *Mother of Oscar*, 214.

23. Christa Saltzinger, *The French Influences on Oscar Wilde's 'The Picture of Dorian Gray' and 'Salome'* (Lewiston, NY: Mellon Press, 1994), 11.

24. Melville, *Mother of Oscar*, 235.

25. Ibid. 250.

26. Max Beerbohm, *Letters to Reggie Turner*, ed. Rupert Hart-Davis (London: Hart-Davis, 1964), 53.

27. Quoted R. K. R. Thornton and Marion Thain (eds.), *Poetry of the 1890s* (Harmondsworth: Penguin, 1997), p. xxv.

28. Quoted H. Montgomery Hyde, *Oscar Wilde: A Biography* (London: Penguin, 2001), 232.

29. J. G. P. Delaney, *Charles Ricketts: A Biography* (Oxford: Oxford University Press, 1990), 96.

CHAPTER 2. The Fabric of Society

1. See W. L. Burn, *The Age of Equipoise: A Study of the Mid-Victorian Generation* (London: George Allen & Unwin Ltd., 1964), and J. F. C. Harrison, *Late Victorian Britain, 1875–1901* (London: Routledge, 1991).

2. Ian Machin, *Disraeli* (London: Longman, 1995), 120.

3. Maurice Cowling, *1867: Disraeli, Gladstone and Revolution: The Passing of the Second Reform Bill* (Cambridge: Cambridge University Press, 1967), 242.

4. Joy Melville, *Mother of Oscar: The Life of Jane Francesca Wilde* (London: Allison & Busby, 1999), 129.

5. David Lowe, 'John Barlas: Sweet Singer and Socialist' (Cupar, Fife: Craigwood Publishing Co., 1915), 8–9.

6. Eric Hobsbawm, *The Age of Capital* (Harmondsworth: Penguin, 1975), 157.

7. Quoted in Paul Simon, *Education and the Labour Movement* (London: Lawrence & Wishart, 1965), 43.

8. Holbrook Jackson, *The Eighteen Nineties: A Review of Art and Ideas* (London: Grant Richards, 1913), 27.

9. Hugh E. M. Stutfield, 'Tommyrotics', in Sally Ledger and Roger Luckhurst (eds.), *The Fin de Siècle: A Reader in Cultural History c.1880–1900* (Oxford: Oxford University Press, 2000), 121.

10. Melville, *Mother of Oscar*, 117.

11. Richard D. Altick, *Victorian People and Ideas* (London: J. M. Dent, 1974), 93.

12. Robert Kee, *The Green Flag* (London: Weidenfeld & Nicolson, 1972), 357.

13. W. E. Vaughan (ed.), *A New History of Ireland*, vol. vi: *Ireland Under the Union, II 1870–1921* (Oxford: Clarendon Press, 1986), 3–4.

14. Kee, *Green Flag*, 357.

15. Richard Symonds, *Oxford and Empire: The Last Lost Cause?* (Basingstoke: Macmillan, 1986), 49.

16. Melville, *Mother of Oscar*, 178.

17. Jane Howarth, 'Gender, Domesticity, and Sexual Politics', in Colin

Matthew (ed.), *The Nineteenth Century: The British Isles 1815–1901* (Oxford: Oxford University Press, 2000), 189.

18. For changes in the law on divorce and marriage, see Lawrence Stone, *Road to Divorce: England 1530–1987* (Oxford: Oxford University Press, 1990); and Carol Dyhouse, *Feminism and the Family in England 1880–1939* (Oxford: Basil Blackwell, 1989).

19. John Ruskin, 'Sesame and Lilies', in *Works*, vol. xviii, ed. E. T. Cook and Alexander Wedderburn (London: George Allen, 1905), 136.

20. Melville, *Mother of Oscar*, 184.

21. Maeve E. Doggett, *Marriage, Wife-Beating and the Law in Victorian England* (Columbia: University of South Carolina Press, 1993), 3.

22. Pat Thane, 'Late Victorian Women', in T. R. Gourvish and Alan O'Day, (eds.), *Later Victorian Britain 1867–1900* (Basingstoke: Macmillan Education 1988), 175–208.

23. George Macaulay Trevelyan, *The Life of John Bright* (London: Constable and Co., 1914), 177.

24. David Cannadine, *The Rise and Fall of the British Aristocracy* (New Haven and London: Yale University Press, 1990), 339.

25 Quoted Joan Perkin, *Women and Marriage in the Nineteenth Century* (London: Routledge, 1989), 83.

26. V. H. H. Green, *Religion at Oxford and Cambridge* (London: SCM, 1964), 304.

27. Jane Garnett, 'Religious and Intellectual Life', in Matthew (ed.), *Nineteenth Century*, 199.

28. Frank M. Turner, *Contesting Cultural Authority: Essays in Victorian Intellectual Life* (Cambridge: Cambridge University Press, 1993), 12–13.

29. Edmund Royle, *Victorian Infidels: The Origins of the British Secularist Movement 1791–1866* (Manchester: Manchester University Press, 1974), 259.

30. Lucy Bland, *Banishing the Beast: English Feminism and Sexual Morality 1885–1914* (Harmondsworth: Penguin, 1995), 99–100.

31. Jeffrey Weeks, *Sex, Politics and Society: The Regulation of Sexual Crime since 1800* (London: Longman, 1989), 91.

32. Havelock Ellis, quoted ibid. 104.

33. Quoted Martin J. Wiener, *Reconstructing the Criminal: Crime, Law, and Policy in England 1830–1914* (Cambridge: Cambridge University Press, 1990), 111.

34. John Sloan, *John Davidson: First of the Moderns, a Literary Biography* (Oxford: Clarendon Press, 1995), 139.

35. Wiener, *Reconstructing the Criminal*, 121–2.

36. Quoted J. J. Tobias, *Crime and Industrial Society in the Nineteenth Century* (London: B. T. Batsford, 1967), 204.

37. Quoted J. J. Tobias, *Nineteenth-Century Crime: Prevention and Punishment* (Newton Abbot: David & Charles, 1972), 138.

38. Quoted David D. Cooper, *The Lesson of the Scaffold: Victorian England* (Athens: Ohio University Press, 1974), 99.

39. Quoted ibid. 84.

40. David Englander, *Poverty and Poor Law Reform from Chadwick to Booth 1834–1914* (London: Longman, 1998).

41. Quoted Keith Laybourn, *The Evolution of British Social Policy and the Welfare State* (Keele: Keele University Press, 1995), 134.

42. Ibid. 139.

43. Henry George, *Progress and Poverty* (London and New York: Dent, Everyman's Library, 1976), 396.

44. See T. W. Heyck, *The Transformation of Intellectual Life in Victorian England* (London and Sydney: Croom Helm; New York: St Martin's Press, 1982).

45. Quoted François Bédarida, *A Social History of England 1851–1990*, trans. A. S. Forster (London and New York: Routledge), 7.

46. Quoted Peter Bailey, *Leisure and Class in Victorian England: Rational Recreation and the Contest for Control 1830–1885* (London: Methuen, 1978), 75.

47. W. Hamish Fraser, *The Coming of the Mass Market* (London and Basingstoke: Macmillan, 1981), 135.

48. C. C. Eldridge, *Disraeli and the Rise of the New Imperialism* (Cardiff: University of Wales Press, 1996), 1.

49. Ibid. 64.

50. R. B. Cunninghame Graham, 'Bloody Niggers', *Social Democrat: A Monthly Socialist Review* (1 April 1897), 104–9.

51. S. M. Ellis (ed.), *The Letters and Memoirs of Sir William Hardman, A Mid-Victorian Pepys* (London: C. Palmer, 1923), 26.

CHAPTER 3. The Literary Scene

1. Lucy Brown, *Victorian News and Newspapers* (Oxford: Clarendon Press, 1985).

2. Quoted Edward Cooke, *Literary Recreations* (London: Macmillan and Co., 1918), 118.

3. John Ruskin, Preface to *Modern Painters*, in *Works*, vol. iii, ed. E. T. Cook and Alexander Wedderburn (London: George Allen, 1903), 9.

4. Matthew Arnold, *Lectures and Essays in Criticism*, ed. R. H. Super (Ann Arbor: University of Michigan Press, 1962), 235.

5. 'A Few Maxims for the Instruction of the Over-Educated', in *The Major Works*, ed. Isobel Murray (Oxford: Oxford University Press, 2000), 570.

6. Quoted Raymond L. Schults, *W. T. Stead and the Pall Mall Gazette: Crusader in Babylon* (Lincoln: University of Nebraska Press, 1972), 29–33.

7. Ibid. 30–3.

8. John Gross, *The Rise and Fall of the Man of Letters: Aspects of English Literary Life since 1800* (London: Weidenfeld & Nicolson, 1969), 95–6.

9. Leon Hugo, *Edwardian Shaw: The Writer and His Age* (Basingstoke: Macmillan, 1999), 47.

10. 'Half an Hour with the Worst Authors', *Pall Mall Gazette*, 43 (15 January 1886), 4; in Richard Ellmann (ed.), *The Artist as Critic: Critical Writings of Oscar Wilde* (New York: Random House, 1968), 24–6.

11. Brown, *Victorian News*, 23.

12. Schults, *W. T. Stead and the Pall Mall Gazette*, 36.

13. In E. H. Mikhail (ed.), *Oscar Wilde: Interviews and Recollections*, 2 vols. (London: Macmillan, 1979), i. 247.

14. H. Montgomery Hyde, *Oscar Wilde: A Biography* (London: Penguin, 2001), 174.

15. Max Beerbohm, *A Peep into the Past, and Other Prose Pieces* (London: Heinemann, 1972), 3–8.

16. See Norman Feltes, *Literary Capital in the Late Victorian Novel* (Madison: University of Wisconsin Press, 1993), 12.

17. See Jacob Korg, *George Gissing: A Critical Biography* (Seattle: University of Washington Press, 1963), 156.

18. For a full account of Wilde's commercial transactions, consult Josephine M. Guy and Ian Small, *Oscar Wilde's Profession: Writing and the Culture Industry in the Late Nineteenth Century* (Oxford: Oxford University Press, 2000).

19. Feltes, *Literary Capital*, 41–8.

20. Quoted Joseph McAleer, *Popular Reading and Publishing in Britain 1914–1950* (Oxford: Clarendon Press, 1992), 20.

21. Quoted ibid.

22. Henry James, 'The Art of Fiction' (1884), in *Selected Literary Criticism*, ed. F. R. Leavis (Harmondsworth: Penguin, 1963), 78–97.

23. R. L. Stevenson, 'A Humble Remonstrance', in *The Works of R. L. Stevenson* (London: Heinemann, 1922), 206–23.

24. For an account of late Victorian 'gothic', see Nicholas Daly, *Modernism, Romance and the fin de siècle: Popular Fiction and British Culture 1880–1914* (Cambridge: Cambridge University Press, 1999).

25. Jack David Zipes, *Breaking the Magic Spell: Radical Theories of Folk and Fairy Tales* (London: Heinemann, 1979); and *The Brothers Grimm: From Enchanted Forests to the Modern World* (New York: Routledge, 1988).

26. Andrew Lang, 'Realism and Romance', *Contemporary Review*, 1886, in Sally Ledger and Roger Luckhurst (eds.), *The Fin de Siècle: A Reader in Cultural History c.1880–1900* (Oxford: Oxford University Press, 2000), 99–104.

27. Quoted Isobel Murray, 'Introduction', *Oscar Wilde: Complete Shorter Fiction* (Oxford: Oxford University Press, 1979), 9.

28. Matthew Arnold, 'On a Study of Celtic Literature', in *Lectures and Essays in Criticism*, ed. R. H. Super (Ann Arbor: University of Michigan Press, 1965), 347.

29. Neil Sammells takes issue with this view in 'Oscar Wilde, the Fairy Tale, and the Critics', in Bruce Stewart (ed.), *That Other World: The Supernatural and the Fantastic in Irish Literature and its Contexts* (2 vols., Gerrards Cross: Colin Smythe, 1998), ii. 228–37.

30. 'Mr Froude's Blue Book', *Pall Mall Gazette*, 49 (13 April 1889), 3; also in Ellmann (ed.), *Artist as Critic*, 136–40.

31. 'Some Literary Notes. By the Editor', *Woman's World* (Feb. 1889); also in Ellmann (ed.), *Artist as Critic*, 131.

32. ' "Henry the Fourth" at Oxford', *Dramatic Review*, 1 (23 May 1885), 264–5.

33. Guy and Small, *Oscar Wilde's Profession*, 70.

34. George Powell, *Nineteenth Century Theatre*, 21/2 (1993), 194.

35. Michael Holroyd, *Bernard Shaw: The Search for Love* (London: Chatto & Windus, 1988), 334.

36. Quoted Jean Chothia, *English Drama of the Early Modern Period 1890–1940* (London: Longman, 1996), 1.

37. Bernard Shaw, 'The Quintessance of Ibsenism', *Major Critical Essays, in Works*, vol. xix (London: Constable & Co., 1930), 3–158.

38. Quoted Chothia, *English Drama*, 9–10.

39. *The Collected Letters of George Gissing*, vol. ii, ed. Paul F. Mattheisen, Arthur C. Young, and Pierre Coustillas (Athens: Ohio University Press, 1991), 276–7.

40. Quoted Peter de Voogd, *Henry Fielding and William Hogarth: The Correspondence of the Arts* (Amsterdam: Rodopi, 1981), 21.

41. Thomas Hardy, 'Candour in English Fiction', *New Review* (11 Jan. 1890), in Ledger and Luckhurst (eds.), *Fin de Siècle*, 116–20.

42. For an account of this see Peter Keating, *The Haunted Study: A Social History of the English Novel 1875–1914* (London: Fontana Press, 1991), 241–51.

43. Karl Beckson (ed.), *Oscar Wilde: The Critical Heritage* (London: Routledge & Kegan Paul, 1970), 72.

44. Ibid. 68–9.

45. Ibid. 75.

46. Ibid. 83–6.

47. Mikhail (ed.), *Oscar Wilde*, i. 247.

48. Virginia Woolf, 'An Essay in Criticism', in *The Essays of Virginia Woolf*, vol. iv: *1925–1928*, ed. Andrew McNeillie (London: The Hogarth Press, 1994), 454.

49. Quoted Richard Ellmann, *James Joyce* (New York, Oxford, and Toronto: Oxford University Press; new edn., 1982), 615.

50. Keith Sagar and James T. Boulton 'Introduction', *The Letters of D. H. Lawrence*, vol. vii (Cambridge: Cambridge University Press, 1993), 7.

51. Lawrence Danson, *Wilde's Intentions: The Artist in his Criticism* (Oxford: Clarendon Press, 1997).

52. A point made in Keating, *Haunted Study*, 243–4.

CHAPTER 4. Wilde and Social Issues

1. Repr. in Karl Beckson (ed.), *Oscar Wilde: The Critical Heritage* (London: Routledge & Kegan Paul, 1970), 229.

2. Ibid. 1.

3. E. H. Mikhail (ed.), *Oscar Wilde: Interviews and Recollections* (London: Macmillan, 1979), ii. 297.

4. Matthew Arnold, 'On the Study of Celtic Literature', in *The Complete Prose Works of Matthew Arnold*, vol. iii: *Lectures and Essays in Criticism*, ed. R. H. Super (Ann Arbor: University of Michigan Press, 1962).

5. Richard Ellmann, 'Oscar at Oxford', *New York Review of Books* (29 March 1984), 23–8.

6. Grant Allen, 'Individualism and Socialism,' *Contemporary Review*, 54 (May 1889); quoted in Josephine M. Guy and Ian Small, *Oscar Wilde's Profession: Writing and the Culture Industry in the Nineteenth Century* (Oxford: Oxford University Press, 2000), 277–9.

7. Isobel Murray, 'Introduction', *The Soul of Man and Prison Writings* (Oxford: Oxford University Press, 1990), pp. xi–xiv.

8. Matthew Arnold, *Culture and Anarchy*, ed. R. H. Super (Ann Arbor: University of Michigan Press, 1965), 115–36.

9. *Speaker* (April 1895); quoted Sally Ledger, 'The New Woman and the Crisis of Victorianism', in Sally Ledger and Scott McCracken (eds.), *Cultural Politics at the Fin de Siècle* (Cambridge: Cambridge University Press, 12995), 24.

10. George Bernard Shaw, *Collected Plays with their Prefaces*, vol. i (London: The Bodley Head, 1970), 126–7.

11. Quoted Sally Ledger, 'The New Woman and the Crisis of Victorianism', in Ledger and McCracken (eds.), *Cultural Politics at the Fin de Siècle*, 25.

12. Quoted John Stokes, *In the Nineties* (Hemel Hempstead: Harvester-Wheatsheaf, 1989), 14.

13. See Joel H. Kaplan, 'A Puppet's Power: George Alexander, Clement Scott, and the Replotting of *Lady Windermere's Fan*', *Theatre Notebook*, 462 (1992), 59–73.

14. *Illustrated London News* (27 Feb. 1893); rpr. in Beckson (ed.), *Critical Heritage*, 125.

15. '"The Cenci"', *Dramatic Review*, 3 (15 May 1886), 151.

16. *The Theatrical World for 1893*, quoted Sos Eltis, *Revising Wilde: Society and Subversion in the Plays of Oscar Wilde* (Oxford: Clarendon Press, 1996), 112.

17. Joris-Karl Huysmans, *Against Nature*, trans. Margaret Mauldon (Oxford: Oxford University Press, 1998), 46.

18. Lucy Bland, *Banishing the Beast: English Feminism and Sexual Morality 1880–1914* (Harmondsworth: Penguin, 1995).

19. Gustav Bouchereau, 'Nymphomania', in Sally Ledger and Roger Luckhurst (eds.), *The Fin de Siècle: A Reader in Cultural History c.1880–1900* (Oxford: Oxford University Press, 2000), 293–7.

20. For an account of the controversy, see John Sloan, *John Davidson: First of the Moderns, a Literary Biography* (Oxford: Clarendon Press, 1995), 119–20.

21. *The Times* (23 Fe. 1893), 8; repr. in Beckson (ed.), *Critical Heritage*, 133.

22. William Archer, *Black and White* (11 May 1893), 290; repr. in Beckson (ed.), *Critical Heritage*, 141–2.

23. William Archer, *World* (20 Feb. 1895); repr. in Beckson (ed.), *Critical Heritage*, 190.

24. *Selected Poems and Prose of John Davidson*, ed. John Sloan (Oxford: Clarendon Press, 1995), 83.

25. William Morris, 'Lectures on Socialism', in *Collected Works*, vol. xxiii (London: Longman Green and Company, 1915).

26. See W. R. Greg's attack on Mrs Gaskell in *Edinburgh Review*, 89 (April 1849).

27. Quoted Humphry House, *The Dickens World* (London: Oxford University Press, 2nd edn., 1943), 46–7.

28. Ann Varty, *A Preface to Oscar Wilde* (Harlow: Longman, 1988), 51.

29. Raymond Williams, *Culture and Society 1780–1950* (London: Chatto & Windus, 1958), 172.

30. Quoted Varty, *Preface to Oscar Wilde*, 55.

31. Philip E. Smith and Michael S. Helfand (eds.), *Oscar Wilde's Oxford Notebooks: A Portrait of a Mind in the Making* (New York: Oxford University Press, 1989), 115.

32. Quoted Stokes, *In the Nineties*, 107.

33. Eltis, *Revising Wilde*, 43.

34. 'Poetry and Prison: Mr. Wilfred Blunt's "In Vinculis"', *Pall Mall Gazette*, 49 (3 Jan. 1889), 3; in Ellmann (ed.), *The Artist as Critic: Critical Writings of Oscar Wilde* (New York: Random house, 1968), 116–20.

35. Walter Pater, *The Renaissance: Studies in Art and Poetry* (London: Macmillan and Co., 1910), p. ix.

36. See Nicholas Daly, *Modernism, Romance and the fin de siècle: Popular Fiction and British Culture 1880–1914* (Cambridge: Cambridge University Press, 1999), 84–116.

37. For discussion of the nineteenth-century dandy as consumer, see Regenia Gagnier, *Idylls of the Marketplace: Oscar Wilde and the Victorian Public* (Stanford, Calif.: Stanford University Press, 1986), 51–99.

CHAPTER 5. Wilde and Intellectual Issues

1. Matthew Arnold, 'On the Study of Celtic Literature', in *Lectures and Essays in Criticism*, ed. R. H. Super (Ann Arbor: University of Michigan Press, 1962), 344.

2. J. A. Symonds, *Studies of the Greek Poets* (London: Smith, Elder & Co., 1879).

3. Philip E. Smith and Michael S. Helfand (eds.), *Oscar Wilde's Oxford Notebooks: A Portrait of Mind in the Making* (New York: Oxford University Press, 1989), 135.

4. Ibid. 162.

5. Frank M. Turner, *Contesting Cultural Authority: Essays in Victorian Intellectual Life* (Cambridge: Cambridge Univeristy Press, 1993), 262.

6. *Athenaeum* (4 Sept. 1880), 301–2; reported in Ellmann, 103–4.

7. Smith and Helfand (eds.), *Oscar Wilde's Oxford Notebooks*, 109.

8. Ibid. 121.

9. Ibid. 110.

10. Ibid. 135.

11. Carole G. Silver, *Strange and Secret Peoples: Fairies and Victorian Consciousness* (Oxford: Oxford University Press, 1999), 139.

12. Max Beerbohm, 'A Lord of Language', *Vanity Fair*, 123 (2 March 1905), 309; repr. in Karl Beckson (ed.), *Oscar Wilde: The Critical Heritage* (London: Routledge & Kegan Paul, 1970), 248–51.

13. J. Edward Chamberlain and Sander Gilman, *Degeneration: The Dark Side of Progress* (New York: Columbia University Press, 1985), 279.

14. Max Nordau, *Degeneration* (London: Heinemann, 1895).

15. E. H. Mikhail (ed.), *Oscar Wilde: Interviews and Recollections* (London: Macmillan, 1979), i. 250.

16. Ibid.

17. Smith and Helfand (eds.), *Oscar Wilde's Oxford Notebooks*, 154.

18. *Athenaeum* (23 July 1881), 103–4; repr. in Beckson (ed.), *Critical Heritage*, 34.

19. *Spectator* (15 Aug. 1881), 54, 1048–9; repr. in Beckson (ed.), *Critical Heritage*, 45.

20. Walter Pater, *The Renaissance: Studies in Art and Poetry* (London: Macmillan and Co., 1910), 236.

21. Turner, *Contesting Cultural Authority*, 45.

22. Matthew Arnold, 'Literature and Dogma', in *Dissent and Dogma*, ed. R. H. Super (Ann Arbor: University of Michigan Press, 1968).

23. *Westminster Review*, 137 (April 1892), 478–80; repr. in Beckson (ed.), *Critical Heritage*, 130.

24. *Lambeth Conferences of 1867, 1878, and 1888* (London: Society for Promoting Christian Knowledge, 1896).

25. Julia Prewitt Brown, *Cosmopolitan Criticism: Oscar Wilde's Philosophy of Art* (Charlottesville: University Press of Virginia, 1997), 88–9.

26. Matthew Arnold, *Culture and Anarchy*, ed. R. H. Super (Ann Arbor: University of Michigan Press, 1965).

27. Pater, 'Winckelmann', in *The Renaissance*, 192.

28. G. S. Street, 'Out of the Depths', *Outlook*, 15 (4 March 1905), 294–5; repr. in Beckson (ed.), *Critical Heritage*, 254.

29. William Blake, 'The Marriage of Heaven and Hell', in *Complete Writings*, ed. Geoffrey Keynes (London: Oxford University Press, 1966), 149.

30. Richard Kearney, 'Introduction', *The Irish Mind: Exploring Intellectual Traditions* (Dublin: Wolfhound Press, 1985).

CHAPTER 6. Recontextualizing Wilde

1. Frank Harris, 'Oscar Wilde' (1915), in E. H. Mikhail (ed.), *Oscar Wilde: Interviews and Recollections* (London: Macmillan, 1979), ii. 424.

2. *Illustrated London News*, quoted Robert Tanitch, *Oscar Wilde on Stage and Screen* (London: Methuen, 1999), 105.

3. W. B. Yeats, 'Introduction', *The Oxford Book of Modern Verse* (Oxford: Clarendon Press, 1936), p. xi.

4. James G. Nelson, *The Early Nineties: A View from the Bodley Head* (Cambridge, Mass.: Harvard University Press, 1971), 301.

5. See Ian Small, *Oscar Wilde: Recent Research* (Greensboro, NC: ELT Press, 2000).

6. Rupert Hart-Davis, *The Letters of Oscar Wilde* (London: Hart-Davis, 1962).

7. John Osborne, 'Preface', 'Introduction', *The Picture of Dorian Gray: A Moral Entertainment* (London: Faber & Faber, 1973), 14.

8. Nicholas De Jongh, *Not in Front of the Audience: Homosexuality on Stage* (London and New York: Routledge, 1992), 35.

9. Leslie and Sewell Stokes, *Oscar Wilde* (London, Martin Secker & Warburg, 1937).

10. Ibid. 41.

11. Alan Sinfield, *The Wilde Century: Effeminacy, Oscar Wilde, and the Queer Movement* (London: Cassell, 1994).

12. Anthony Powell, *A Buyer's Market* (London: Heinemann, 1952), 149.

13. Quoted Tanitch, *Wilde on Stage and Screen*, 383.

14. Bryan Forbes, *Ned's Girl* (London: Elm Tree Books, 1977); quoted Tanitch, *Wilde on Stage and Screen*, 274.

15. Quoted Joel Kaplan, 'Wilde on the Stage', in Peter Raby (ed.), *The Cambridge Companion to Oscar Wilde* (Cambridge: Cambridge University Press, 1997), 262.

16. Noel Coward, *After the Ball* (London: Chappell, 1954).

17. De Jongh, *Not in Front of the Audience*, 33–4.

18. See Michael Coveney, *The Citz: 21 Years of the Glasgow Citizens Theatre* (London: Nick Hern Books, 1990), 176–9.

19. Joel H. Kaplan, 'Staging Wilde's Society Plays: A Conversation with Philip Prowse', *Modern Drama*, 37 (1994), 192–205.

20. Peter Raby, 'Wilde's Comedies of Society', in Peter Raby (ed.), *The Cambridge Companion to Oscar Wilde* (Cambridge: Cambridge University Press, 1997), 154.

21. Michael Billington, *Guardian* (22 Feb. 2002), 18.

22. Peter Hall, 'Oscar and his Plays', Programme, *Lady Windermere's Fan*, Theatre Royal Haymarket (2002).

23. Osborne, 'Introduction', *The Picture of Dorian Gray*.

24. For an account of the performance history of *Salome*, consult William Tydeman and Steven Price (eds.), *Wilde: Salome* (Plays in Production; Cambridge: Cambridge University Press, 1996).

25. Quoted Tanitch, *Wilde on Stage and Screen*, 28.

26. James C. Robertson, *The Hidden Cinema: British Film Censorship in Action, 1913–1975* (London and New York: Routledge, 1989), 122.

27. Roy Carr, *The Rolling Stones: An Illustrated Record* (London: New English Library, 1976), 47.

28. Tom Stoppard, *The Invention of Love* (London: Faber & Faber, 1997), 96.

29. Bernard Shaw, *Our Theatres in the Nineties*, vol. i (London: Constable and Co., 1931), 10–11.

30. A point made by Neil Sammells, *Wilde Style: The Plays and Prose of Oscar Wilde* (London: Longman, 2000), 8–9.

31. Terry Eagleton, *Saint Oscar and Other Plays* (Oxford: Blackwell, 1997), 24.

32. Sammells, *Wilde Style*, 121.

33. Ibid. Wilde's body was moved to Père Lachaise from Bagneux in 1909.

34. Norbert Kohl, *Oscar Wilde: The Works of a Conformist Rebel*, trans. David Henry Wilson (Cambridge: Cambridge University Press, 1988).

FURTHER READING

CONTEXTUAL MATERIAL

Politics and Nationalism

Eldridge, C. C., *Disraeli and the Rise of the New Imperialism* (Cardiff: University of Wales Press, 1996).

Kee, Robert, *The Green Flag* (London: Weidenfeld & Nicolson, 1972).

Laybourn, Keith, *The Rise of Socialism in England, c. 1880-1952* (Stroud: Sutton Publishing, 1997).

White, Terence de Vere, *The Anglo-Irish* (London: Gollancz, 1972).

Woodcock, George, *Anarchism: A History of Libertarian Ideas and Movements* (Harmondsworth: Penguin, 1962).

Sexual Politics: Feminism and Gender

Bland, Lucy, *Banishing the Beast: English Feminism and Sexual Morality 1885-1914* (Harmondsworth: Penguin, 1995).

Dyhouse, Carol, *Feminism and the Family in England 1880-1939* (Oxford: Basil Blackwell, 1989).

Hale, Lesley A., *Sex, Gender and Social Change in Britain since 1880* (Basingstoke: Macmillan, 2000).

Ledger, Sally, 'The New Woman and the Crisis of Victorianism', in Sally Ledger and Scott McCracken (eds.), *Cultural Politics at the Fin de Siècle* (Cambridge: Cambridge University Press, 1995).

Mason, Michael, *The Making of Victorian Sexual Attitudes* (Oxford: Oxford University Press, 1994).

Perkin, Joan, *Women and Marriage in Nineteenth-Century England* (London: Routledge, 1989).

Weeks, Jeffrey, *Sex, Politics, and Society: The Regulation of Sexual Crime since 1800* (London: Longman, 1989)

—— *Coming Out: Homosexual Politics in Britain from the Nineteenth Century to the Present* (London: Quarto, 1977).

Philanthropy and Social Reform

Englander, David, *Poverty and Poor Law Reform from Chadwick to Booth 1834-1914* (London: Longman, 1998).

Jones, Gareth Stedman, *Outcast London* (Harmondsworth: Penguin, 1971).

Laybourn, Keith, *The Evolution of British Social Policy and the Welfare State* (Keele: Keele University Press, 1995).

Crime and Punishment

Cooper, David D., *The Lesson of the Scaffold: Victorian England* (Athens: Ohio University Press, 1974).

Stokes, John, 'Our Dark Places', in his *In the Nineties* (Hemel Hempstead: Harvester-Wheatsheaf, 1989).

Tobias, J. J., *Nineteenth-Century Crime: Prevention and Punishment* (Newton Abbot: David & Charles, 1972).

Wiener, Martin J., *Reconstructing the Criminal: Culture, Law, and Policy in England 1830–1914* (Cambridge: Cambridge University Press, 1990).

Science, Religion, and Evolution

Chamberlain, J. Edward, and Gilman, Sander (eds.), *Degeneration: The Dark Side of Progress* (New York: Columbia University Press, 1985).

Haley, Bruce, 'Wilde's Decadence and the Positivist Tradition', *Victorian Studies*, 28/2 (1985), 215–29.

Heyck, T. W., *The Transformation of Intellectual Life in Victorian England* (London and Sydney: Croom Helm; New York: St Martin's Press, 1982).

Levine, George, *Darwin Among the Novelists: Patterns of Science in Victorian Fiction* (Cambridge, Mass., and London: Harvard University Press, 1988).

McLeod, Hugh, *Religion and Society in England 1850–1914* (Basingstoke: Macmillan, 1996).

Smith, Philip E., and Helfand, Michael S. (eds.), *Oscar Wilde's Oxford Notebooks: A Portrait of Mind in the Making* (New York: Oxford University Press, 1989). (Contains Wilde's 'Commonplace Book' and 'College Notebook'.)

Turner, Frank, *Contesting Cultural Authority: Essays in Victorian Intellectual Life* (Cambridge: Cambridge University Press, 1993).

Aestheticism, Leisure, and Commodity Culture

Bailey, Peter, *Leisure and Class in Victorian England: Rational Recreation and the Contest for Control 1830–1885* (London: Methuen, 1978).

Freedman, Jonathan, *Professions of Taste: Henry James, British Aestheticism, and Commodity Culture* (Stanford, Calif.: Stanford University Press, 1990).

Gagnier, Regenia, *Idylls of the Marketplace: Oscar Wilde and the Victorian Public* (Stanford, Calif.: Stanford University Press, 1986).

Richards, Thomas, *The Commodity Culture of Victorian England: Advertising and Spectacle 1851–1914* (Stanford, Calif.: Stanford University Press, 1990).

BIOGRAPHY AND CRITICISM

Beckson, Karl (ed.), *Oscar Wilde: The Critical Heritage* (London: Routledge & Kegan Paul, 1970).

—— *The Oscar Wilde Encyclopedia* (New York: AMS Press, 1998).

Behrendt, Patricia Flanagan, *Oscar Wilde: Eros and Aesthetics* (London: Macmillan, 1991).

Brown, Julia Prewitt, *Cosmopolitan Criticism: Oscar Wilde's Philosophy of Art* (Charlottesville: University of Virginia Press, 1997).

Cave, Richard Allen, 'Wilde Designs: Some Thoughts about Recent British Productions of His Plays', *Modern Drama*, 37 (1994), 175–81.

Clements, Patricia, 'Wilde: The Brotherhood of the Arts', in her *Baudelaire and the English Tradition* (Princeton: Princeton University Press, 1985).

Coakley, Davis, *Oscar Wilde: The Importance of Being Irish* (Dublin: Town House, 1994).

Cohen, Philip, *The Moral Vision of Oscar Wilde* (London: Associated University Press, 1978).

Danson, Lawrence, *Wilde's Intentions: The Artist in his Criticism* (Oxford: Clarendon Press, 1997).

Dellamora, Richard, 'Oscar Wilde, Social Purity, and *An Ideal Husband*', *Modern Drama*, 37 (1994), 120–38.

Dollimore, Jonathan, 'Different Desires: Subjectivity and Trangression in Wilde and Gide', *Textual Practice*, 1 (1987), 48–67.

Eagleton, Terry, 'Oscar and George', in his *Heathcliff and the Great Hunger* (London: Verso, 1995), 320–41.

Ellmann, Richard, *Oscar Wilde* (London: Hamish Hamilton, 1987; reissued Harmondsworth: Penguin, 1988).

Eltis, Sos, *Revising Wilde: Society and Subversion in the Plays of Oscar Wilde* (Oxford: Clarendon Press, 1996).

Frankel, Nicholas, *Oscar Wilde's Decorated Books* (Ann Arbor: University of Michigan Press, 2000).

Gagnier, Regenia (ed.), *Critical Essays on Oscar Wilde* (New York: G. K. Hall & Co., 1991).

Guy, Josephine M., 'Oscar Wilde: Traditional Iconoclast', in her *The British Avant-Garde: The Theory and Politics of Tradition* (Hemel Hempstead: Harvester-Wheatsheaf, 1991).

—— and Small, Ian, *Oscar Wilde's Profession: Writing and the Culture Industry in the Late Nineteenth Century* (Oxford: Oxford University Press, 2000).

Hyde, H. Montgomery, *The Trials of Oscar Wilde* (New York: Dover, 1973).

—— *Oscar Wilde: A Biography* (London: Penguin, 2001).

Kaplan, Joel H., 'A Puppet's Power: George Alexander, Clement Scott, and the Replotting of *Lady Windermere's Fan*', *Theatre Notebook*, 46/2 (1992), 59–73.

—— 'Staging Wilde's Society Plays: A Conversation with Philip Prowse', *Modern Drama*, 37 (1994), 192–205.

—— and Stowell, Sheila, *Theatre and Fashion: Oscar Wilde to the Suffragettes* (Cambridge: Cambridge University Press, 1988).

Knight, G. Wilson, 'Oscar Wilde', in his *The Christian Renaissance* (London: Methuen, rev. edn. 1960).

Knox, Melissa, *Oscar Wilde: A Long and Lovely Suicide* (New Haven and London: Yale University Press, 1994).

Kohl, Norbert, *Oscar Wilde: The Works of a Conformist Rebel* (Cambridge: Cambridge University Press, 1988).

McCormack, Jerusha (ed.), *Wilde the Irishman* (New Haven and London: Yale University Press, 1998).

Martin, Robert K., 'Oscar Wilde and the Fairy Tale: "The Happy Prince" as Self-Dramatization', *Studies in Short Fiction*, 16 (1979), 74–7.

Mikhail, E. H. (ed.), *Oscar Wilde: Interviews and Recollections*, 2 vols. (London: Macmillan, 1979).

Nassaar, Christopher, *Into the Demon Universe: A Literary Exploration of Oscar Wilde* (New Haven: Yale University Press, 1974).

Osborne, John, 'Introduction', *The Picture of Dorian Gray: A Moral Entertainment* (London: Faber & Faber, 1973).

Pine, Richard, *The Thief of Reason: Oscar Wilde and Modern Ireland* (Dublin: Gill & Macmillan, 1995).

Powell, Kerry, *Oscar Wilde and the Theatre of the 1890s* (Cambridge: Cambridge University Press, 1990).

Raby, Peter, *Oscar Wilde* (Cambridge: Cambridge University Press, 1988).

—— (ed.), *The Cambridge Companion to Oscar Wilde* (Cambridge: Cambridge University Press, 1997).

Rowell, George, 'The Truth About *Vera*', *Nineteenth Century Theatre*, 21/2 (1993), 94–100.

Sammells, Neil, 'Oscar Wilde, the Fairy Tale, and the Critics', in Bruce Stewart (ed.), *That Other World: The Supernatural and the Fantastic in Irish Literature and its Contexts* (Gerrards Cross: Colin Smythe, 1998), ii. 228–37.

—— *Wilde Style: The Plays and Prose of Oscar Wilde* (London: Longman, 2000).

Sandulescu, C. George (ed.), *Rediscovering Oscar Wilde* (Gerrards Cross: Colin Smythe, 1994).

Satzinger, Christa, *The French Influences on Oscar Wilde's 'The Picture of Dorian Gray' and 'Salome'* (Lewiston, NY: Mellon Press, 1994).

Shewan, Rodney, *Oscar Wilde: Art and Egotism* (London: Macmillan, 1977).

Sinfield, Alan, *The Wilde Century: Effeminacy, Oscar Wilde, and the Queer Movement* (London: Cassell, 1994).

Small, Ian, 'Oscar Wilde', in his *Conditions for Criticism: Authority, Knowledge and Literature in the Late Nineteenth Century* (Oxford: Clarendon Press, 1991).

—— *Oscar Wilde Revalued: An Essay on New Materials and Methods of Research* (Greensboro, NC: ELT Press, 1993).

—— *Oscar Wilde: Recent Research: A Supplement to 'Oscar Wilde Revalued'* (Greensboro, NC: ELT Press, 2000).

Stokes, John, *Oscar Wilde: Myths, Miracles and Imitations* (Cambridge: Cambridge University Press, 1996).

Tanitch, Robert, *Oscar Wilde on Stage and Screen* (London: Methuen, 1999).

Tydeman, William, and Price, Steven (eds.), *Wilde: Salome* (Plays in Production; Cambridge: Cambridge University Press, 1996).

Varty, Ann, *A Preface to Oscar Wilde* (Harlow: Longman, 1988).

Willoughby, Guy, *Art and Christhood: The Aesthetics of Oscar Wilde* (London: Associated University Presses, 1993).

Worth, Katharine, *Oscar Wilde* (London: Macmillan, 1983).

WEBSITES

http://www.literaryhistory.com/19thC/WILDE.htm   Links   to   literary
essays and articles, biographies, online texts, and other Oscar Wilde sites.

http://65.107.211.206/victorian/decadence/wilde/wildeov.html   The Victorian Web section on Oscar Wilde containing a biography, the social and
political context of the period, sections on imagery and characterization,
and links to related websites.

http:homepages.gold.ac.uk/oscholars   Founded in June 2001, an electronic
journal published monthly for the exchange of information on current
research, publications, and productions concerning Oscar Wilde and his
circle.

http://www.1890s.org/sub/wilde.htm   Links to sites for general information, societies, journals, discussions, photographs, and exhibitions and
online images of illustrations by Aubrey Beardsley.

www.oscarwilde.com   Website for the 1997 film *Wilde* starring Stephen Fry,
audio clips of Fry reading extracts from 'The Selfish Giant', *De Profundis*,
and *The Ballad of Reading Gaol*, introduction to Wilde, quiz, and links.

www.humnet.ucla.edu/humnet/clarklib/wildphot   Original photographs of
Wilde and his circle owned by the Clark Library.

http://www.indecorous.org/wilde/   Up-to-date news and archive of Oscar
Wilde stories, previews, and reviews of films and plays, and a biography.

www.sfmuseum.org/hist5/bierce   Columnist Ambrose Bierce's denunciation of Wilde's 'opulence of twaddle', printed following a lecture in San
Francisco in 1882.

http://users.ox.ac.uk/~sedm1657/oscar.html   Photographs and links, Oscar
Wilde Society at Oxford University.

http://www.law.umkc.edu/faculty/projects/ftrials/wilde/wilde.htm   Essays,
transcripts, manuscripts and letters, images, relating to the three legal trials
with Wilde's writings while on trial and in prison.

http://www.upword.com/wilde/dorgray.html#wb   Link to online texts,
Koen Van Cauwenberge's dissertation on *De Profundis*, and an image of
Wilde's burial site.

http://www.showgate.com/tots/gross/wildeweb.html   List of Oscar Wilde
sites on the web.

ONLINE TEXTS

http://www.bibliomania.com/o/o/frameset.html   Online texts and study
guides, a general introduction to Wilde and links.

http://www.hoboes.com/html/FireBlade/Wilde/   Complete online texts
of *The Importance of Being Earnest*, *The Picture of Dorian Gray*, 'The Selfish Giant', and poetry with links to other useful sites.

http://www.planetmonk.com/wilde/   Online collection of texts indexed and divided into chapter links including 'The Happy Prince', 'The Portrait of Mr W. H.', *A House of Pomegranates*, and *The Picture of Dorian Gray.*

http://www.everypoet.com/archive/poetry/Oscar_Wilde/oscar_wilde_contents.htm   Wilde's poetry online.

http://www.ucc.ie/celt/et19wilde.html   Works in HTML or plain text versions.

http://www.burrows.com/found.html   Extracts from Wilde's speeches given during a tour of America in 1882 on the aesthetics of design in architecture.

FILM, OPERA, AND BALLET
ADAPTATIONS

The following lists some of the significant adaptations of Wilde's work for the cinema, opera, and ballet (media other than films are indicated in bold type), and films about Wilde. For a comprehensive chronology of Wilde in performance, readers should consult Robert Tanitch's *Oscar Wilde on Stage and Screen* (London: Methuen, 1999).

Oscar Wilde (GB; director Gregory Ratoff, 1960, with Robert Morley in the title role and Ralph Richardson as Sir Edward Carson).

The Trials of Oscar Wilde (GB; in US *The Man with the Green Carnation*; director Ken Hughes, 1960, with Peter Finch as Wilde and James Mason as Edward Carson).

OW (**ballet** by Joe Layton, performed by the Royal Ballet Company at Sadler's Wells Theatre, London, 1972).

Oscar (**ballet** by Domy Reiter-Soffer, performed by the Irish National Ballet in Cork, Ireland, 1989).

Wilde (GB; director Brian Gilbert, 1997, with Stephen Fry as Wilde and Jude Law as Lord Alfred Douglas).

Der Zwerg ('The Dwarf', **opera** version of 'The Birthday of the Infanta' by Alexander von Zemlinsky, with libretto by Georg Klaren, Opera House, Cologne, 1922, conducted by Otto Klemperer).

The Canterville Ghost (US; director Jules Dassin, 1943; with Charles Laughton as the Ghost).

The Shadow and the Sea (adaptation of 'The Fisherman and his Soul'; US; director Charles Guggenheim, 1963).

Eine Florentinische Tragödie ('A Florentine Tragedy', **opera** by Alexander von Zemlinsky, with libretto by Max Meyerfeld, Opera House, Stuttgart, 1917, conducted by Max von Schillings).

The Happy Prince (GB; animated film by Peter Pearce, 1960).

The Happy Prince (British **opera** with music and libretto by Malcolm Williamson, at the Farnham Festival, 1965).

The Happy Prince (premiere of British **musical** by Sue Casson at Buxton Opera House, 1992).

An Ideal Husband (GB; director Alexander Korda, 1947; with Michael Wilding as Lord Goring and Paulette Goddard as Mrs Cheveley).

Idealny Muzh (Russia; director Viktor Georiyev, 1981).
An Ideal Husband (GB; director Oliver Parker, 1999).
An Ideal Husband (GB; director Bill Cartlidge, 1999).

The Importance of Being Earnest (GB; director Anthony Asquith, 1952, with Michael Redgrave as John Worthing and Edith Evans as Lady Bracknell).
Found in a Handbag (premiere of Allon Bacon's **musical** at Theatre Royal Margate, 1957).

Lady Windermere's Fan (GB; director Fred Paul, 1916).
Lady Windermere's Fan (US; director Ernst Lubitsch, 1925, with Ronald Colman as Lord Darlington).
The Young Lady's Fan (adaptation of *Lady Windermere's Fan*: China; director Shen Hung, 1926).
Historia de una Mala Mujer (adaptation of *Lady Windermere's Fan*, English title *The Story of a Bad Woman*: Argentina; director Luis Sanlavsky, 1948).
The Fan (adaptation of *Lady Windermere's Fan*: US: director Otto Preminger, 1949, with George Sanders as Lord Darlington).

Flesh and Fantasy (adaptation of 'Lord Arthur Savile's Crime': US; director Julien Duvivier, 1943).

The Nightingale and the Rose (premiere of **ballet** by Anton Dolin, music by H. Fraser-Simon, at the London Coliseum, 1927).

Dorian Grays Portræt (Denmark; director Alex Strom, 1910).
Portret Doriana Greya (Russia; director Vsevolod Meyerhold, 1915).
The Picture of Dorian Gray (GB; director Fred W. Durrant, 1916).
Das Bildnis des Dorian Gray (Germany; director Richard Oswald, 1917).
The Picture of Dorian Gray (Hungary, 1918; with Bela Lugosi as Lord Henry Wotton).
The Picture of Dorian Gray (US; director Albert Lewin, 1945; with George Sanders as Lord Henry Wotton and Angela Lansbury as Sibyl Vane).
The Secret of Dorian Gray (American title of West German/Italian production; director Massimo Dallamano, 1970; with Herbert Lom as Lord Henry Wotton and Richard Todd as Basil Hallward).
The Picture of Dorian Gray (premiere of **opera** by Lowell Liebermann at the Opera House, Monte Carlo, 1996).

The Remarkable Rocket (Canada; animated film; diector Gerald Potterton, 1975).

Salome (**opera** by Richard Strauss premiere at the Royal Opera House,

Dresden; director Wilhelm Wirk; conductor Ernest von Schuch, 1905; British premiere at the Royal Opera House, London; director Louis Verande; conductor Thomas Beecham, 1910).

Salomé (**ballet** by Mikhail Fokhine, performed at St Petersburgh by Ida Rubenstein, 1908).

Salome (Italy; director Dr Garriazzo, 1913).

La Tragédie de Salomé (**ballet** by Boris Ramonov, music by Florent Schmitt, by Les Ballets Russes at the Théâtre des Champs-Élysées, Paris, 1913).

Salome (US; director J. Gordon Edwards, 1918).

Salome (**ballet** by Flemming Flindt, music Peter Maxwell Davies, Cirkus Theater, Copenhagan, 1978).

Salome's Last Dance (GB; director Ken Russell, 1987).

The Selfish Giant (Canada; director Peter Sander, 1972).
The Selfish Giant (GB; director V. H. McGrath, 1973).

A Woman of No Importance (GB; director Denison Clift, 1921).
Une femme sans importance (France; director Jean Choux, 1937).
Una mujer sin importancia (Spain; director Luis Bayon Herrera, 1945).

INDEX

Ackerman, Robert Allan 182

Acton, Lord 45

actresses 21, 29, 43, 67, 80–1, 89, 90, 91, 105, 171, 179

Adam Bede (Eliot) 40

adultery 40, 43

advertising 10, 57, 58–9, 66, 134

aestheticism 4, 10, 11, 15, 17, 36–7, 46, 60, 100, 150; in all cultural areas 191; communal spirit of 163–5; consumerism and 135; ethics and 160–1; insouciance 69; poor and 125–6; rationalism and 152–3; romance novels 77

Afghanistan 101

agriculture 32, 39, 42

Alexander, George 20, 25, 69, 72, 89, 106, 108, 168

Alexander II, Tsar of Russia 87

Alexander III, Tsar of Russia 87

Allen, Grant 103, 104–5

Allen, Maud 182

altruism 122, 123, 140

American Civil War 37–8

anarchism 15, 34–5, 37, 87, 102, 104, 126, 128, 129

ancient Greeks 3, 4, 125, 139–40, 152, 164

Andersen, Hans Christian 80, 82

Anglo-Boer War 102

animal magnetism 141–2

Anouilh, Jean 179

anthropology 152

Antoine, André 88

aphorisms 94–5, 118

Archer, William 90–1, 110, 117

architecture 57

aristocracy 44–5, 49, 107, 172, 173, 177

Aristotle 140, 152, 153

Armstrong, Revd Richard 49

Arnold, Dr Thomas 60, 157

Arnold, Matthew 5, 6, 17, 37, 46, 47, 55, 61, 62–3, 64, 73, 100, 104, 147; on aestheticism 125–6; on Celtic and Anglo-Saxon qualities 83, 139; on communal spirit 165; on gospel of 'Culture' 157–8, 159, 163; on ideal of art 153

art 16–17, 73, 135, 137, 153, 164; biblical 112; criticism 17, 62, 63; Hegel on 154; New Hedonism 19; revelation of the spirit 155; treatment of 181

art nouveau 36

Arts and Crafts Movement 73, 134

Athenaeum 156

athleticism 60

avant-garde 73, 74

Bagehot, Walter 122

Balfour, A. J. 39

Balzac, Honoré de 78

baptism 163

Barlas, John 18, 35

Barratt, Thomas 58

Barrett, Lawrence 68

Barrett, Michael 53

Barrie, J. M. 81, 82

Baudelaire, Charles 15, 17, 78, 105–6, 154, 166

BBC 178, 186

Beale, Edmond 33

Beardsley, Aubrey 19, 23, 68, 70, 71, 74

Beaton, Cecil 174

Beck, S. William 67

Beerbohm, Max 19, 23, 26, 69, 168

Beerbohm Tree, Herbert 21, 89, 168, 176, 177

Beere, Mrs Bernard 21

Benson, S. H. 58

Bentley, Eric 186

Berkoff, Steven 182

Bernhardt, Sarah 21, 29, 89, 90, 180

Besant, Annie 48, 112, 125

Besant, Walter 71, 123, 124

Biograph 64, 69

birth prevention (control) 48, 112

'Birthday of the Infanta, The,' *see House of Pomegranates, The* (Wilde)

Black, William 82–3

blackmail 24

Blackwood, William 71, 75

Blackwood's Magazine 36, 62, 97

Blake, William 128, 160, 166, 189
blasphemy laws 47
'Bloody Sunday' (1887) 34–5, 37
Blunt, Wilfred Scawen 129
Bodichon, Mrs Barbara 41
Bodley Head (publishing house) 71–2, 73, 74
bohemianism 18, 36–7, 168–9
bombings 38
Booth, William 55
Bouchereau, Gustave 112
Boucicault, Dion 65
Bourget, Paul 78
boycotts 39
Bradlaugh, Charles 48
Bright, John 44, 52
British Empire 59–60, 60, 102–3, 129
Broccoli, Albert R. ('Cubby') 183
Brontë, Charlotte 46, 76, 150
Brooke, Rupert 102
Brothers Grimm 80
Broughton, Lord 41
Browning, Robert 47, 84
Browning Society 158
Buckle, H. T. 152
Bulwer-Lytton, Edward 181
Burgess, Guy 183
burlesque 81
Burns, John 34, 130
Butler, Josephine 48
Butt, Isaac 38

Campbell, Lady Archibald 105
'Canterville Ghost, The', *see Lord Arthur Savile's Crime and Other Stories* **(Wilde)**
capital punishment 51, 52–3, 127, 131
Capital Punishment Within Prisons Bill 52, 53
capitalism 31
Carlyle, Thomas 33, 37, 61, 62, 78–9, 80
Carroll, Lewis 80
Carson, Edward 25, 39, 98, 188
Cartlidge, Bill 179
Cassell and Company 66, 75
Cavendish, Lord Frederick 14, 39
Celtic school of literature 19, 21, 82–4, 139
censorship 21, 87–98, 111, 171, 175, 183
Century Guild Hobby Horse (quarterly periodical) 73
Chamberlain, Joseph 59

Chameleon (undergraduate magazine) 27, 118
Chapman and Hall (publishers) 75
charity 121–3
Charity Organization Society 33
Chartist movement 31
Chekhov, Anton 177
child custody 42, 43, 107–8
child prostitution 48, 66
children 42; literature for 76, 79, 80; in penal system 52, 130–1
Christ figure 27, 165–7
Christian Socialist action groups 121
Christianity 129, 157–9, 159, 163
Chuang Tzu 126
circulating libraries 75, 92–3
Citizens' Theatre, Glasgow 176–8
Clarke, Sir Edward 25, 185
Clifford, William Kingdom 143
Cobden, Richard 52
Colenso, Bishop 157
Coleridge, Samuel Taylor 97, 132
collectors 136
Colman, Ronald 173
commodity culture 10, 73–4, 190
community 163–5
Conrad, Joseph 120, 168
consumerism 56, 58–9, 134–8, 190
Contagious Diseases Act 48
Cook, Edward T. 66
Cook, Thomas 57
Corelli, Marie 114
COS (Charitable Organization Society) 54
Court and Society Review 62
Courtney, W. L. 66, 68
courtship 118–19
Coward, Noel 174–5
Crane, Walter 86
crime 115, 126, 127, 149–50
criminal anthropology 127
Criminal Law Amendment Act (1885) 45, 49
Crockett, S. R. 82
Cruikshank, George 80, 92
curtain-speeches 21, 69
cycling 58

Daily Chronicle 28, 52, 62, 99, 127, 130, 131, 133
dandyism 8, 13, 15–16, 58, 116, 125, 126, 171, 172

Danson, Lawrence 170
Dante Aligheri 2
Darwin, Charles 42, 54, 115, 140, 144, 157
Davidson, John 50, 56, 113, 120
day-trippers 57
De Quincey, Thomas 128
decadence 19, 36, 49, 74, 150, 153, 191
Decadents 166
Dial (magazine) 18
Dickens, Charles 47–8, 50, 52, 77, 80, 92, 121, 122, 123, 136, 142, 150
Dilke, Sir Charles 33, 34, 43
Disraeli, Benjamin 32, 33, 59, 150, 167
divorce 40–1, 43, 46
Divorce and Matrimonial Causes Act (1857) 40–1, 46
Dostoevsky, Fyodor 127–8
Douglas, Lord Alfred (Bosie) 22–5, 26, 27, 28, 29, 30, 148–9, 172, 183, 186
Dowden, Ernest 97
Dowie, Menie Muriel 105
Doyle, Arthur Conan 64, 69, 76, 136
D'Oyly Carte, Richard 11
Dramatic Review 62
Drumlanrig, Lord 24
Du Cane, Sir Edmund 51, 127
du Maurier, George 10, 12
Dublin 1–2, 14, 39, 44
Duchess of Padua, The (Wilde) 20, 68, 99
Dunne, Father Cuthbert 30

Eagleton, Terry 188
earnestness 43, 117, 140
economic depression 32
Edinburgh Review 36, 76, 122
education 55–6, 61–2, 116
Edward, Prince of Wales (later Edward VII) 11, 33, 43, 45, 47
effeminacy 172–3
Egerton, George 42
electric lighting 31
Elementary Education Act (1870) 61
Eliot, George 50, 77, 107
Ellis, Havelock 49
Ellmann, Richard 102, 186
Eltis, Sos 128
Emerson, Ralph Waldo 103
Encyclopaedia Britannica 140
English Players, The 173
entertaining 56–7

Established Church 158–9, 162–3
ethics 156–67
Evangelicalism 47–8, 56
Evans, Edith 174, 187
evolution 40, 42, 139, 140, 143, 157
Ewart, William 52
examinations 55
Examiner of Plays 88, 89, 175

Fabian Society 36, 55, 88, 103, 125
fairy-tales 79–80, 120–1, 122, 151, 161, 166
faith healing 47
Faithfull, Marianne 185
'fallen women' literary theme 106, 107, 114
fashion 58
feminism 41, 42, 43, 48–9, 67, 112
Fénéon, Felix 128
Fenianism 37–8, 52–3
Field Day Theatre Company 188
Fielding, Henry 52, 92
films: Wilde's life 170, 182–3, 186; Wilde's plays 171, 173, 174, 179, 191
fin de siècle 74, 168–9
Finch, Peter 182–3, 184
Firth, Peter 171
Fish, Arthur 67
'Fisherman and his Soul, The,' *see House of Pomegranates, The* (Wilde)
'Five Pirates' trial (1864) 52
Flaubert, Gustave 77
flogging 52
folk-tales 79–80, 84, 86
football 58
Foote, George William 47
Forbes, Archibald 65
Fort, Paul 89
Fortnightly Review 62, 68, 93, 94, 97, 104, 123
France: bohemianism 37; influence on English literature 76–7, 87; power of suggestion 142; theatre in 88, 90; Wilde revivals in 179
Franco-Prussia war 33
Freeman, E. A. 39
Freemasonry 7
French Symbolists 15, 17, 84, 89, 112, 128, 153
Frith, William Powell 11, 12
Froude, J. A. 83–4, 85
Fry, Stephen 170, 186, 187

Furnell, John 183

Gambon, Michael 186
Gaskell, Elizabeth 122
Gautier, Théophile 15, 105–6, 136
gay rights movement 170
gender 105–6, 116–17, 118–19, 189
geology 46
George, Henry 34, 55, 122
German fairy-tales 82
German Romanticism 80, 97
Germany 31–2, 38
Gide, André 18, 99
Gielgud, John 171, 174
Gilbert, W. S. 46, 56, 63
Gilbert and Sullivan 11, 190
Gilpin, Charles 52
Gissing, George 50, 58, 60, 68, 69, 76, 92,
    122, 123, 151
Gladstone, Herbert J. 52
Gladstone, William 32, 33, 38, 43, 45, 59
Godwin, E. W. 17, 43, 105
Goethe, Johann Wolfgang von 139, 140
golf 58
gothic novels 79
Gothic Revival 153
Gower, Lord Ronald Sutherland 45
gradualism 36, 125
Graham, R. B. Cunninghame 34–5,
    59–60
Grand, Sarah 42, 105
Grant, Richard E. 175
Gray, John 18, 22, 68, 74
Great Exhibition (1851) 10, 31, 56, 134
Great Famine (Ireland) 1, 31, 54
Greg, W. R. 122
Grein, Jacob T. 88, 182
Griffiths, Trevor 188
Guardianship of Infants Act (1886) 42,
    107–8, 109

Haggard, Rider 60, 76, 77
Hall, Peter 179–80
Hallam, Arthur 97
Happy Prince and Other Tales, The
    (Wilde) 80–1, 87, 120–1, 122–3, 166,
    186
Hardy, Thomas 42–3, 50, 53, 69, 82, 92,
    102, 106, 114, 151
Hare, David 188
Harris, Frank 68, 168
Harrison, Frederic 46

Hart-Davis, Rupert 99
Havergal, Giles 176–7
Hawk (tabloid newspaper) 65
Hawkesworth, John 186
hedonism 159–60
Hegel, Georg Wilhelm Friedrich 15,
    153–4
Hellenism 3, 4, 125, 139–40, 142, 153
Henley, William 85, 93
heredity 150–1
history 151–2
Hoffmann, E. T. A. 80, 82
Hogarth, William 92
holidays 56, 57
Holland, Vyvyan 177
Holyoake, George 48
Home Rule 14, 18, 32, 35, 38–40, 45, 59,
    129
homoeroticism 164
homosexuality 19, 22–3, 25, 27–8, 29, 60,
    93–4, 95; change in the law on 175,
    185; in *Importance of Being Earnest*
    118, 175, 176; legislation on 49;
    recognition of 171–3; 'temporary and
    curable madness' 149–50; upper class
    45; Wolfenden Commission 183
honours system 44
Hood, Jacomb 86
Horne, Herbert 73
House of Commons 32, 35, 90, 93
House of Lords 34
House of Pomegranates, A **(Wilde)** 71,
    74, 81, 120–1, 146–7, 161, 166
Housman, A. E. 186
Hughes, Ken 183, 185
Hughes, Thomas 60
Hugo, Victor 21, 181
humanitarianism 165
Humphreys, Charles 24
Hutchinson, George 76
Huxley, T. H. 46
Huysmans, J.-K. 95, 112, 137, 141
Hyde, H. Montgomery 183
Hyndman, Henry Mayers 34, 122
Hytner, Nicholas 175

Ibsen, Henrik 21, 43, 88, 89, 90, 110, 113,
    115
ice-skating 58
Ideal Husband, An **(Wilde)** 20, 22, 29,
    69, 114–17, 163, 168; conscience/
    cowardice link 141; film versions 174,

179, 191; philanthropy ridiculed in
124; revivals of 178, 179–80; satire of
tabloid journalism 65

illustrators 74, 80, 86

ILP (Independent Labour Party) 36, 55,
88

Image, Selwyn 73

imperialism 38, 39, 40, 59–60, 129

Importance of Being Earnest, The
(Wilde) 20, 22, 24, 29, 69, 72, 117–19,
189; demise of traditional power 32;
gay subtext 118, 175, 176; heredity in
151; musical adaptation of 175; press
as running joke in 63; revivals of 168,
176–7, 179, 187, 191; satire on
Established Church 162–3

Independent Theatre, London 88,
182

individualism 103–4, 115, 125, 126, 140,
143, 148, 150, 153, 163–5

industrialization 31–2

insanity 113

Intentions (Wilde) 71

Invincibles, The (terrorists) 14

Ireland 14, 32, 37–40, 59; Great Famine
1, 31, 54; literature 82, 83–4, 189; mass
emigration 1; political patriots 129;
poverty 54; society in 44

iron and steel industry 31

Irving, Henry 90

Italy 38

Jackson, Emily 42

Jackson, Holbrook 36, 168

Jagger, Mick 185

James, Henry 31, 72, 77, 78, 81, 95–6,
136, 192

James, Jesse 127

Jane Eyre (Brontë) 150

Jennings, Alex 175

Johnson, Lionel 22

Jones, Henry Arthur 181

journalism 40, 61, 62–8, 96

Jowett, Benjamin 154

Joyce, James 40, 96–7, 173

Jubilee celebrations 34, 58–9, 60

Jude the Obscure (Hardy) 43, 50

juvenile offenders 52, 130–1

Kailyard literature 82

Kaufman, Moisés 188

Keats, John 73

Kelmscott Press 73

Kemp, Lindsay 182

Kiberd, Declan 189

Kingsley, Charles 80, 121, 123

Kipling, Rudyard 60

Knowles, James 45

Korda, Alexander 174

Kropotkin, Peter 35, 129

Labouchere, Henry 49

Lady Chatterley's Lover (Lawrence) 97,
98

Lady Windermere's Fan (Wilde) 20, 69,
72, 106–8, 162, 163, 168, 173, 174–5,
175, 178, 179–80

laissez-faire liberalism 31, 50, 103

Lambeth Conference of Anglican bishops
(1888) 162

landowners 32, 34, 38, 122

Lane, John 58, 71–2, 96, 169

Lang, Andrew 68, 80

Langtry, Lillie 11, 16, 43, 58

Law, Jude 187

Law Amendment Society 41

lawn tennis 58

Lawrence, D. H. 6, 96–7

Le Gallienne, Richard 19, 68, 99, 169

Lecky, William 152

Leclerq, Pierre 107

Leeds Mercury 66

left-wing politics 33, 34–5

leisure 56–7, 60

lesbianism 49

Liberal Party 32, 33, 36, 38, 59

Liberal Unionists 45

Liberty and Property Defence League
103

libraries 75, 92–3

Linton, Mrs Eliza Lynn 104–5

Lippincott's Monthly Magazine 93

literacy 61, 62

literature: animal magnetism in 141–2;
censorship of 91–8; children's 76, 79,
80; commodification of 73–4; criticism
of philanthropy in 122; expansion in
consumerism 58–9; 'fallen women'
theme 106, 107, 114; fragmentation of
61, 75–6; heretical lyricism in 47; ideal
of aristocratic ease in 69; Irish 82,
83–4, 189; 'loss of faith' theme in 157;
manliness in 60; nature *versus* nurture
theme in 150–1; 'New Woman' 42–3,

95, 104–5, 113–14, 115–17;
non-realistic forms of 76–87; as a
profession 71; Pygmalion story in 136;
redemptive suffering in 50; Salome
iconography 111–12
Little Dorrit (Dickens) 47–8
Lloyd, Otho 18
lobby groups 32–3, 41
Lom, Herbert 171
Lombroso, Cesare 127, 149, 150
London society 11, 44–5
*Lord Arthur Savile's Crime and Other
Stories* (Wilde) 74, 81, 104, 136–7
Louÿs, Pierre 23
Lubitsch, Ernst 173
Lugné-Poë, Aurélien 91, 181
Lugosi, Bela 171
Lyell, Sir Charles 46

Mac Liammóir, Micheál 183
McClure's Magazine 68
MacDonald, George 80
Mackmurdo, Arthur 73
McLaren, Laura 67
Maclean, Donald 183
Macmillan and Sons (publishers) 75, 86
Maeterlinck, Maurice 21, 181–2
Magdalen College, Oxford 5, 6
Mahaffy, John Pentland 4, 152
Mallarmé, Stéphane 15
Malthusian League 112
Mann, Tom 34, 35–6
marriage 41–2, 109–10, 111, 114–17,
118
Married Women's Property Act (1882)
41, 111
Martin, Thomas 130
Marx, Eleanor 34
Marx, Karl 33, 123
mass culture 56
Massingham, H. W. 130
masturbation 9
materialism 125–6
Mathews and Lane (publishers) 58, 74–5
Matrimonial Causes Act (1884) 41
Maturin, Charles (great-uncle) 2, 28, 79,
127
Maupassant, Guy de 77
Maurice, F. D. 121
Meagher, Thomas 37
Mearns, Andrew 54
Meinhold, J. W. 79

Melmoth the Wanderer (Maturin) 2, 28,
79, 127
mental illness 149
Merimée, Prosper 136
Mesmer, Franz Anton 142
Meyerhold, Vsevolod 171
'Michael Field' (poet) 105
middle class 18; entertaining 57;
marriage 109–10; morality 21, 44;
radicalism 33, 35; women 41, 43, 67
Miles, Frank 11
Mill, John Stuart 50, 62, 158
Millais, John 11
Milner, Alfred 66
misogyny 119
Mitchel, John 14, 37, 38
Modern Painters (Ruskin) 63
Modjeska, Helena 11
monasticism 113
Moore, Augustus 65
Moore, George 88, 92–3, 96
morality 43, 44, 48–9, 93–4, 108–11, 112,
115, 117, 156
Moreau, Gustave 112, 114
Morley, John 68
Morley, Robert 172, 182, 184–5
Morris, Clara 88
Morris, William 34, 35, 59, 73, 74, 100,
103, 120, 123, 126
Morrison, Jim 190
Morrison, Revd William Douglas 130
Most, Johann 87
motherhood 41–2, 107–9, 110–11
Mudie's Select Library 75, 92
Müller, Friedrich Max 7, 152
Mulrenin, Bernard 2
Munte, Lina 91
Murray, John 71
Myers, Frederic 158
myth-making 152

Naden, Constance 105
Napoleon III, Emperor of France 33
Nation (nationalist journal) 1
National Land League 39
National Observer 36
National Union of Gas Workers 36
National Vigilance Association 48, 93
nationalism 37–40, 83, 100–1
natural selection 157; *see also* evolution
Neeson, Liam 188
Nevill, Lady Dorothy 44

Neville, John 183
New Hedonism 19, 37, 141
New Journalism 63–6, 96
New Testament 81, 102, 103, 111, 166
'New Woman' literature 42–3, 95, 104–5,
    113–14, 115–17
Newdigate Prize for English verse
    (Oxford University) 9, 11
Newman, John Henry 4, 5, 6, 7, 46, 55
Newnes, George 76
newspapers, *see* press
Nicholson, John Gambril 118
Nightingale, Florence 40
nihilism 128
Nineteenth Century (periodical) 17, 45,
    62, 64, 68
Nonconformists 33, 43, 44
Nordau, Max 149, 150, 155
Norton, Mrs Caroline 41
nouveaux riches 44–5
Nutt, Alfred Trübner 86
nymphomania 112, 113

Obscene Publications Act (1857) 91
O'Connor, Ulick 188
Oliphant, Mrs 82
Oliver Twist (Dickens) 50, 150
Omar Khayyam Club 69
Origin of Species, The (Darwin) 54
Orton, Arthur 44
Osborne, John 171, 173, 181
Oscar Wilde (play) 172
Osgood, McIlvaine and Co. 71, 86
O'Shea, Kitty 40, 43
Ovid 135–6
Oxford Magazine 39
Oxford University 4–9, 27, 66, 152

Pacino, Al 182
Paley, William 157
Pall Mall Gazette 48, 63, 64, 65, 68, 92,
    99
Paris 3, 14–15, 29, 30, 88, 89, 128, 190
Paris Commune (1871) 33
Parker, Charley 24
Parker, Lynne 175
Parker, Oliver 179, 191
Parliamentary Reform Act (1867) 33,
    34
Parnell, Charles Stewart 14, 38, 39–40,
    43, 129
pastimes 58

Pater, Walter 7, 14, 15, 17, 73, 84, 95,
    100, 135, 141, 153, 155, 156, 163,
    165–6
pathology 149
Patience, or Bunthorne's Bride (comic
    operetta) 11, 190
Patmore, Coventry 41
patriotism 101–2, 129
Pattison, Mark 55
pedestrianism 58
Pemberton-Billing, Noel 182
penal system 27, 49–50, 126–34; reform
    51–3, 99, 130–4
Pentonville prison 27
Père Lachaise cemetery, Paris 190
Petrie, George 79
philanthropy 49, 55, 56, 121–4
philology 152
philosophy 140–54
Phoenix Park assassinations (1882) 14,
    39
picketing 35
Picture of Dorian Gray, The (Wilde)
    85, 115, 181; censorship battles over
    91, 94–8; collecting in 137–8; criticism
    of 64, 86–7, 145; decoration of 74;
    dramatization of 171–2, 173; evolution
    in 140–1; fantasy tale of 78, 79;
    hereditary destiny in 150; influence of
    Melmoth the Wanderer on 28; love as
    imitation in 148; model for Lord
    Henry Wotton character 45; moderate
    sales of 86; New Hedonism in 18–19,
    159–60, 161; psychology of influence
    in 142–6; royalty agreement on 71; six
    new chapters added to 72, 86
Pigott, Richard 40
Pike, L. O. 51–2
Pinel, Philippe 149
Plato 17–18, 140, 142
Playgoers' Club 19
poetry 73, 84, 92, 97, 101–2, 105, 113,
    118, 128, 129, 139, 154, 155
politics 32–7, 100–4
Poor Law (1834) 54
Portora Royal School, Enniskillen 2–3
post-colonialism 188
poverty 54–5, 122
Powell, Anthony 173
Pre-Raphaelite Brotherhood 4, 7, 8, 73,
    153
Preminger, Otto 174

press 10; 'battle of the Oscars' 183; capital punishment providing morbid interest 53; celebrity interviews in 68–9; criticism of *Dorian Gray* 86–7, 93–4, 96; cult of celebrity 169; gloating at Wilde's imprisonment 26; growth of 62; interest in Wilde's American tour 14; new leisure 56; Parnell and the 39–40; penal reform letters 28, 99, 130, 131, 133; racial stereotyping in 39; satirized by Wilde 63; war against decadence in 36; Whistler/Wilde exchanges in 16–17; *see also* journalism
Prewitt Brown, Julia 170
Prison Acts 51
prize fighting 58
property 15, 41
prostitution 48, 49, 50, 53, 60, 66
protest rallies 34–5, 37
Protestants 38–9, 113, 188
Proudhon, Pierre-Joseph 15, 35
Prowse, Philip 176–8
psychology 149
public executions 51, 52–3, 127, 131
public health 57
publishers 71, 72, 74, 75–6, 86, 93
Punch 10, 12
Punch and Judy shows 42
punishment 27, 49–50, 51–2, 126–34
puritanism 112, 153
Pygmalion story 136

Queensberry, Lady 23, 29
Queensberry, Marquess of 24, 26, 58, 98
Quiller Couch, Arthur T. 68

racism 39, 60, 103
Radcliffe, Mrs Ann 79
radicalism 32–4, 100–4
railways 31, 57
rare book trade 73–4
rationalism 139, 152
Reading Gaol 27–8, 29, 51, 130–1
realism 76–7, 119–20, 124–5, 132–3, 175, 176–7, 181
Redgrave, Corin 170, 188
Redgrave, Vanessa 179
Reform League 33
Reform Union 33
Reinhardt, Max 182
religion 45–8, 154, 156–67

Renaissance 112, 153
Renaissance, The (Pater) 7
Renan, Ernest 63, 144
rent boys 23, 24, 25, 26
Republic (Plato) 17–18
republicanism 14, 33, 34, 100–1
Retté, Adolphe 128
Review of Reviews 65, 113
Rhymers' Club 19, 73
Richard, Keith 185
Richardson, Joely 179
Ricketts, Charles 18, 19, 21, 27, 74, 86, 180
riots 34–5, 37, 47
Robert Elsmere (Ward) 157
Robertson, T. W. 181
Rolling Stones 185
Roman Catholic Church 4, 7, 8, 30, 37, 113, 169
romance novels 77–9
Roscoe, Thomas 92
Rosebery, Lord 24, 27
Ross, Robert 18, 23, 24, 25, 29, 30, 69, 133, 182, 186
Rossetti, Dante Gabriel 4, 47
Rough Magic troupe 175
Royal Irish Academy 79
Ruskin, John 7, 14, 17, 33, 37, 41, 42, 61, 62, 63, 73, 77, 80, 107–8, 114
Russia 129

sabbatarianism 47–8
Saint Oscar (Eagleton play) 188–9
Salisbury, Marquess of 44
Salome (Wilde) 21, 74, 89–91, 96, 111–14, 180–2
Salvation Army 55
Sammells, Neil 190
Sanders, George 171
Sardou, Victorien 21, 181
Saturday Review 63
Schreiner, Olive 42
science 45–6, 79, 139–56, 149, 159
Scots Observer 93
Scott, Clement 107
Scott, George C. 171
Scribe, Eugène 181
séances 158
sectarianism 38–9
Seeley, Sir John 34
self-gratification 159–60
self-help 54–5

self-realization 50, 147–9, 150, 159, 165–6

self-reliance 103

'Selfish Giant, The', *see Happy Prince and Other Tales, The* (Wilde)

sensation novels 75, 79

Settlement Movements 33, 121–2

sex laws reform 48, 175, 185

sexual abstinence 18

sexual politics 104–19

sexuality 91–2, 95–7, 118

Shairp, Mordaunt 171

Shakespeare, William 84–5, 92, 94, 97, 118, 133–4, 142, 164

Shannon, Charles 18, 19, 74, 86

Shaw, George Bernard 13, 19, 21, 36, 72, 108; Celtic school 83, 104; censorship 87, 89, 91; on female purity 116; on heightened histrionics 81; journalism 64, 65, 67; on Life Force 189; review of Wilde 188; on socialism 103

Shelley, Edward 71

Shelley, Mary 79

Shelley, Percy Bysshe 139, 140

Sherard, Robert Harborough 16, 18

Sheridan, Richard Brinsley 108

Sherlock Holmes stories 76

Shirley (Brontë) 46

Sickert, Helena 67

silent films 173

Smiles, Samuel 54

Smith, W. H. 75, 92

smoking 57

Smyth-Pigott, Edward 87, 90

social change 53–6

social criticism 61, 62, 68, 126

Social Democratic Federation (SDF) 34, 35, 122

social mobility 10–11

Social Purity Alliance 49

socialism 15, 34–6, 55, 59, 99, 103, 122, 129, 165

Socialist League 34, 55

Society of Authors 71, 123

Somerset, Lord Arthur 93–4

sonnets 97, 142

Soul of Man, The (formerly 'The Soul of Man under Socialism') (Wilde) 10, 40, 89, 90, 94, 99, 103, 115; Christ figure 27, 165, 166; contemplation 161; imprisonment 129; individualism 165; poetry 128; property 15; self-

realization 50; social conscience 123, 124, 125, 126, 127

Speaker (journal) 68, 105

Spectator, The 156

Spencer, Herbert 127, 140, 141, 155

Spirit Lamp (undergraduate magazine) 27

sports 58, 60

St James Theatre 20, 24, 25

St James's Gazette 93, 94, 96

'Star-Child, The', *see House of Pomegranates, A* (Wilde)

Stead, W. T. 48, 64, 65–6, 68, 113

steamships 31

Stendhal 127

Stepniak, Sergei 35

Stevenson, Robert Louis 75, 77, 79, 95

Stoker, Bram 114

Stokes, Leslie and Sewell 172

Stoppard, Tom 179, 186

Strahan, Alexander 76

Strauss, Richard 182

strikes 32, 35, 36

Stutfield, Hugh 37

subscription libraries 75, 92–3

suburbs 31, 57

suffrage 40

Sunday Trading Bill 47, 48

Swinburne, Algernon 4, 5, 47, 128

Symbolist movement 15, 17, 18, 21, 74, 84, 89, 112, 128, 153, 154, 180

Symonds, John Addington 139

Synge, J. M. 168

Taylor, Alfred 23, 24, 26

Taylor, Tom 181

technological innovation 19, 47, 59, 134, 191

telepathy 158

television 178, 186

Tennyson, Alfred Lord 45–6

Terry, Ellen 43, 80–1

Tess of the D'Urbervilles (Hardy) 53, 106, 107, 114

Thackeray, William Makepeace 65, 82, 92, 114–15

theatre: censorship 87–91, 111; curtain-speeches 21, 69

Third Reform Act (1884) 34, 122

Thompson, Henry Yates 66

Thorne, Will 36

Tichborne Case (1867–75) 44

Times, The 39, 56, 113
Tom Brown's Schooldays (Hughes) 60
Tory party 32
tourism 57
Tractarians 46
trade unionism 35–6
Trafalgar Square protest rally (1887)
    34–5, 37
Travers, Mary 2, 44
treadmill punishment 27, 51
Trevelyan, John 183
Trinity College, Dublin 3–4, 5, 6, 38,
    152, 188
triple-deckers 75
Turgenev, Ivan 127
Turner, Reggie 23, 25, 186
Tyrell, George 47

Ulster 38–9
Unionists 38–9, 59
United States: anarchists 102; censorship
    laws 175; industrialization 31, 32;
    press 64; Wilde's lecture tour 7,
    13–14, 38, 39, 100, 127, 135, 190;
    Wilde's posthumous success 87
universities 46, 55
upper class 44–5, 49; London society 11,
    44–5; marital infidelity 43; travel for
    57; Wilde's irreverence towards 173–4;
    women's property rights 41
urbanization 19, 31, 57, 62, 122, 191
utilitarianism 34

Valistes (bohemian circle) 18
Vanity Fair (Thackeray) 114–15
venereal disease 48
Vera: or The Nihilists (Wilde) 13, 20,
    87–8, 101, 128
Verlaine, Paul 15
Victoria, Queen 2, 31, 33, 34, 40, 43, 58,
    59
Villiers de l'Isle-Adam, Philippe-
    Auguste, Comte de 113
Vizetelly, Henry 93
voluntary organizations 54
Vortex, The (Coward play) 174

Wainewright, Thomas Griffiths 105, 128,
    135
Wallace, William 154
Walpole, Robert 88
Ward, Lock and Co. 71, 72, 86

Ward, Mrs Humphry 157
Watson, William 169
Watts, G. F. 43
Waugh, Evelyn 174
Webb, Sidney and Beatrice 51
welfare reform 53–5
Wells, H. G. 69
Wemyss Reid, Thomas 66, 67, 68
West, Mae 175
Westminster Gazette 37, 162
Whistler, James MacNeill 8, 11, 16, 20,
    64, 169
White, William Hale 157
Whitman, Walt 13
Wilde, Constance, née Lloyd (wife) 16,
    18, 22, 23, 24, 27, 29, 36, 41, 58, 183
Wilde, Cyril (son) 17, 23
Wilde, Isola (sister) 1, 3
Wilde, Lady Jane, née Elgee (mother) 1,
    2, 6, 9, 14, 22, 23, 27, 33, 38, 41, 79,
    100

WILDE, OSCAR FINGAL O'FLAHERTIE
    WILLS

character: aestheticism 4, 7, 9, 10, 17, 36,
    77, 100, 125–6, 160–1, 191–2; business-
    like approach to writing 71–2, 74–5,
    86; cultural superiority 6; dandyism 8,
    13, 15–16, 58; gifted raconteur 99,
    123; homosexuality 18, 22–3, 27, 72,
    97–8; intellectualism 139; literary
    fastidiousness 68; republicanism 14,
    100–1; self-publicist 64, 68, 190;
    self-realization 147–9, 150; warmth
    and humour 162, 180
interests: childhood 127–8; fairy-tales
    79; fashion 8, 13, 15–16, 58;
    Hellenism 3, 4, 125, 139–40
life: Anglo-Irish background 188, 189;
    birth and childhood 1; Catholicism 4,
    7, 8–9; closure of plays 168; death and
    burial 29–30; death of sister 3;
    dramatizations of 170, 182–3, 186,
    188; editorship of *Woman's World* 16,
    43, 66–8, 104–5; education 2–9; exile
    28–9, 168; finances 7–8, 11, 23, 26, 29,
    39; forbidden from seeing children
    again 42; influence of Paris 14–15;
    inner circle 11, 19–20, 23, 45;
    interviews 68–9; lecture tour to
    America 7, 13–14, 38, 39, 64, 100, 127,
    135, 190, 192; libel action against
    Marquess of Queensberry 24–5, 98;

marriage 16, 17, 23; penal reform 28–9, 52, 53, 65, 94, 99, 130–4; petition for early release 149–50; prison experiences 129–30; public scandals 23–4; relationship with Lord Alfred Douglas 22–4, 29, 148–9; satirized 10; theatrical success 20–1; trials and imprisonment 26–8, 49, 60, 105, 188–9; true age 5, 25

opinions: anti-authoritarianism 126–34; importance of the miraculous 47; Irish nationalism 39–40, 100–1; journalism 40, 63–5; philanthropy 56, 123–4; prison 126–34; radicalism 34, 35, 36, 100–4; regional writers 82–3

WORKS:

essays: 'Pen, Pencil and Poison' 105, 116, 118, 128, 135; 'The Critic as Artist' 17, 103, 117–18, 127, 143–4, 145, 153, 154–5, 158, 161, 164; 'The Decay of Lying' 126, 128, 153, 154, 155, 157–8; 'The Portrait of Mr W. H.' 78, 97–8, 116, 142, 143, 164; 'The Rise of Historical Criticism' 9, 151–2, 155; 'The Truth of Masks' 20, 106, 167, 181

plays and fiction: art as revelation of the spirit 152–5; book-as-object 73–4; censorship of 87–98, 111; constant revision of plays 72; consumerism theme in 134–8; cowardice/conscience link 141; criticism of 19–20; diversity of effect 85–6; education 56; film versions 170, 171, 173, 174, 179, 191; musical versions 174–5, 182; non-realistic forms 77–8, 80–2, 85–7, 119, 161, 189; plagiarism accusations 16, 20; play reviews 20–1; politics 100–4; populist label 169; posthumous success of 87; psychology of influence 141–6; religious philosophy 156–67; revaluation of 170, 176–80, 182–92; revivals of plays 168, 170–2, 173, 176–82; sexual politics 43, 104–19; social conscience 119–26; stagecraft

181–2; working timetable 69–71; *see also under individual titles in bold*

poetry: 'Ave Imperatrix' 101–2; *The Ballad of Reading Gaol* 28–9, 53, 99, 131–4; 'Libertatis Sacra Fames' 100–1; *Poems* (1881) 74, 156; 'Requiescat' 3; 'The Harlot's House' 16; 'Wasted Days' 9

prose apologia: *De Profundis* 23, 28, 55–6, 83, 123, 129, 130, 135, 147–8, 165, 166, 167, 170

Wilde, Sir William (father) 1, 2, 7–8, 39, 44, 79

Wilde, Vyvyan (son) 17, 18, 23

Wilde, Willie (brother) 1, 2, 23, 27

Williams, John 67

Williams, Raymond 126

Wilson, Henry ('cousin') 1, 8

Wolfenden Commission 183

Woman of No Importance, A (Wilde) 20, 21, 22, 108–11, 116, 124, 168, 177

Woman's World (monthly magazine) 16, 43, 66–8, 104–5

women: education 116; magazines for 67; motherhood 41–2, 107–9, 110–11; new leisure activities 58; 'New Woman' literature 42–3, 95, 104–5, 113–14, 115–17; rights for 40–3, 108; sexuality 112–14

Wooldridge, Charles Thomas 28–9

Woolf, Virginia 96–7, 169

working class 36, 54–5

World (society magazine) 64, 66, 67, 90–1

Yates, Edmund 64

Yeats, W. B. 6, 19, 27, 57, 84, 169, 189

Yellow Book (illustrated quarterly) 58, 74, 97, 105, 113, 169

Young Ireland movement 1, 14, 37, 128, 129

'Young King, The', *see House of Pomegranates, A* (Wilde)

Zola, Émile 77, 87, 93

American Literature

British and Irish Literature

Children's Literature

Classics and Ancient Literature

Colonial Literature

Eastern Literature

European Literature

History

Medieval Literature

Oxford English Drama

Poetry

Philosophy

Politics

Religion

The Oxford Shakespeare

A complete list of Oxford Paperbacks, including Oxford World's Classics, Oxford Shakespeare, Oxford Drama, and Oxford Paperback Reference, is available in the UK from the Academic Division Publicity Department, Oxford University Press, Great Clarendon Street, Oxford OX2 6DP.

In the USA, complete lists are available from the Paperbacks Marketing Manager, Oxford University Press, 198 Madison Avenue, New York, NY 10016.

Oxford Paperbacks are available from all good bookshops. In case of difficulty, customers in the UK can order direct from Oxford University Press Bookshop, Freepost, 116 High Street, Oxford OX1 4BR, enclosing full payment. Please add 10 per cent of published price for postage and packing.